July, 04

ALL THINGS

Collected Columns & Essays

CONSIDERED

MICHAEL COREN

*To Tracy,
Blessings,
M.C*

Fenn Publishing Company Ltd.
Bolton Canada

To Bruxy Cavey

ALL THINGS CONSIDERED
A Fenn Publishing Book / March 2001

Michael Coren can be contacted via his website www.michaelcoren.com

Publisher: C. Jordan Fenn

Fenn Publishing Company Ltd.
Bolton, Ontario, Canada

Distributed in Canada by H. B. Fenn and Company Ltd.
34 Nixon Road, Bolton, Ontario, Canada, L7E 1W2

visit us on the World Wide Web, at www.hbfenn.com

Canadian Cataloguing in Publication Data

Coren, Michael
All things considered

Columns written for the Toronto Sun.
ISBN 1-55168-252-4

I. Title.

PS8555.O614A16 2001   081   C00-932971-4
PR9199.3.C67A16 2001

Printed and bound in Canada

Introduction

Why publish a collection of columns, essays and reviews that have already appeared in print in various newspapers and magazines? To be candid, all writers enjoy seeing their journalistic work appear in the more permanent form of a book. On a more practical level, however, the reason for this compilation is that so many people have asked for it. When I speak in public, when a particular column appears somewhere, when people read me in a newspaper or watch me on television for the first time, I am asked if there is somewhere they can buy a book of my journalism. Now I can give them an answer.

In fact this is my second such collection. The first one appeared more than five years ago and there is much in it of which I am extremely proud. But we move on, we change, we evolve. At least most of us do. Since that book appeared my life has been transformed on several levels. At the risk of sounding holy – the very worst sin, it appears, in our contemporary society – I experienced a Christian conversion and such an event informs everything someone does, thinks and writes. I am not the same person and I am certainly not the same writer.

Because of this some commentators have suggested that I have gone soft, by which they mean that I no longer call myself a conservative. Well, hardness or softness has little to do with it. Quite simply I refuse to be locked into any political definition, particularly one that is by its very nature meagre and inadequate. In fact on the basic moral issues of which people these days seem so frightened – sexuality, abortion, family, faith, virtues – I see no need to compromise. Truth is truth, whatever the papers and the television might say in their infinite wisdom.

I was tempted to update and edit these pieces but that seemed somehow dishonest. They stand as my views on a specific subject at the particular time that they were written and that, surely, is how they should be judged. There may also be some repetition of style, even of the occasional phrase, but this is inevitable if someone is writing a hundred columns a year.

To tamper with a column with the aid of hindsight would be cowardly. As would be writing too long an introduction to somehow explain or justify. Here they are. My words, my thoughts, my statements. I hope that many of you like them and I hope that many of you don't. Bland consensus, writing only what people want to hear, promoting self and friends are all too common in modern journalism and all too repugnant to me. On this I will not and cannot change.

Michael Coren

Acknowledgements

First an apology. To all those whose names should be here and are not, please forgive me. The head sometimes forgets what the heart always remembers. To Lorrie Goldstein, Lynda Williamson and everybody at the Toronto Sun I owe much gratitude. Sense and sensibility. Or to put it another way, editors who listen. Many thanks also to the Calgary, Edmonton and Winnipeg Suns and The London Free Press. Most of the book reviews here reprinted appeared in The National Post, and my gratitude goes to Noah Richler, Andy Lamey and Aida Edemariam. The Boomer magazine has been most generous in publishing my extended essays and Beth Marlin in particular has shown me great kindness and understanding. To the following I shall always be in debt. Dick Gray, David Mainse, Fred Glover, Bill Carroll, Paul Godfrey, Diane Francis, Steve Jalsevac, Brian Inkster, Father Jonathan Robinson, Lorne Freed, Dave Wilson, Chris Corkery. And finally to Bernadette, Daniel, Lucy, Oliver and Elizabeth – you know.

H. G. Wells and the Coming of the Scientists

The time is almost sixty years ago. The place a leafy European suburb. A group of men gather around the table and share a joke about one of their colleagues. He is the only one amongst them who isn't a man of science, isn't a doctor. He is a handsome man, with his blonde hair, blue eyes and carved features. Gifted too, and the head of state's favourite politician. But he simply isn't one of them. They have spent years at various universities studying chemistry, biology, physics and the related disciplines that compose the magnificent world in which they place so much hope. They are pioneers, knights of progress, disciples of the scientific muse.

Because they are rooted in science, soaked in its genius, they know that whatever they think and say is wise and, more than this, ethical. Science has to be ethical because it represents the future and the future has to be better than the past. Simple logic. I breathe therefore I am. The arrogance of the living. The dictatorship of chronology. So they discuss, drink coffee, smile and come to a unanimous conclusion about what they must do.

The handsome rival was SS commander Reinhard Heydrich, the head of state was Adolf Hitler and this was the Wannsee Conference, in which the Final Solution of the "Jewish problem" was decided upon and planned. Men of science could find no moral objection to what they were about to do. And frankly, I am not particularly surprised.

Fast forward to the present and a good, gentle, caring man who would shudder at the thought of Nazism and death camps walks into a small room in a hospital and sits down next to a pretty young woman. She is pregnant, was happy beyond belief but is now frightened. She can see on the doctor's face that something is wrong. He explains to her that the tests have revealed that her child, if born, would not be, well, would not be normal. He gives

1

his best "I know how you feel" look and explains that science is a wonderful thing. She does not have to proceed with the pregnancy. Interestingly enough he starts to scientific language. Her baby is no longer a baby, it is now a fetus. Science, he says, can give you a choice.

Actually he is right. Science has given us a choice, but it is choice without responsibility. Now I am not for a moment making a qualitative comparison between a Nazi warlord and a contemporary obstetrician. I am simply saying that the more we can do because of the expansion of science, the more we should root ourselves in an unchanging moral code. But we don't.

Simply because we "can" do certain things does not mean that we "should" do them. Not a week goes by without another aspect of scientific capabilities clashing with existing virtues. Sex-change operations, so-called population control, chemical contraceptives, genetic experiments. We look up as children in a planetarium, fascinated and excited but terribly confused. We look for a hand to hold but there is nobody there. And the culture tells us not to worry, merely to trust in science and leave the morals to the men in white coats.

What is so extraordinary about all this is that the father of the whole enterprise, the whole notion of rule by science, was in fact a short, plump Englishman with a high-pitched voice and a bad moustache. H.G. Wells is better known for writing science fiction novels such as The Invisible Man, The Time Machine and The War of the Worlds than for changing the world. But not only in his scientific politics but also in his greater attitudes and opinions Wells was in many ways the very first modern man. So welcome to the world of H.G. Wells.

There is an anecdote about Wells that exemplified his character more than a dozen memoirs. The bar of a London theatre in the 1920s. Herbert George Wells, a literary doyen of the greatest celebrity, when that really meant something, sips a blended brandy. A breathless young student approaches Wells, holds out his hand and exclaims, "Mr. Wells, you probably don't remember me ..." "Yes I bloody well do" replies Wells, and runs from the theatre.

Rude, nasty, selfish. Yet since his death in 1946 Wells has been treated rather kindly by biographers, rather too kindly. He was a bully who wanted to use science to control the world, he was a bitter anti Semite, he was a misogynist who treated woman in an appalling fashion and he was a racist whose ideas of human experimentation were personally absorbed by Hitler, Stalin and the generations of social engineers who followed them.

There are several reasons why Wells has got away with it for so long. The first is that as a man who was dedicated to science and progress he could apparently do no wrong. The second is that he was a socialist, and we all know that it is only people on the right who are capable of being blackguards, don't we. The third is that a great many people of influence agreed and agree with him. For example, Wells wanted to strictly control the "breeding" of people of colour in Africa and Asia. Imagine that. Yet today western governments will only give aid to such countries if they agree to allow widespread abortion and promote contraception. So very different? I can't see it. Remember that we could feed these people twice over and not even notice any financial hardship.

The dramatist George Bernard Shaw knew Wells for many years. Describing his ideas and behaviour he wrote, "Multiply the total by ten; square the result. Raise it again to the millionth power and square it again; and you will still fall short of the truth about Wells – yet the worse he behaved the more he was indulged; and the more he was indulged the worse he behaved."

Shaw, however, was something of a friend who killed with kindness. Hilaire Belloc, that champion of Catholicism, was more direct. "Mr. Wells means to say all that is in him, and if there is not very much in him, that is not his fault." It is hardly surprising that Belloc was an enemy, but it is extremely surprising that so many feminists have adored Wells down the ages. From his contemporaries, to the mothers of Planned Parenthood, and even to modern feminist writers, Wells is treated as a hero. His book Ann Veronica was and still is considered a seminal work. Indeed it is in print precisely because of the devotion of Britain's largest feminist publishing house.

"The thing to do is to go out into the world; leave everything behind, wife and child, and things; go all over the world and come back experienced" he announced to a group of friends one evening." One onlooker asked what would happen to the wives. "The wives will go to heaven when they die," he said. Wells did not believe in heaven.

Such were Wells' own domestic arrangements. When Amy Catherine Robbins married Wells she was told by her husband that she would have to change her name. Not only her surname. Her Christian name was not to Wells' liking and from now on she would be called Jane. She acquiesced, partly because she knew that Wells would leave her if she resisted and partly because of the undoubted hold he had over women. Lots of them.

Rebecca West was a leading feminist of her age. She was forced to leave London when she gave birth to Wells' illegitimate child because the presence of the boy might embarrass his father. West was both emotionally and physically abused by her "lover" and was frequently publicly humiliated by him when he would shout and laugh at her in crowded restaurants and explain to people at adjacent tables that his mistress had grown ugly. He even had his wife referee between rival mistresses, forcing her to decide with whom he should next be unfaithful.

Another woman, Hedwig Verena Gatternigg, attempted suicide in Wells' front room and he spent more time in trying to keep the story out of the press than in trying to save her life. Amber Reeves, a young and innocent woman, was violated by Wells and then left to take care of her pain and her child. "For all my desire to be interested I have to confess that for most things and people I don't give a damn," he wrote in his autobiography.

He did care about Jews. "I met a Jewish friend of mine the other day and he asked me what would come of his people," Wells wrote. "That is exactly what is matter with them – my people." That man's people were about to be exterminated in The Holocaust. Writing of The First World War Wells stated "Throughout those tragic and almost fruitless four years of war, the Jewish spokesmen were most elaborately and energetically demonstrating that they cared not a rap for the troubles and dangers of English, French, Germans, Russians, Americans or of any other people but their own. They kept their eyes steadfastly upon the restoration of the Jews."

It was pointed out to Wells that the first volunteer for the American forces in Europe was Jewish, that there were numerous Jewish winners of the Iron Cross, that Jews were in fact over-represented in the fighting armies. His response was sullen aggression. "There was never a promise; they were never chosen; their distinctive observances, their Sabbath, their Passover, their queer calendar, are mere traditional oddities of no present significance whatsoever."

Eleanor Roosevelt called Wells a fool and a bigot and tried to have him banned from the U.S.A. Leon Gelman, President of the Mizrachi Organisation of America wrote at the time, "Wells is brazenly spreading notorious lies about the Jews. His violent language betrays a streak of sadism that is revolting. If any man who professes to be an enlightened human being can preach such heinous distortions, then mankind is doomed to utter darkness." Quite so.

Which leads us to Wells the social engineer. In massively best selling books such as Anticipations and A Modern Utopia Wells wrote that he believed the world would collapse and from this collapse a new order should and would emerge. "People throughout the world whose minds were adapted to the big-scale conditions of the new time. A naturally and informally organised educated class, an unprecedented sort of people." A strict social order would be formed. At the bottom of it were the base.

These were "people who had given evidence of a strong antisocial disposition", including "the black, the brown, the swarthy, the yellow." Christians would also "have to go" as well as the handicapped. Wells devoted entire pamphlets to the need of "preventing the birth, preventing the procreation or preventing the existence" of the mentally and physically handicapped. "This thing, this euthanasia of the weak and the sensual is possible. I have little or no doubt that in the future it will be planned and achieved."

The people of Africa and Asia, he said, simply could never find a place in a modern world controlled by science. Better to do away with them than tell them lies. "I take it they will have to go," he said of them. Marriage as it is known would have to end but couples could form unions based on mutual needs and desires. They would list their "desires, diseases, needs" on little cards and a central authority would decide who was fitted for whom.

Population would be rigidly controlled, with forced abortion for those who were not of the right class and race and a firm control of family size even for the "acceptable" population. Religion would be unnecessary and banned, children would be raised in communes and all would be well. The old and the ill would, naturally, have to be done away with and doctors would be given the authority to decide who had a right to love, who had a duty to die.

Remember that Wells was an internationally best selling author before television, before radio was popular. He sold literally millions of copies of his books, translated into numerous languages.

He was a star of his age, and he dominated the literary and cultural world from as early as 1900, right up until the Second World War. His warning of the horror of future air-war, for example, is thought by historians to have made a huge contribution to Britain's reluctance to rearm against Germany in the 1930s.

Stalin knew of Wells' importance and relished his work. He met with Wells and enjoyed the encounter so much that he cancelled the rest of the day's activities so he could listen to the great man for even longer. Hitler thought that Wells spoke and wrote for the "new man" and should be listened to by the modern world.

Wells was pleased at this adulation and continued to write about his favourite subject, about the future and how it should develop. In his The Outline of History he offered similar views, but perhaps didn't do all of the work himself. During the writing of the book he delivered a lecture to a group of young people. One of them inquired about a folder of papers in Wells' car. "Today I've motored from Stonehenge, and you may care to know that I've polished that off in forty minutes." The student was surprised, reminding Wells that Stonehenge had baffled experts of hundreds of years. "Very likely, but anyway I've settled it to my satisfaction. I've left a couple of experts behind, they have a fussy kind of knowledge that looks well in a footnote."

In other words he was a plagiarist. Other people were doing the work for him and he was taking the credit and the cash. I suppose we should not be surprised. What should surprise us is the lasting influence of man who is not really read any more. People who couldn't name a book by Wells have been raised in a context and an environment where his ideas are increasingly acceptable. He was an authentic man of vision. He influenced the future, and he described the future. Vision indeed. Trouble is, it is a dark and horrible vision that comes into sharper focus by the day.

Life Amongst the Richlers

I have just finished paying back the best publisher in the country a very large advance for a very large book. It's taken me eighteen months to do and it almost killed me. It could have been worse. Stoddart Publishing asked for not a penny of interest, thus giving me what was really an extremely generous, interest-free loan. They also forgave me, calming my contrition with a "Hey, it happens." The book was a biography of Mordecai Richler, with the full co-operation of the subject.

I just couldn't do the thing. I tried, goodness how I tried. If for nothing else because of the money. There was even more due when the book was finished. I'd written several other biographies and they'd done quite well. Translations, foreign publishers, good reviews. But they were all of dead British authors. This one was of a most definitely living Canadian. Every time I thought I had the thing under control another loose end would appear, another unresolved problem.

Oh please! Who the hell am I kidding here? I was tired of the man, tired of his work, tired of the project. And that could only have resulted in a bad book, one that would not have either him or me any justice at all.

When Richler agreed to let me write the book he faxed me that I mustn't tell people about "me being voted best cross-dresser of the year when I went to the Purim Ball dressed as Queen Esther." I wish I could have, because it might have been one of the more interesting aspects of the book. Because when it comes down to a genuine analysis the author of, amongst other, The Apprentice-ship of Duddy Kravitz, St.Urbain's Horsemen, Oh Canada! Oh Quebec! and the Jacob Two-Two books is, well, is a little dull.

Now I know that this statement will annoy, because we tend to guard our Canadian institutions as though they were freshly laid eggs. But I'm not sure if Mordecai himself would argue very much with the comment. He almost prides himself on an enlightened ordinariness. In other words, pretentious he is not. A stable and inspiring marriage, good friends, a beautiful home and a fine family. Take, for example, the reasons why he works. He certainly has that visceral need to express himself but he also works out of sheer practicality. None of the contrived angst and anger of so many contemporary novelists.

I went with him to a speech he gave at a Toronto synagogue, where the audience could easily have been taken from one of his more satirical novels. Why, I asked after this somewhat painful experience, did you agree to do it? "Because I've got one of the kids getting married soon and it's a very expensive business." Honest, nice. He then took me and his eldest son out for a late night drinking session for which he insisted on paying.

If we are brutally candid I think all of us could point to a Richler essay or column and say that it seemed a little on the perfunctory side. Critics, in fact, argue that his columns in the National Post seldom say anything that is original or even particularly interesting. Not completely fair, but not completely untrue either.

Mordecai Richler's prism is still that of 1950s Jewish Montreal. A very small and only partly engaging aspect of the great human carnival that should composes the back cloth for any writer, in Canada or elsewhere.

He was born in that Jewish Montreal in 1931 and his autobiography can be found in several of his books. Two errors can be embraced here. To believe that the books are all based on personal experience, and to believe that none of them are. Most of Richler's friends are to be found somewhere in his novels, especially if you look deeply enough.

Have no doubts, those friends certainly do. Richler has a circle of close ones who are long-term and loyal, an indication of the man's character. I interviewed several, and the typical reaction was guarded in the extreme. Jack Rabinovich is an old pal of Richler's Montreal days. And he has a very nasty dog. As I knock on the door I hear this hound from hell, this Baskerville reject, screaming to get at me. "He's a guard dog," says Jack, holding the mutt back as the door is opened. "Don't pet him." Then put the bloody thing away. Instead the dog sits by my side, and when I casually move my hand he nips at it. "I told you he nips."

Rabinovich does that "friend of Mordecai" thing where he tells me absolutely nothing of any value. I'm bored, smiling, listening, thinking "I've wasted my time again", and my mind wanders. I don't mean that the guy gives me very little, I mean that he gives me nothing. I still have the tape, and my questions are okay. Not great, but okay. Rabinovich just keeps saying that Richler is a good man and a fine friend. Absolutely nothing more. And remember, Richler has told his buddies that he has approved me, that they can talk.

I suppose you'd expect more from the man who gave us The Giller Prize, that inflated but entertaining literary award named after Rabinovich's widow, Doris Giller, who for many years worked in the books section of The Toronto Star. She too knew Richler. Once, when I used to review books at the Star, she said to me, "You know why I speak my mind, you know why I don't care?" No, I answered. "Because I'm from fucking Montreal, that's why. Because I'm from fucking Montreal."

I've never really understood this. What had a fairly unremarkable city got to do with someone allegedly speaking her mind? This was, by the way, after Giller had screamed at someone because I had written a favourable review of a biography of the president of Syria. I can only assume that they don't like the Syrian president in Montreal and are "not afraid" of speaking their minds about it.

Perhaps this was my problem. I just didn't get Montreal. I'd grown up in London, England, in the middle of a swirling community of Jews, Irish and cockneys. Extraordinarily fertile. Sorry, but in comparison Montreal is nothing more than a bland suburb. Yet to understand Richler one has to understand his home.

This is where he saw his parents split up, his weak but good-natured father dominated by a powerful and difficult wife. She would eventually write a memoir, in which she failed to mention her son the novelist at all. Richler had not seen his mother for years when she died in just a few years ago. Nor did he attend the funeral. I asked him why.

"It would have been hypocrisy," he says, showing no emotion. "I hadn't seen her or heard from her for so long. To suddenly show up when she was dead would have been unfair to all the people there who had been with her." And he stops. As his way. No small talk, no filling in the gaps. Some people think this is rudeness. Don't think so. He just doesn't care that much. He's said what he wanted to say, now onto the next part of the conversation.

He has said little about his parents in any interviews, though her does refer to his mother in his novels. According to his children Richler loved his father and helped him out financially when things were difficult. But his mother he did not like, perhaps grew to despise as he and she grew older. He has a brother too, living in New Brunswick. There is no relationship. There was also a first wife, something many people don't realise.

"We were both kids, both stupid. It was never going to work." There's no grudge here, no emotion at all really. Had they ever met since?

"We spoke on the phone when we were in the same city, but she has her life, I have mine. It would be dishonest to ask for anything more."

Honesty is key in Richler. I was told a story by a member of his family about a screenplay he never wrote. He was offered a large amount of money to write a script for a movie company. He said he wasn't interested. They said they'd give him the money just to keep him as part of the team. He said he couldn't take it. No work, no money.

It's an ethic that informs everything he does, and probably goes some way to explaining why his marriage to Florence has been so good for so long. Friends mock him about the number of times he calls he wife, a former model who, according to one of her sons, was once proposed to by Sean Connery. When I tell Richler of this he looks surprised. "I didn't know that. Really?" Back to the friends and their joke. They say he calls Florence when he arrives at Montreal airport, calls her again to say he's arrived at the other airport, calls her to say he's made it to the hotel. You get the picture. And it's a refreshing one.

Florence certainly provides stability and certainty. She also has her feet firmly on the ground, not easily won over by what is often the sheer flummery of the Canadian literary community. She's also not Jewish. There is a famous incident, caught on film, when a member of an audience to which Richler is speaking asks him in less than conciliatory terms why he married a gentile. Richler put the question and the questioner down so quickly and so finally that you almost feel for the poor fool.

But here's the contradiction. On the one hand he has no time for organised religion and constantly makes fun of Jewishness and Judaism. But he takes offence at what he sees as the anti-semitism latent in Quebec nationalism. Some say his book Oh Canada! Oh Quebec! was harmful, saw Jew-haters around every block and was profoundly out-of-touch with contemporary realities.

"I don't think so" he defends. "It's more that people don't like to be reminded of what is around them." Has he suffered lately because of his being Jewish? "Some guy drove past me slowly in Montreal, looked me up and down and said 'Hey, it's the Jew'." Was that so bad? "Bad enough."

He divides his time between Montreal, a sumptuous country home in the eastern townships and a home in London. I remember a professionally cynical arts journalist from the Globe and Mail asking incredulously why he would spend the winter in London. Richler stared her down and said, simply, "Why not!" Pause. Stop.

This Globe journalist of whom I speak is a gifted, experienced writer. Yet before the interview with Richler she was physically trembling and she asked me if I would come with her and help out. Offer protection. Richler has this effect on people. He frightens them. Are you rude, Mordecai? Are you rude to people, are you short with them? A quick "No." And he smiles.

Okay, he's being funny. But there's something to say here. He definitely can be rude, foolishly so. He is paid good money to give speeches and take questions. Usually he does his job but there have been times when he's been bloody-minded, not giving appropriate answers to people who are fans, people who pay the dollars that keep Richler in the lifestyle to which he has become accustomed. We can refuse to suffer fools while still having the manners to suffer the gauche.

I remember when I introduced him to my wife and children. Charm itself. Real charm. This wasn't forced. He seemed genuinely pleased to be meeting these children who had no idea who he was. Perhaps that was why. He was always kind to me as well. But although he agreed to me writing the book and was flattering about my work he obviously didn't like the process of being interviewed. I once asked him why he had agreed to me doing the thing in the first place.

"Someone is going to do it I suppose. And the last thing I want is for some academic to write my biography." I think he believed that I was enough of an outsider to do the job. I flatter myself that he regarded me as enough of a free spirit to capture the essence of Mordecai Richler.

I didn't, and I still haven't. His son Daniel, a novelist in his own right and a respected television broadcaster, says that "he is a very private man. There's an element of closing the door of the house and being completely at home and at peace. Remember, he spent his early years in a family that we'd probably call dysfunctional today. Off he goes to Europe when he is very young, something of a maverick. Does all the things that young writers are supposed to do. Then he makes it. Makes it quite big.

"He might have wanted to change the world in the beginning but now he's more content. He's happy, probably happier now than ever before. I think if there is any essence of Mordecai it is contentment, being happy."

Daniel is the oldest of the children, Florence's son by her first marriage. There are two other boys and three girls. Close? "We are, but we're also a normal modern family with all of the problems that a normal family encounters" says Daniel Richler. He stops for a moment, gathers his thoughts. "Look, he can hurt. You see. He can hurt. Hurt me when he didn't say very much about my book. It did well, I put a great deal of work into it. He was so bloody reticent about it. I still don't know if he's read it or not" and he trails off.

Brother Jake, a journalist at the National Post, is more protective. We speak for more than two hours at a bar and I hear nothing that tells me very much about his father. Just like my interviews with close friends in Toronto and Montreal. Polite, nominally helpful but they give nothing more than what seems like a party line.

Which me brings me back to why I gave up the project and why I said that I became tired of the man. Because I couldn't really find him. Only one person close to Richler gave me information that explained him and he swore me to secrecy. No book is worth the breaking of a word. Nor by "the man" do I mean the bad stuff, the malodorous stuff. I mean the guts, not the gossip.

I could speculate. I could say that Richler's lack of parental love made him what he is. That his novels are some sort of attempt to keep alive the world of his father. That there is a strange coldness about his relationships with many close to him and that his warmest love is in his writing. That his drinking and smoking and rudeness is merely a bandage over a deeper loneliness. Not sure if that gets us anywhere.

We sit drinking beer at his home in the Quebec countryside. Conversation is difficult. I throw him what is surely perfect Richler material. Ever hear of Ted Kid Lewis, Mordecai? "No." He was a world champion boxer from just round the corner from where I grew up. Real name was very long and very Yiddish. One of those great Jewish fighters who dominated boxing before the war. Anyway, when the British fascist leader Oswald Mosley came on the scene, before he was an out-and-out anti-Semite, Lewis was his bodyguard. Can you believe it? Amazing, eh.

Now this is Jewish legend, under belly story-telling, political contradiction. Richler will bite and the conversation will flow. Can't fail.

Quite a guy, I say, quite a guy. Mordecai Richler looks at me and says nothing. Says absolutely nothing. It was then, yes, it was then that I realised that I would be paying a very large advance back to my publisher.

Marnie Rice Profile

There are none so silent as the Canadian lambs. The Oak Ridge Division of the Mental Health Centre, Penetanguishene, Ontario. The place where the bad guys are locked away. The really bad guys. The guys who rape and murder children, who kill everybody around them because they are hearing voices. Not criminally responsible due to insanity. Bad guys.

The juxtaposition is startling. The natural, serene beauty of the lake, bordered by verdant forests, all wrapped in a quintessentially rural tranquillity. And on this hill, overlooking the silver and the green, is a cold building with huge, iron barred doors. The guard at the front jokes that I look like one of the prisoners and that if my wife doesn't see me for five days she might want to call the facility. I have the impression that he gives this line to every visitor. And that every visitor is made more than a little uneasy by the suggestion. But then I am reassured. As I enter through yet another door I notice a large sign. "This is a non-smoking facility." It's going to be okay. I'm in Canada.

I am here to see the person in charge of Oak Ridge, a woman named Marnie Rice, who has revolutionised the study of psychopaths and their ways, who has delved deeper into the lives and lusts of sexual lunatics than most of us would dare to imagine. But first I have the tour.

The place was built in 1933 to separate the mentally ill criminals from the rest. Everyone here uses hospital terminology. The people locked away are patients and not prisoners and they live in rooms and not cells. There are no guards, only nurses. There are 140 men here. And suddenly one of them stops me to have a conversation. "Wanna hear my story?" he asks. The person in me does not, the journalist in me disagrees. "You'd be amazed the way I've been screwed" my new friend insists, his tattoos distending with indignation. My guide thinks that we should now continue our tour. Hannibal is left to his lunch.

The bad guys who are female bad guys go to St. Thomas, where there is a medium security "hospital". Although research is beginning to show that women are as violent as men, they aren't as strong and don't use weapons as often, so the consequences of their violence are less damaging.

The majority at Oak Ridge have been charged with murder or attempted murder. Some of them have committed a series of murders. The rest are here for crimes against the person, often of a sexual nature. And there is the occasional arsonist for good measure. There are psychopaths, psychotics, paranoid schizophrenics and a few manic-depressives. The average stay is five to six years but most leave to go to a medium security prison. Actual freedom takes a very long time.

While their stay here is hardly pleasant it could be worse. They are allowed under the law to refuse treatment and to not even speak to the staff. Many of them have VCRs in their rooms. I ask what they watch. "Oh, anything they want," replies my guide. Anything? "Yeah, anything." Pornography? "Yeah, they watch a lot of that." I'm amazed. "They have the same rights as any other citizen. They order pornography, even if it's misogynistic or brutal, as long as it's legal." Where do they get the money? "Relatives, savings, legal cases."

Long pause. Breath of incredulity. Legal cases? "They're a very litigious lot. There was a wild-cat strike here among the nurses. The patients were in their rooms all day and they sued the union. The union's lawyers decided to settle out of court. I think it was about $4000 a man."

Just as I think I have heard everything I am proved wrong. "They can vote as well. We had an all-candidates meeting." Stop. "They were particularly interested in the free trade issue." Anything else? "They're considered financially competent and have outside bank accounts where they can earn interest. They're also allowed as many phone-calls as they like as long as they have the money." I was wrong. There are many more silent than the Canadian lambs.

Finally to the office of Dr. Marnie E. Rice, the winner of numerous scientific research grants and of the 1995 American Psychological Association's Award for Distinguished Contribution to Research in Public Policy. An associate professor at Queen's and McMaster and the Director of Research at Oak Ridge. She's fifty, looks younger, and wears a blue dress with tiny white spots and a large broach on her right white lapel. There are framed degree certificates on the wall, rubbing shoulders with a large picture of two children walking hand-in-hand through a glade. Lots of deliciously normal photos of family and friends and beside them a button with the words "Psychologists Need Understanding." Very disarming.

The inevitable question is, well, inevitable. What is a nice woman like this doing here with men who rape children, strangle them and throw their bodies in the garbage? "At university I thought I'd like to work with kids. I began with autistic children, the most difficult to work with. At the time I was graduating my husband and I were looking for a place to settle. I saw an advertisement for a psychologist at a maximum security hospital for men in Penetanguishene. My husband had been taken on at a law practise up here so I thought, hey, it might work. I came for a tour and it just sort of grabbed me, back in 1975. I remember seeing a ward with some of the most regressed men, some very retarded people. The place was just so dismal, every patient was like an animal in a zoo. I suppose it was partly their way of trying to put me off, the men in charge who didn't want a woman working here. They would have the patients perform for me, singing, standing on their heads, it was such a horrible place, I thought surely I could do some good here."

From the vulnerability of autistic children to the repugnance of mass murderers. "Yeah, well it was hard in a way but it was amazing to me how easy it was to like these guys. They seemed more like the victims than anything else. You would read about their backgrounds and you would understand. When you heard what they did, how horrible it was, you thought you could never like them, but not after you met them and found out about them. Since then, though, my interest has turned almost completely to the psychopathic personality and it's more difficult to like these guys."

This is Marnie Rice's speciality, her expertise, the subject in which she is a world leader and shaper. A psychopath is a person with a complete a lack of empathy, an inability to appreciate things from another person's view, at least at an emotional level. They don't feel any remorse or guilt, they are easily bored, they demand constant excitement, they're irresponsible, very Machiavellian and tend to be sexually promiscuous. They're also superficially charming so they quite easily convince people that they're sincere. They leave women them pregnant and alone, they exploit business relationships. The ones who break the criminal law become infamous and hated. The ones who only break the moral law often become famous and admired.

"That's true," says the doctor. "The offenders are the violent ones. We don't know much about the non-violent ones because they don't get arrested. It's part of the reason that they're so fascinating. I started researching psychopaths after a programme was put in place here in the late 1960s. They put patients together to take care of each other as a way of treating their behaviour. The programme specifically took psychopaths and put them in a 24 hour, year by year programme with other patients. People came from all over world to see it and it had a great reputation for a very low recidivism rate.

"We decided to have another look. We looked at every guy who had been in the programme for two years and we matched them to guys with the same backgrounds and records who had been to an ordinary prison. The results?" She laughs. "On release the psychopaths did worse. They were learning better ways to con people, better ways to use their charm and glibness to achieve their own ends. Virtually every one who left the programme went on to commit another violent crime. It did show that they could be changed. For the worse."

So there is a realist here, not the owner of a heart that bleeds so red and readily. "The mixture of psychopathy and deviant sexual preference produces time bombs, extremely high risk guys. We've achieved a lot in being able to predict whether they will re-offend. We can do that very well indeed. The problem is, we can't change them for the better. There are things you can do to them that will actually make them even more likely to re-offend on release."

Though she is too modest to say it, this is important, a breakthrough. "You see, it was thought that in psychology it was all about degree. Everybody has a bit of egotism, for example, and everybody has a bit of psychopathy. We found out that this is not true. You are either a psychopath or you are not. There are no in-betweens. The first few years of life will decide whether you will live out the tendency or not. So because you were born with it does not mean that it is immutable – the first few years will turn the switch on or turn it off. If you're born to a loving, nurturing family and a caring society there is a better chance that the switch will not be turned on. So in other words you are better off with Canada and its social system than the United States and their system. Just look at the rates of violence down there."

The research methods that were developed at Oak Ridge begun in Toronto. They are thoroughly Canadian. And they consist of attaching a set of wires to a man's penis and measuring his response to abnormal sex. Oddly enough we haven't seen this achievement commemorated in a Heritage Moment on the CBC, with Peter Gzowski's voice proudly intoning "And it's Canadian."

Marnie Rice laughs. "Quite. Well we're always looking for control subjects, Michael." I mumble something about having to wash my hair. "We attach a gauge to the penis and show slides or tell stories. We learn what these guys find sexually arousing. We also test guys from the community to see what normal men like. They have the biggest arousal to adult women and have less and less arousal to younger women until there's no arousal at all. The offenders are the exact contrary. Similarly with the rapists. Consenting sex doesn't arouse them the way that rape does. Real rape by the way, not as it's portrayed in pornography. Normal men don't like the rape at all. I know it all sounds bizarre but it does seem to precisely predict what happens when guys get out of here."

What about the normal men from the community who turn out to be not so normal men from the community? "Rare. But it has happened. We put an ad in the local paper, without being specific, that we need people to be tested. Once they get here we explain the details and they don't have to go through with it, they're paid anyway. Most of them stay. Twice the results were not what they should have been. With one of the men he knew he had a certain tendency and we offered him counselling if he wanted it. With the other, he was totally unaware. We said nothing."

But I have to say something. The research is fascinating, the results are intriguing, but the conclusions are obvious. The true psychopaths simply cannot be released.

"Of the guys who are in here, some have committed an enormous number of offenses so if we can deal with them we will deal with a huge number of crimes that society worries about. Two thirds of those I see are men who have offended against

children. The worst of the paedophiles are the psychopathic paedophiles, because they have no remorse or empathy." She looks
up, rubs her dress with her hands. "No, I could not justify send-
ing these men back into society. I would not be able to defend not
using capital punishment against a Bernardo, I wouldn't even try.
But as a society we can judge ourselves by the way we treat our
worst members.

"We've tried all sorts of things. We try noxious smells connected to illegal sexual preferences, we try shock treatment. It's
not reliable. Neither is chemical castration. You use a drug that
will suppress sexual desire by suppressing the sex drive across
the board. They hate this so much that as soon as they can get out
of taking it they will. There's no good way of knowing if they're
not taking testosterone at the same time, getting it illegally. And
of course the psychopaths are better at lying about this than anyone else. Even physical castration doesn't work – they can get
testosterone in other ways. And the body produces testosterone
in places other than the gonads."

We've covered child murder, the rape of old women, the gruesome and the grotesque. I am wilting, she is still smiling. "No I
don't turn off the work when I get home and yes the kids do tell
me to get a life. You know there's only been a small number of
men I couldn't work with. Most of them have such terrible backgrounds that there is always at least a tiny area for empathy or
sympathy. Of course that can lead to the danger of manipulation
and indeed we've had female clinicians here who have fallen in
love with these guys. You can know everything about psychopathy and still fall for them, or for some of them. I myself had to
overcome the knowledge that some of these guys were looking at
me in a certain way, particularly in the past, and doing goodness
knows what in their cells and in their minds. But I've never really
been frightened. There was one time when a guy, who died pretty
soon after, grabbed me and put his arms round my neck but all
the other patients helped me. I've only been assaulted once," she
says, with a nonchalance that is either impressive or ridiculous.

Marnie Rice walks me to the door, and to the next door and to
the next door. The guard makes a similar joke to the one he made
when I arrived some hours earlier and the good doctor wishes me
goodbye. I return the comment to this optimist in a polluted sea
of pessimism and realise that it is people like this, people of hope,
who make the agony of hopelessness almost bearable.

C. S. Lewis Centenary

He liked to be called Jack. Plain Jack. It suited his character, or so he thought. Certainly those who knew him said that he looked like an ordinary high-street butcher. Until he spoke and until he wrote. Oh, and how he wrote. Mere Christianity, The Screwtape Letters, Surprised by Joy and The Lion, The Witch and The Wardrobe among so many others. C.S. Lewis, Clive Staples, one of the finest popular communicators of the Christian message and the Christian life.

Lewis was born one hundred years ago, November 1898 in Belfast, Northern Ireland. As such this is his centenary and, commercialism being what it is, we are in the middle of a thunderstorm of books and videos. But it is a sweet rain and it is a joy to be made wet. Lewis would have laughed at such antics, always considering himself to be an ordinary teacher and an ordinary Christian.

In fact he was a most extraordinary teacher. A lecturer at both Oxford and Cambridge University, he was considered one of the finest minds of his generation by fellow professors. His "English Literature in the Sixteenth Century Excluding Drama" and "The Allegory of Love" are still considered to be academic masterpieces. But it is Lewis the Christian who changed the world. His genius was the ability to convey highly complicated and complex ideas in a straightforward and understandable manner. Like some grand knight of common sense he charged through the ranks of cluttered thinking, double-talk and atheism, seldom taking any prisoners.

"There are two equal and opposite errors into which our race can fall about the devils" he wrote. "One is to disbelieve in their existence. The other is to believe, and to feel an excessive and unhealthy interest in them. They themselves are equally pleased by both errors, and hail a materialist or a magician with the same delight."

Of the increasingly common statement that Jesus might have been a great moral teacher but was not the son of God Lewis pointed out that this contradicted Christ's own claims. "A man who was merely a man and said the sort of things Jesus said would not be a great moral teacher. He would either be a lunatic – on the level with the man who says he is a poached egg – or else he would be the Devil of Hell. You can shut Him up for a fool, you can spit at Him and kill Him as a demon; or you can fall at His feet and call Him Lord and God. But let us not come with any patronising nonsense about His being a great human teacher. He has not left that open to us. He did not intend to."

Lewis declared himself a Christian in 1929, "perhaps the most dejected and reluctant convert in all England." It was as though he had tried to avoid the inevitable, considering every argument against Christianity, forcing himself to take on all of the objections his fertile mind could produce. Each one he overcame. By the time his intellect was well and truly won over his emotional being simply fell into place.

From this point on everything he wrote was informed and enlivened by his Christianity. But Lewis was too subtle and too clever to knock people over the head with his faith. He knew that talking was far more effective than shouting. In 1950 "The Lion, The Witch and The Wardrobe" was published, the first of seven books in the Narnia series. The Christian metaphors and imagery are obvious to most adults but to children the stories are merely delicious and unforgettable. As such they have sown the seeds of belief in innumerable young minds. Certainly in mine. When as a little boy I read of a great lion king called Aslan giving his life for a bad child, of his coming to life again, of his defeating an evil queen, of a magical world that we all could enter, I could only weep with excitement. Thirty years later I weep with gratitude.

In 1952 Lewis's "Mere Christianity" appeared. The title reflected the author's attempt to remove Christianity away from those who would adapt it, alter it, dilute it, change what is pure and pristine into something that is confused and confusing. Again, he did not pepper his prose with quotes from the scriptures because he knew that this would have a limited effect with the majority of his readers. It is seldom advisable to use Biblical statements to argue with people who do not believe in the Bible. What he did do was to show that a belief in God was logical and that from this belief an acceptance of Jesus Christ was unavoidable. He reversed the equation offered by the secular world, that it is the thoughtless who become Christians, the thoughtful who reject it. Simply, he summed up the arguments like an angel:

"There is no need to be worried by facetious people who try to make the Christian hope of Heaven ridiculous by saying they do not want to spend eternity playing harps. The answer to such people is that if they cannot understand books written for grown-ups, they should not talk about them. All the scriptural imagery (harps, crowns, gold, etc) is, of course, a merely symbolical attempt to express the inexpressible. People who take these symbols literally might as well think that when Christ told us to be like doves, He meant that we were to lay eggs."

In the 1950s Lewis met and fell in love with Joy Davidman, an American convert from Judaism. The marriage was beautiful but brief and Joy died in 1960. The movie Shadowlands chronicled some of the magnificence of the relationship but managed to expunge most of the Christianity from the story. What brought them together, what sustained them during the agony of cancer and what saved Lewis after the loss was a commitment to Jesus Christ. Just as in Lewis's day, the entertainment industry is not comfortable with such a notion.

After Joy's death Lewis wrote a short book entitled "A Grief Observed", an exploration of his own feelings following his wife's death. "Grief still feels like fear," he said. "Up till this time I always had too little time. Now there is nothing but time. Almost pure time, empty successiveness." He told friends he could no longer remember Joy's face. Until it came to him that she was there all along, just waiting. Her face shone again in his mind and God's love and certainty overwhelmed his pain.

Though his remaining years were never as happy as those spent with Joy he wrote and lectured, becoming a famous man in Europe as well as North America. He died in 1963, on the same day as President Kennedy. Because of this his death received less coverage than it might. Something that would have pleased Jack Lewis. Yet his funeral in Oxford was well attended, with so many people grieving. But grief was quite unnecessary. Lewis had known that what was to come was far greater than what we have already known. And he was reunited with Joy. As for the lion Aslan, some say they heard him roar all day, from Oxford to the ends of the Earth.

Gore Vidal: A Biography

By Fred Kaplan – Doubleday, 850pp

The scene is London's River Thames, the Parliament buildings juxtaposed with Dickensian warehouses in that quintessentially British practicality. A patrician American talks to a camera as he gives his thoughts on the novelist Angus Wilson. "His contribution to this country was great," says the man in the expensive suit. "Compare this Wilson to the Prime Minister, Harold Wilson, and you'll see who left the greater legacy." Unexpectedly a passing boat releases a foghorn fart. Unflappable, our hero the commentator turns to the lens and say, simply, "Sorry Harold." Smiles, turns and walks away.

Gore Vidal is clever. No serious person would doubt that for a moment. Less clever than he thinks he is. No serious person "should" doubt that for a moment. But the Americans, for all their protestations, still fall headlong for what they see as class and elitism. Witness the triumph of the Kennedy boys. Vidal detests the reality of the United States, and the Americans love him for it. Fred Kaplan positively adores him for it.

The biographer of Thomas Carlyle and Charles Dickens, Kaplan is more comfortable with the nineteenth-century than with times modern, but with Vidal that will do nicely. Although born in 1925, he has cultivated the manners and morals of the Victorian liberal artist. His speech, his writing, his distance from the people all place him in the school of Washington Irving and Henry James rather than in the club of Norman Mailer and Philip Roth.

He grew up in Washington, an emerging witness to the courtship and statecraft of a maturing super-power. His father was a director of Roosevelt's cabinet, his grandfather, Thomas Gore, was Oklahoma's first Senator. Kaplan is meticulous in explaining the influence on Vidal of his grandfather. The old man's intellect and wit moulded his grandson, the patrician surroundings of home smoothed the edges, a succession of boarding schools probably developed an inchoate homosexuality. Kaplan is a product of his age and never deals with Vidal's sexual preference with anything other than slavish approval. Sad but predictable.

After a non-combatant role in World War Two, a career in literature seemed inevitable. Vidal never seriously considered any other occupation, because unlike most American novelists he was never financially needy. A novel based on his wartime experiences, Williwaw, appeared in 1946, followed two years later by The City and the Pillar, perhaps the first mainstream work of fiction to deal with homosexuality. He was also earning a reputation as a raconteur and a political commentator, assuming the mantle of the philosopher king who spat down barbs from on high.

He could and can be genuinely witty. On Ronald Reagan, "A triumph of the embalmer's art." On corporal punishment, "I'm all for bringing back the birch, but only between consenting adults." On friendship, "Whenever a friend succeeds, a little something in me dies." Amusing, but not profound. More "Cheers" than Chesterton.

There were big and bigger novels, many of them with a historical context. Burr and Lincoln were sharp and illuminating, Live from Golgotha and Hollywood less so. But it was Myra Breckenridge in 1968, about a man who dies and returns to life as a woman, that established Vidal as the craftsman he most certainly is. Play-offs level for sure, but not quite Stanley Cup. Kaplan disagrees. "He was writing from deeper, more spontaneous sources than had readily been reachable in previous attempts. For the first time he was decisively and totally liberated from the narrow realism from which he had started."

The reviews were generally positive, and the critics gave Vidal the ultimate literary fillip, they said he was anti-establishment. Vidal ran with it, forming friendships with other famous types who were, apparently, foes of the ruling class. The relationships with Paul Newman and Truman Capote are particularly well chronicled, as is the infamous feud with conservative doyen William F. Buckley. What characterized Vidal and his fellow foes of the system is that, ironically, they were establishment from their toes to their ties.

Vidal ran for office, appeared in movies, wrote more books and essays, and then went to live in Italy. What Kaplan fails to grasp, or to admit, is that his subject is so uncomfortable with America as to actually despise it. Probably because he just doesn't understand it.

Nothing revealed this more explicitly than a nasty little piece he wrote about the relationship between Jews and homosexuals entitled The Pink Triangle and the Yellow Star, His tone was so vehement and intolerant that if it had come from, say, a conservative author, he may have been ostracized as an anti-Semite. Vidal displayed a grotesque ignorance of the Holocaust and an equal lack of knowledge of his country. He claimed that American Christians hated both Jews and, his term, "Fags" equally, so that the two groups ought to form an alliance.

Vidal should have known that The New York Review would never have published such a fatuous work, but his reaction to their refusal merely demonstrated more, shall we say, ambivalence towards his would-be allies. Vidal didn't understand American Christians, American Jews, American blacks and even American homosexuals. But he does understand himself, and rather likes what he knows.

So does Fred Kaplan, a little too much. "American writers want to be not good but great; and so are neither," said Vidal. Kaplan is actually a good biographer, but in spite of massive research and work, he has let hagiography smother his art. He is not great.

Literary Converts

By Joseph Pearce – Ignatius, 452pp

I used to throw rocks and bottles at British author Joseph Pearce. He was a young fascist leader, I was a young half-Jew from London's east-end. Politics, soccer team, tribe, political demonstrations. Violence and rhetoric. Something the liberal bourgeoisie have never understood. This was the working class at war and play, far less harmful in fact than the well-groomed whim of a lawyer or politician.

Two decades later and I am no longer throwing missiles and Joseph Pearce is no longer preaching racism. Although we have never met we grew up in almost identical economic circumstances, only a few miles from one another, the same age. Now both of us find ourselves as orthodox believers within the Roman Catholic Church. A hard-knock conversion on a rocky road, a tug rather than a twitch upon the thread.

The similarities continue. I write books, so does Joseph Pearce. And he writes them extremely well. The biographer of G.K. Chesterton and J.R.R Tolkein, his latest offering is an account of people of letters becoming people of faith. It is also the finest single volume on the subject I have encountered.

The thesis is straightforward. The twentieth-century witnessed an extraordinary number of conversions of great writers from cynicism and secularism to a crisp and conservative Christianity, usually of a Roman Catholic kind. Indeed there is a crescendo-like quality to the book, as conversion follows conversion with something approaching inevitability, even invincibility.

Some of the conversions are familiar to us. That grand knight of paradox, G.K. Chesterton, spending years defending Catholicism before he becomes a Catholic. Evelyn Waugh lowering his guard of condescension so as to join what his hero Hilaire Belloc, a cradle Catholic who figures large in the book, referred to as an essentially proletarian institution. Waugh was once asked how he could be so disagreeable and still be a Catholic. "Imagine" he replied, "how bad I'd be if I wasn't a Catholic!"

There is Grahame Greene's agonised path to Rome, though according to Pearce he was a more faithful believer than his most recent biographers have stated. Some of the best and brightest of their generation are here. Ronald Knox, Compton MacKenzie, Alfred Noyes, Malcolm Muggeridge and R.H. Benson. The latter was the son of the Archbishop of Canterbury, the most important Anglican in the world.

The opening chapter begins with the turn of the nineteenth and twentieth centuries, and flies in the face of contemporary sexual politics. Oscar Wilde is exploited today as some sort of homosexual Hercules, a martyr for the love that dare not speak its name but now never shuts the hell up. In fact Wilde was not really homosexual at all and only "used" young men because he had venereal disease and was frightened of infecting his wife. More than this, however, Wilde became a Catholic. The lion of decadence became the lamb of Christianity.

He was joined in the Church, and this I did not know, by his nemesis the Marquis of Queensbury. The old aristocrat was known for three things. The rules of boxing, the attack upon Oscar Wilde that sent the poet to prison, and militant atheism. Yet he too bent the knee. An extraordinary vision. The voices of God hatred and God mockery joined together in a melodious chorus of worship.

Pearce chronicles all this with a fine style. Of the great T.S. Eliot, the American convert to Anglo-Catholicism whose efforts to appear English bordered on the absurd, he writes, "The problem was that he had become naturalized without becoming natural". He is also perceptive. Writing of a debate between the Edith Sitwell and Alfred Noyes he discovers that the press "reported that Sitwell, the champion of modernity, spoke without notes, whereas the old-fashioned Alfred Noyes delivered his text from a ponderous manuscript. It was, of course, the other way round." How little has changed.

"Taken as a whole" writes Pearce, "this network of minds represented a potent Christian response to the age of unbelief." He is right. To paraphrase G.K. Chesterton, when people stop believing in Christianity they do not believe in something else, they believe in everything else. That, of course, is the crisis of our time, and a crisis that Joseph Pearce predicts so poignantly in this startlingly necessary book. I'm rather glad none of the rocks and bottles found their target.

The Muted Voice: Religion and the Media

By Michael W. Higgins – Novalis, 99pp.

Winston Churchill always denied saying that "an empty cab arrived at the House of Commons and the leader of the Labour Party got out." It was witty enough, accurate enough to be the great man. But perhaps it was just a little too lacking in courtesy.

Fifty years later an empty parcel arrives at my home. Inside is a copy of The Muted Voice by one Michael Higgins. I lack Churchill's wit, but I am often quite accurate and I have no time for misplaced courtesy.

For those of us who care deeply about the place and state of faith in the Canadian media a thorough and balanced literary exploration is long overdue. Thus the outrage over this offering. Consisting of three lectures delivered by the President of St.Jerome's University in Waterloo, this booklet is less a wasted opportunity than a downright insult to the informed and the inquisitive.

That the media is largely indifferent to faith issues is surely axiomatic. It is only when the more rancid flavours of faith tickle the taste buds of the secular culture that anybody takes notice. Dirty vicars, homosexual ordination or women dressing up as priests.

Any serious analysis of the problem would be welcomed. But Higgins' purview is so limited as to be stifling. The author appears to live in a world bound on one side by the Globe and Mail and the CBC, on the other by a handful of fashionable Anglicans and liberal Catholics. His chapters concern television, radio and print. But where is the meat, be it kosher, Halal or good old Baptist bacon?

We need statistics, we need interviews with faith leaders, we need the opinions of editors, we need alternatives. In short, we need a serious book that will demand change.

Instead Higgins gives us no solutions and in fact forms very few questions. He simply bemoans the fact that his sort of religion is not given enough space in the media, when in fact his type of religion receives more than most. If any branch of faith is treated kindly in the media it is the twig of well-connected liberal Christianity.

He judges television, for example, according to his own limited experiences on various shows and then contemptuously disregards them as being inadequate. He might be right. But he simultaneously splatters disgust towards, amongst others, "bible-thumping televangelists." An ugly phrase that immediately closes the debate about the subject. Higgins might not like TV preaching, but no intelligent person can dismiss one of the phenomena of religious television with a gutter insult. The author is part of the problem.

This is elitism at its worst. Snobbery without cleverness. In between all those references to himself are the unforgivable "Methinks", "Veteran scribe" and "That's how I became a scriptwriter." Oh Lord.

Higgins ignores those faith communities genuinely victimised by the media. Serious Catholics with a pro-life and pro-family position, committed evangelicals who are invariably abused in the press, practicing Moslems routinely painted as fools or terrorists.

The stories of these folk remain to be told. They concern class and race stereotypes, nasty prejudice and sheer hypocrisy. If Michael Higgins had left the comfort of his complacency he would have found the aching truth about faith and the Canadian media

Perhaps the last word on this little effort should go to, well, to the last word. The CBC's Michael Enright gives a blurb on the back, lauding the book as "logical" and "startling." This is the same man who described the Roman Catholic Church as the greatest criminal organisation in the world outside of the mafia. Poor Professor Higgins. He just doesn't get it.

Anne Morrow Lindbergh: Her Life

By Susan Hertog Doubleday. 561pp

Fly away Charles; fly away Anne; fly back Charles; fly back Anne. Anne Morrow Lindbergh that is, the wife of the great aviator Charles Lindbergh and author and flight pioneer in her own right. This extraordinary woman withdrew all cooperation from Susan Hertog in the writing of this biography and now finds herself in the middle of a bubbling literary controversy about who said what to whom and why. Which will do nothing to damage the sales of the book but might make it slightly difficult for American freelance journalist Hertog to find further willing subjects for her biographical attentions.

There is absolutely no doubt that the author spent more than a decade on the project and did her homework with a massive diligence. Some, however, have wondered whether Hertog really knew her subject. Intimacy is certainly implied in the book, but apparently Anne Lindbergh never fully cooperated with Hertog and eventually forced the biographer to remove all direct family quotations from the work and did not allow her access to personal papers.

Ten interviews were certainly granted, along with some conversations with the Lindbergh family. But according to the Lindberghs this was because matriarch Anne was told that the book would be a feminist study of the women of the family, not a biography. As soon they discovered otherwise they broke off all contact. Hertog in turn says that the nature of the project was made clear from the very beginning.

Oh dear oh dear. How these clever types do squabble. But why? Quite clearly Lindbergh was afraid that her husband's links to the Nazis would once again be explored, and that Hertog might find one or two other German-speaking skeletons in the cupboard. She needn't have worried.

If anything this competent and readable book takes Anne Lindbergh's side, placing her firmly in the role of victim in her husband's political flirtations and describing her as a feminist and a pioneer. In the author's hands she is a cultured and sensitive woman who was certainly as accomplished as her husband and abundantly more sensitive when it came to political and social trends.

The daughter of the U.S. Ambassador to Mexico, this intensely busy and vibrant woman left her family to attend college before 1920 had shown its face, and at the age of twenty-three met and fell for the dashing Mr. Lindbergh.

Although they were deeply in love they were in fact quite unsuited to one another. She had said that she always wanted to "marry a hero" and this she did. But Charles was away being, well, being heroic, for much of the time and his wife's sense of isolation was sometimes overwhelming. She would almost drown in her loneliness. Her life jacket was writing. She was a good poet, a better prose stylist. In fact her 1955 opus Gift From The Sea not only changed her life, it changed that of her biographer. She became a devotee precisely because she read this book.

But first came the flying, when Anne was sometimes her husband's co-pilot and navigator. She also flew solo, and according to her biographer almost relished the danger. Out of this came her first book, North to the Orient and later Listen! The Wind. These were the good days, the grand days, the together days.

It was the kidnapping and death of Anne Lindbergh's baby son, Charles Junior, in 1932 that changed so much. The Lindberghs were stars in the somewhat muddy firmament of 1930s America. He broke flying records, she helped him and chronicled the events. They were beautiful and rich. And vulnerable.

Hertog is magnificent here. "Anne thought she heard a baby cry, but before she could speak, she was told it was the shrill of a cat. Later, Anne was certain it was the howl of the wind." That wind blew through the Lindbergh household and never stopped its bitter journey. They were devastated, so was America.

After the slaughter of the innocent the family retreated, building a wall around their other children. They were convinced, and Hertog believes they were right, that it was the press and the publicity that had killed their beloved little son.

As for Charles' politics, Anne was embarrassed by her husband's penchant for the Nazis but in truth he rejoiced in the Ger-

man defeat, more concerned with the Soviet menace than anything else. He died in 1974 but Anne flew and wrote on. There
were volumes of autobiography and novels, there was financial
assistance to students, colleges and societies. "My passport photo
is one of the most remarkable photographs I have ever seen – no
retouching, no shadows, no flattery – just stark me" she once
said. Which makes it all the more strange that she would object to
this jubilantly fair and balanced biography. My condolences to
Ms. Hertog.

Hostage to Fortune

Lisa Jardine and Alan Stewart – Hill and Wang, 637pp

There is something both delicious and compelling about decline. The decay of grandeur, the melting away of glory, the aching absence of success. If any monarch epitomised the shining triumph of the English way it was Elizabeth, the first of that name. This was pure Anglo-Saxon genius, not the contrived achievements of later centuries. Pirates and princes, anarchists and governors, poets and killers. The second half of the sixteenth-century was England's era. She kicked away at mighty Spain with the Protestant world cheering and even half the Catholic globe admiring the little country's crazed tenacity. Drake and Raleigh, Shakespeare and Marlowe.

There is an anecdote that symbolises the quintessence of the age. One of the Virgin queen's greatest sailors is outnumbered five to one by the Spaniards. He sinks three of the enemy's ships but is finally captured. He is mortally injured but the men of Spain still move away from him as he comes on board their craft. They are as frightened as they are respectful. He sits, pours a glass of wine down his throat and then proceeds to eat the glass and laugh at his foe and his predicament. The escapade is turned into a poem back in London, and it glows like a Tudor turquoise.

Francis Bacon has cried out for a thorough and up-to-date biography for thirty years now and in this work he has it. He was born in 1561, and was thus a young man in his prime when the Spanish Armada was defeated, when the London theatres were at their busiest and the Elizabethan Renaissance was splashing over Europe. As the son of the queen's Lord Keeper he witnessed the major events of the day and met Elizabeth herself. But Bacon was of that second generation of Elizabethans, those who stood on the shoulders of the men who had really stared at greatness.

The queen died in 1603 and was succeeded by a dribbling pederast from Edinburgh, James VI of Scotland, the first of England.

This was the man who fondled his young boys in court, the king who had Sir Walter Raleigh executed. The year before Bacon died James' son Charles came to the throne. He was to lose his throne and his head to the Puritans under Oliver Cromwell.

Thus, decline. The scene was set for anyone with an eye and a mind. Bacon had one of the finest eyes and perhaps the best mind of his generation. Trained as a lawyer, he entered Parliament in his early twenties and was soon involved with the power blocs at court. He was given generous support by the Earl of Essex, but later played a key role in the trial and execution of the man for treason. Elizabeth never completely trusted Bacon, partly because of his homosexuality, and although he was one of the two or three most powerful men in England by the end of her reign, it was under James that he became first attorney general and then Lord Chancellor.

As a politician he was sly and cold but as a judge he was incisive and deeply clever. He rulings and decisions laid a foundation for constitutional and, to a lesser extent, civil law in England and, by extension, Canada. As the authors demonstrate, his legal abilities could have been the result of his not actually liking people very much, leaving him free to judge with a genuine objectivity.

He was also a scientist, whose theory of scientific classification and work on differentiating between the natural and supernatural world was ahead of its time. And he wrote. Oh how he wrote. His essays, History of Henry VIII and De Sapientia Veterum are astounding even for an age that normalised the brilliant.

He also dabbled in the occult, took drugs, used stolen bodies for medical research and perhaps collaborated with Shakespeare on some works and is one of the candidates put forward by those people obsessed with the idea that Shakespeare didn't write Shakespeare. Bacon didn't write the works of Shakespeare, and even if he did, a movie called Bacon In Love would have been dreadful for a whole host of reasons!

What Jardine and Stewart have done is to provide a contemporary analysis of an historic man. Here was a soul trying to make a living. "Francis was obliged to make a working career for himself in the law – a career which constantly interfered with his beloved intellectual pursuits ... The ideal scenario, however, would have involved no demands of employment on Francis Bacon's time whatsoever."

Peppered through the book are Bacon's attempts to find easy money as government employee, royal favourite or high-priced lawyer. An individual version of a legal dream-team, but with twice the wit. He took on cases and stabbed friends in the back purely for money. The book shows how his life became a back-stairs existence, partly because of his sexuality and his dabbling in magic, but also because he was simply better than the mediocrities who peopled the court of James I and had to hide from their resentment. He was, we learn, effectively born twenty years too late.

The cause of Bacon's death is disputed but the most likely, and Good God I hope it is the most authentic, version concerns Bacon trying to stuff a dead hen with snow, to see if it would keep. It did, he didn't. He caught a cold and his weak health let him down. By the time of his death he was financially secure but politically outcast.

He was a nearly man for all seasons. His achievements are mainly in the legal, whereas they should have been in the intellectual. Given a good monarch he could also have been a statesman of historical proportions. Yet nobody more embodies the growing darkness, cloudy intrigue and brilliant if empty philosophy of the age like Bacon. He was, then, perhaps the first truly modern man. Here chronicled by the truly first modern biography of him.

The Unmasking of Oscar Wilde

By Joseph Pearce – Harper Collins, 301pp

Oh how we have learnt recently the importance of being Oscar. Festivals, movies, plays and unbridled devotion. The importance, that is, of being Oscar Wilde. The author of, amongst others, Lady Windermere's Fan and The Picture of Dorian Gray. The accepted line is that Wilde was a gentle giant of the intellect, an inspired wit and raconteur whose homosexuality led him into battle with a callous British establishment. The bad guys won and Wilde went to prison, where he was broken beyond repair.

Not quite so, says British historian and biographer Joseph Pearce in his new biography of the man. Certainly Wilde was the painted butterfly of the late nineteenth-century, but to view him as some sort of political activist is quite ridiculous. In fact Wilde was not really homosexual at all, only frequenting a notorious male brothel after developing venereal disease and being told by his doctor that he could never again have a sexual relationship with his wife.

His affairs were sordid and sad, often with semi-literate boys who "pleasured gentlemen" for cash and betrayed them as soon as they left the building. If there was perhaps one homosexual love in Wilde's life it was with the son of the Marquis of Queensbury, a spoiled aristocrat known as Bosie. Once again, according to Pearce this is not the tale we have been told in recent years.

That politicised image concerned Bosie's brutal father persecuting Wilde and forcing him into incarceration. It is true that Queensbury was capable of baseness, but he was obliged to watch as the fat, 40-year-old Wilde paraded Bosie, young enough to be his own, around London as a play thing. Not easy for a father to tolerate. More than this, it was Wilde, not Queensbury, who eventually launched a legal battle for libel. It is simply that Queensbury won.

Another aspect of the life usually hidden to the point of exclusion is that after prison Wilde rejected his earlier ways, apologised for them and embraced Roman Catholicism. Rather than some grand icon of decadence he actually became a gentle knight of orthodoxy. "Much of my moral obliquity is due to the fact that my father would not allow me to become a Catholic", he told a journalist. "The artistic side of the Church would have cured my degeneracies."

Pearce has in many ways given us a life of Wilde for the new century. He celebrates the man's undoubted literary gifts but refuses to bow down to the gods of political correctness. Which is entirely appropriate, because the last person who would have done so would have been one Oscar Wilde.

If the great Irishman is deserving of study because of his genius, his young lover and eventual cause of shame, Lord Alfred Douglas, is of interest for entirely different reasons. The nickname Bosie was merely a play on Boysie, a title given to Douglas when he was tiny. There is something strangely appropriate about it.

There have been books about the man in the past, but nothing of the scope and ambition of Douglas Murray's effort. The youth of the author guaranteed the book celebrity status before it was even produced. Douglas Murray is still at university in Britain, and was hard at work on the book whilst still in his teens. So impressed were publishers on both sides of the Atlantic that the industrious Mr. Murray became a very wealthy young man indeed.

And good for him. Because this is a thorough, well-rounded and startlingly readable account of a severely troubled figure. He was an impressive youngster, talented as athlete as well as poet and thought to be the most beautiful man at Oxford University. Opportunities fell at his feet like raindrops from some loving sky. Until he met the storm that was Oscar Wilde.

There is, according to Murray, mutual exploitation in what happened next. Clearly Wilde devoured Bosie's youth and looks and lived vicariously through this bright young thing. Equally Bosie bathed in Wilde's reputation and also used the notoriety of the relationship to ridicule his father. Wilde was old enough to know better, Bosie was young enough to know best.

Contrary to what has been considered true until now, we are told here that Bosie remained loyal to Wilde through trials, prison and subsequent shunning by fashionable society. But what Murray explains so well is that the entire Wilde episode took up only a few years of Bosie's life. Wilde died in 1900, Bosie lived for almost another half-century. In short, what did he do?

Strangely enough he too converted to Roman Catholicism, but not before rejoining literary society and becoming friends with George Bernard Shaw and the massively overrated artists and writers of The Bloomsbury Group. He launched and edited a small circulation magazine, wrote poetry and occupied a place on the periphery of intellectual society. He also followed Wilde in another way, in that he served a period in prison.

The reason was a libeling of Winston Churchill, against whom he had launched a virtual vendetta some years earlier. By 1924 Churchill, in and out of political office, had turned enough cheeks and decided to sue. Bosie was nothing if not irresponsible and his accusations against Churchill of political corruption resulted in a cell and a badly fitting striped suit.

In a way it was indicative of Bosie's life after Wilde. Attempts at fame and success resulting in failure and sometimes in a quite pernicious darkness. He was intensely jealous of those around him and as his age increased and his looks declined he lashed out with an increasing absurdity. He faced other libel cases, fell headlong into a rancid anti-semitism, became almost permanently and sometimes hysterically unhappy.

He died in 1945, largely forgotten and largely deserving of it. "A deeply flawed personality, perhaps," writes Murray. "A quarrelsome snob or bigot, even. Douglas was a highly complex, but in many ways still loveable figure who, against all odds, has found a place in the history of letters and politics."

Murray is actually being somewhat generous. But then he has a right to be. He has glimpsed through that cloud of unknowing to give us a clear view of a paradoxically significant figure of recent history. We ought to be grateful. So should Lord Alfred Douglas.

The Doctor and the Detective: A Biography of Sir Arthur Conan Doyle

By Martin Booth – McClelland & Stewart, 371pp, $42.99

I learnt when I was writing my biography of Arthur Conan Doyle that few authors inspire as much passion, and pomposity, as the creator of Sherlock Holmes. To many people this fine author and better man may as well still be living. He takes on the role of a favourite relative who needs an admiring younger nephew's protection. "What! They took a shot at Uncle Arthur. Doris, hand me my revolver and pack me a good lunch."

It is not, of course, Doyle himself to whom these people devote themselves but the consulting detective with a magnifying glass and a sidekick. Holmes has outlived his creator, and the whims of literary taste, more effectively than perhaps any other figure in the history of fiction. As Doyle has faded into a miasma of pipe smoke Holmes has emerged with an increasingly sharp focus.

As British author Martin Booth makes clear this is precisely what Doyle did not want. He killed off Holmes because he was tired of the man and was obliged to resurrect him only due to public and commercial pressure. Doyle wanted to be taken seriously as an author of so much more than detective stories. He was proud of his historical romances involving medieval knights and Napoleonic generals, of his science-fiction works and, most of all, his journalistic writing about the supernatural.

Born into a Roman Catholic Edinburgh family, Doyle was raised by a dominant mother and a passive, physically and mentally ill father. The clan was poor but proud. Doyle was given a private education and trained as a doctor.

It is these formative years that Booth explores so delightfully well. Doyle the robust, sporty schoolboy constantly raising his fists for the sake of honour. Doyle the troubled youth hurt and bewildered by his father's alcoholism and instability. Doyle the medical student. It was as the latter that he came under the influence of Dr. Joseph Bell, a man who used deduction to solve medical mysteries. He was also rather tall and had a long nose. You'd have to be Watson at his most dim not to see the influence. Booth tells us of Doyle's tough time in general practice and of his embrace of adventure and travel as a form of emotional compensation. He set sail on a whaler, for example, drinking in the stories of the hardened sailors along with the seawater and the bad rum. Back in England there was the approach of despair, perhaps depression. Until he wrote what he considered a forgettable tale that begun with a former army surgeon meeting with a most extraordinary private investigator.

"I am not, repeat not, Sherlock Holmes and he is most certainly not me", said Doyle to anybody who would listen. Too late. The success of the books makes Harry Potter look like, well, like Harry Potter. The relationship between author and creature is best depicted by a contemporary cartoon showing Doyle manacled to a tiny Holmes, unable to break out of a lucrative but ultimately painful incarceration.

The tragedy of the man's life, and this is something that the author explains with a jubilant intelligence, is that whilst Doyle thought himself a great author who should be remembered for other works, his non-Sherlockian oeuvre now appears dated and dusty.

But it is the phenomenon of Doyle the spiritualist that presents the most difficulties. For a man who exposed atrocities in the Belgian Congo, who was knighted for his medical work during the Boer War, who defended the underdog and the underbelly, he was a most gullible fellow when it came to ghouls and fairies.

Simply, Doyle was a spiritualist of spiritualists. Photographs by Yorkshire schoolgirls of gossamer winged figures convinced him. Mediums talking to cousin Maud who had been dead a decade won him over. A close friendship with Harry Houdini broke apart because the escapologist continually exposed fake s_ances. "Arthur, believe me", said the New Yorker, "these aren't real."

"Perhaps to you", replied Doyle.

The only film footage we have of him, and fascinating it is, shows the plump, smiling author dismissing Holmes and promoting the cause of his life, that of spiritualism. Here Booth is perhaps too much the cynic. One doesn't have to follow Casper to appreciate Doyle's search for the life beyond. It has to be remembered that virtually everyone after 1918 had lost a close relative in the bloody quagmire of that horribly misnamed war to end wars. Doyle was no exception.

To a very large extent when he died in 1930 Doyle was a disappointed man. His books had made him wealthy but he had lost the rhythm of his times. Like some knight of old who had somehow strayed into decaying modernity, he was severely out of place and out of fashion. Yet to the last there was truth and decency. This was a man worth knowing. And this is very much a book worth reading.

Karl Marx

By Francis Wheen – Fourth Estate, 431pp

Any biographer of Karl Marx faces an inexorable problem. Marx is not a man, he is a cause. To offer an opinion of him is not to pass judgement on a philosopher or an economist, but to proclaim a view of the last century of history. It is the triumph of British journalist and author Francis Wheen that he has given us the most satisfying and, as near as is possible, objective life of Marx in living memory. Simply, reality in place of rhetoric. And, important this, readability. Anyone who has looked at other studies will appreciate the true meaning of prolix. Why use one word when a political statement will do. As the great screenwriter Robert Bolt said of bringing the great dead to life, "You've got to be able to smell them as if they were standing next to you in a crowded room."

Marx was paradox personified. The child of privilege who claimed to speak for the poor. The Jew who fell headlong into anti-Semitism. The snob who preached equality. Finally, beyond his life, the idealist whose followers slaughtered their way through entire continents.

He was born in 1818 into the German middle-class, his father a lawyer who had abandoned Judaism for the more comfortable state religion of Lutheran Christianity. The conversion was entirely political. Contrary to what some would have us believe Marx suffered hardly any persecution because of his Jewish ancestry, attended the prestigious universities of Bonn and Berlin and even indulged in dueling, that traditional pastime of the Germanic ruling class.

More than this, and here Wheen is most perceptive, when Marx fell in love with Johanna Bertha Julie Jenny von Westphalen, the daughter of an extremely Prussian aristocrat, he was met not with disdain but with a genuinely liberal enthusiasm. So what did the kid have to complain about? Not a lot.

What the book reveals so bitingly is that Marx was almost child-like in his irresponsibility and naïveté. His wife cared for him as if she were a mother, paying his creditors, sobering him up and making sure he changed his dirty clothes when it became acutely necessary – proving that the great Mr. Bolt had a point. In later life he would not even have finished any of his books if he were not being constantly scolded by wife, children and friends.

So Marxism was not the result of experience but of imagination. The German universities of his time were drenched in Hegelianism and nobody has ever seriously doubted the fact that Marx "borrowed" much of his philosophy from the father of objective idealism. Added to this was timing. Between Marx's birth and his final years at university there were revolutions of some sort in almost every country in Europe. From Britain's minor "Peterloo Massacre" of protestors to France's major upheaval of 1830, the European digestive system was not handling the food of change at all well.

What impressed Marx was not the success of all this but its quintessential failure. Power changed hands, but the hands were always finely groomed. Wheen's "tremendous show-off and sadistic intellectual thug" applied a weird logic to humanity and developed a theory of history and of political change. It was if his writing could barely keep pace with the events it described and predicted. In 1848 came, in effect, world revolution, with those laborious barricades being piled up again in half-a-dozen world capitols. Marx was kept busy.

Germany became understandably less accommodating to the man when he called for the people to rise up and murder their rulers so Marx moved to England, to bathe in the sunlight that was the financial, moral and intellectual tutelage of Friedrich Engels. "A penniless, deracinated exile in a strange land might seem to need all the friends he can muster; but not Marx. The only ally he required was Engels – who, faithful as ever, moved to London, loins girded for battle with the backsliders and traitors."

Engels was rich. Because daddy was rich. And if Engels' dad was rich, Karl Marx was rich. In London's British Museum he wrote some of his better work and the relatively tolerant nature of British society enabled him to become politically active once again. Not that he was ever successful. Wheen presents a lisping, long-winded extremist who was never wrong and had absolutely no understanding of compromise.

Once again, paradox and contradiction. In Wheen's biography, and surely in life, this was the heart of the man. He was loyal and loving to his one wife. He was loved by his children who called him "Moor" because of his swarthy looks and rode him like a horse. Yet at the same time he could casually call for the British police, who allowed him his freedom, to be clubbed to death and also scream gutter insults about Jews and blacks.

Finally comes the legacy. It is banal to remind ourselves that Marxist countries have not applied true Marxism and so on, but when Francis Wheen goes further. He is convinced that Marx did not himself believe in his work as being scientific. Marx should be thought of as an artist, the author explains, not as a shaper of world events. How darkly tragic that Lenin, Stalin, Mao, Pol Pot and the other war criminals failed to grasp the fact.

Personally, in spite of this jubilantly intelligent book, I'd still rather watch brother Groucho than read comrade Karl. More laughs, less blood. And a better understanding of human nature.

Ireland

It's not really about the politicians. Not about Tony Blair or Bertie Ahern, David Trimble or Gerry Adams. It's not really about government, not really about the experts, not really about religion and not really about power. It's not even really about Ireland. It's about Billy and Liam.

Billy's father had always wanted to be a policeman. He was raised on stories of Sherlock Holmes and catching the bad guys. So as soon as he was old enough he joined the Royal Ulster Constabulary. But Billy's dad failed almost every exam, only just made it past the physical requirements and if truth be told was accepted because of the shortage of recruits. While his comrades carried sub-machine guns and patrolled the streets Billy's dad merely handed out parking tickets.

"What does ya da do?" Billy's friends would shout, laughing because they knew the answer. Billy just smiled. He was very proud of his father and loved him very much.

The morning the IRA active service unit set out they knew exactly what to do and why they were doing it. It was because of the forced Irish diaspora, because of the famine of the last century, because of the British conquest and the brutality of the invaders, because of Roman Catholics being treated in the past as second-class citizens. And they did it. Fired bullet after bullet into the plump body of Billy's dad.

When Billy's mum was told of the murder she did not cry. Instead she sat down and stared at the fire-place. For hours. Billy did cry but tried to be brave for his mother. He limped over to the woman and put his skinny arms around her. He limped because he had been handicapped, physically and mentally, from birth and lived vicariously through the father of whom he was justifiably proud.

So close and so very far from Billy, Billy's mum and the heavily framed photographs of Billy's dad lived Liam and his family. Liam once supported Sinn Fein but he later decided to reject the IRA and all its works. He was still a defiant republican who wanted a united Ireland but he wanted it through the ballot box.

Until Liam was nineteen-years-old he had never actually known a Protestant. Of course he had seen them and spoken to them, even spent a day with them when a well-meaning organisation had tried to bring two different high schools together so as to build bridges. It didn't work. But suddenly Protestants, unionists, loyalists, had a name and a face. The name was Liz and the face was beautiful.

Liam met Liz at work. He knew she wasn't Catholic almost immediately, in that extraordinary way that Ulster people do. But he could not stop thinking about her. They had lunch together and Liam was amazed to discover that Liz believed in compromise and peace and, surprise of surprises, agreed that Catholic grievances had to be heard.

There were a few minor problems when they begun dating but far fewer than both had anticipated. A generation earlier and the couple may well have been forced to emigrate. To somewhere like Canada. But this wasn't so bad, and Liam's buddies were more interested in the way Liz smiled than in the way she prayed.

Liam was drinking in a different pub, a rural pub, the night it happened. The men who burst in had sworn an oath on the Bible to uphold the freedom of Ulster. They had grown up in poverty, in a protestant neighbourhood where unemployment and drugs were as common as British flags. They joined the Ulster Volunteer Force because they had seen the ripped and smashed victims of the IRA lying on the street, had seen the results of bombs placed in family stores and street corners.

They screamed as they pumped their guns into the mass and mess of people. One of those killed was, ironically, a Protestant. Another was Liam. Liz left Northern Ireland and swore she would never return.

So much blood. So much bloody history. So much to be forgotten by everybody concerned.

Again, it's not about the politicians but about Billy and Liam and the other 3200 dead in 30 years. And because of that the peace deal has to work and has to win.

Postit

In case you missed it, we have just completed Freedom To Read Week. This annual event enables some of the rich and famous to read from previously banned books and explain the horrors of censorship. It is perhaps significant that many of these champions of freedom were the same people who not so long took part in a notorious conference where jokes were made about conservative writers being tortured and imprisoned. But then consistency is terribly difficult. Or, to put it another way, there is an enormous difference between a genuine belief in liberty of expression and in an obsessive desire to change the nature of society to suit your own ends.

Be that as it may, the likes of Adrienne Clarkson, Veronica Tennant, Katherine Govier, John Sewell and John Ralston Saul proudly read from censored works and condemned those who believe in controlled access to certain books in their communities. The fact that many of these people, described by some zealots as "neanderthals and fascists", are concerned parents who love and care for their children is, it seems, irrelevant. As is the perfect right of small communities to impose their own standards on their own society.

But the obvious liberal narcissism is less important than the sheer daftness of all this. Put simply, we do not have some inalienable right to read anything we want. We have, for example, placed restrictions on racist hate-literature for some years and the vast majority of people would argue that such censorship has been largely painless and mostly beneficial to our way of life and to the well-being of the population. Child pornography is similarly illegal and, again, most people accept this as a moderate and wholesome position for the state to take.

As to the argument about who does the censoring, the answer is not as complex as some would have us believe. The same peo-

47

ple who frame, create and impose the other laws of the land. If customs officers are not qualified to make decisions about literature we must hire better educated customs officers. And hire more of them. Yet I really wonder if someone requires a profound education to prevent the wholesale distribution of, for example, Dennis Cooper?

In his book "Frisk" Cooper graphically describes the kidnapping, rape and sexual murder of a teenager. The boy's penis is sawn in half, his excrement is eaten, his bloody corpse is "kicked around for a while" by a group of friends, he is decapitated and the killers then masturbate over the body, which is later dumped in a canal. The murderers laugh at what is going on and find the slaughter to be sexually fulfilling. This particular boy is only one of many young victims.

And does one have to possess a doctorate in medieval literature to believe that the work of one Ann Wertheim might be harmful to many people, especially the powerless, in our society? She describes a case of incest where a young, vulnerable victim is shown as enjoying herself as her father rapes her, beats her and forces her to perform oral sex. In a compilation book that included this story the editors wrote that when they read the material "several of us nearly fainted from intense levels of sexual heat."

The reason I refer to these authors in particular is because their writings have been stopped by our customs officers at the border and both, along with many similar texts, have become fashionable causes for free speech extremists. Oddly enough I have yet to hear the likes of Adrienne Clarkson and Veronica Tennant publicly reading from the collected works of Dennis Cooper. But then it is much easier to pretend that censorship is about the foolish banning of Catcher In The Rye and Lord Of The Flies when it is in fact about the healthy censorship of books where the rape and murder of children is presented as being erotic, gratifying and rather hip.

It is not really that difficult to know where to draw the line and most people seem to agree where it should be drawn and how we should draw it. It is just that there are some out there who seem intent on turning that line into a circle of confusion. How sad.

Let the Teacher Teach

Blaise Thompson is a confused and frustrated man. A faithful and observant Roman Catholic, he trained as a teacher and spent some happy years in Ontario's Separate System. Until, that is, in 1995 when things seemed to change. Five years later this extremely gentle, somewhat unassuming 40-year-old is bruised, hurt and unemployed. It is a story worth telling.

Thompson was teaching French, English and Religious Studies as Nicholson Catholic College in Belleville, Ontario. All seemed fine, and peers and students were satisfied with his performance. So much so that the school principal's daughter was one of Thompson's students. It was generally considered that Thompson was a good teacher.

Then the regime at the school changed and a new vice-principal arrived. Thompson's yearly evaluations became radically different from what those he had received in the past. His performance was, he was told, unsatisfactory.

He was criticised for strange, even ridiculous things. One example being that he did his teaching with the classroom door closed. "I have no idea what that was about", he says. "All I know is that it was anarchy outside and the children couldn't hear anything." Another complaint was that he gave out too much photocopied material, again something he simply did not understand.

But the central issue seemed to be that he taught from the Catholic Catechism. This book, translated into numerous languages and an international best seller, is a quite beautiful summary of the Church's teaching. But, frankly, extreme liberals who like to call themselves Catholics hate it with a passion.

Thompson was reprimanded for, it seems, teaching Roman Catholicism in a Roman Catholic school. A complaint was made that he described homosexuality as a disorder and a sin. "I did", he says. "And that is Catholic teaching. I taught hundreds of classes and only mentioned it once, when Sodom and Gomorrah came up, but yes, I did mention it."

It seems that five or six children out of the sixty he taught did not like the reference. "They can think whatever they like," explains Thompson, "but this is school. I'm the teacher, and I can't just play into the self-esteem nonsense. I have a job to do. I also have to teach the faith upon which the school is based, and that concerns objective truth and not the feelings of a child on a particular day of the week."

The authorities at the school did not see it this way. So consistent were Thompson's bad evaluations that he was even denied the pay increase routinely given to his colleagues. Then a most extraordinary event occurred. Blaise Thompson was called into the school office and told he was being put on sick leave. "But I'm not sick!" he said, I'm actually extremely healthy." Yes you are sick, he was told in no uncertain terms.

A psychiatrist who had never met Thompson stated that he was a paranoid schizophrenic suffering from delusions of grandeur. In other words, that he was profoundly mentally ill. The doctor had concluded this from reading Thompson's letters to his vice-principal concerning his evaluations and from discussing Thompson with the woman in question. It must be stressed that at no time did the psychiatrist and Blaise Thompson actually meet, yet an evaluation was given that could have sent Thompson to a mental hospital.

He was then examined by a neutral doctor who said, incredulous at what was going on, that there was absolutely nothing wrong with the man. "I was amazed, it was like I was in some sort of nightmare," says Thompson. " It was like a Soviet horror case. But at least I was in a union. I had to be, it's compulsory."

But the Ontario English Teachers' Association seemed less fraternal than Thompson had hoped. They almost seemed to side with the employer and gave what Thompson describes as "no real help at all."

More than this, because the union had carriage rights over any legal action Thompson was not allowed to hire a private lawyer to fight his case. When he tried, the lawyer was barred from the room.

So he is in a grotesque limbo. Sick leave ended, he cannot find another teaching job with such a stigma hanging over him. He lost his home and moved in with relatives. His wife, the mother of their three children, had to go out to work.

The strain on the marriage became too great. Blaise Thompson's wife left him, with the children. He now lives in an apartment with his father and tries desperately to understand what he did wrong.

Is the story unique? Yes and no. The intensity of the tale is unusual but faithful Catholic teachers across this country find it difficult to teach in an increasingly secular and militantly liberal Catholic school system.

Whether you are Catholic or not, religious or not, Blaise Thompson's case must concern you. Because it is about fairness, justice and truth. About an ordinary man who was made a victim. If him now, who next? It is a question Blaise Thompson asks almost every day of the week.

Art Attack

Great news. The Brooklyn Museum of Art and its champions in the liberal elite are defending the gallery's right to exhibit a picture of the mother of Jesus Christ embellished with clump a of elephant dung and two dozen cutout pictures of buttocks from a pornographic magazine.

I say again, great news. And great news that the work, entitled The Holy Virgin Mary, was painted in the first place. This is exciting, uplifting and, most than all, extremely encouraging. I couldn't be happier.

Why? Simple. As the decaying artistic establishment breathes its last and flickers down to a well-deserved death it attacks the targets by which it feels more threatened. It attacks God and religion. If such people ignored Jesus, ignored Mary, ignored faith, then we really would be in trouble. Because then we wouldn't matter. But it's now abundantly clear that to people like the Brooklyn art dodgers, God and His people matter more than anything else on earth.

Cardinal John 0'Connor has asked Roman Catholics to join him in condemning the painting and New York Mayor Rudolph Giuliani has threatened to remove the museum's public grant of more than $7million. The former is a sincere man but the latter leaves a little to be desired. If Christ and His mother stand for anything it is a support for the poor and the disadvantaged – by the way, I use the present tense on and with purpose. The pipmaster of the big apple has shown precious little regard for this particular constituency.

Of course public funding must be removed from such galleries and such artists, just as it should be from the Canadian versions, but the cash should in turn be given to those who really need it and not be turned into some manipulative and crass vote-catching gimmick.

This latest proof that God terrifies and intimidates sick and immoral people, however, is only one in a long chain of examples. In the past few years we have had both Piss Christ and Piss Pope, consisting of pictures of Jesus and the head of the Roman Catholic church soaked in urine. These came to tour in western Canada and were roundly defended.

We were also treated to an illustration of a priest having oral sex with the crucified Christ, which won an arts award in a competition judged by a Canadian. Recently there was a controversy over a play portraying Christ as a homosexual, in which Jesus is said to be the "King of the queers." The same production featured Jesus having sex with His apostles.

Going back to the sixties, when all of this anger received its post-war impetus, a homosexual magazine in Britain ran a story describing a Roman soldier masturbating as he watched Christ dying on the cross. The publication was sued in a trial that divided the United Kingdom.

And now this. But those who are shocked by it all must surely understand that this is the very intention of the trash's confused creators. Such men and women lack the genius of a Picasso, lack the brilliant powers of provocation of an Oscar Wilde, lack the sheer talent of a Tolstoy. So, like children in the schoolyard they scream at what they fear. In fact they are really still swearing at their parents and hoping that someone will take notice.

They tried punching away at capitalism, until they realised that big business was often their friend more than their enemy. They kicked against the American way, until they found out that they would starve anywhere else in the world. Then they discovered what really scared the hell out of them and what couldn't be seduced. Universal truth, unchanging morality, the eternal difference between right and wrong, light. Yes, light. These painters and playwrights are not scared of the dark, they are scared of the light.

Instead of becoming so upset and outraged about a picture that nobody will really care about or remember moments after they see it, those who believe in God and in virtue should celebrate yet another victory. The other side is absolutely terrified, and the best weapons they can find are a lump of dung and a few pictures of people's bums. Hey, it's going to be all right after all.

The Pope and WWII

A book has just been published that claims to give the final word on the role of the Roman Catholic Church and the Vatican during World War Two. Entitled "Hitler's Pope: The Secret History of Pius XII", it is an unbridled and often polemical attack upon a man and an institution that simply do not deserve such contempt.

Author John Cornwell rather gives away his biased intentions with the title of his volume, and in all honesty it's a little hard to take the stuff seriously after that. His claim that the Pope was anti-Semitic and that the Vatican did little to help the Jews is based on a single letter written by Pius XII in 1919 and an account of a handful of Vatican officials who certainly weren't on the side of the angels.

No surprise that such a book should appear at this particular time. It's open season on RCs and Catholic-bashing is the last acceptable prejudice of the millennium. Not only acceptable, it's almost fashionable.

A few facts. Before he became Pope Pius, Cardinal Pacelli drafted the papal encyclical denouncing Nazi racism and had it read from every pulpit. Hitler was said to have screamed in anger when he heard.

The Vatican used its assets to ransom Jews from the Nazis, ran an elaborate escape route and hid Jewish families in Castel Gondolfo, the Pope's summer residence. All this is confirmed by Jewish experts such as B'nai B'rith's Joseph Lichten.

Because of the presence of the Pope, the Jews of Italy had a far higher survival rate than in most other countries. Indeed the World Jewish Congress donated a great deal of money to the Vatican in 1945 and Rabbi Herzog of Jerusalem thanked Pope Pius "for his lifesaving efforts on behalf of the Jews during the occupation of Italy." When the Pope died in 1958 Golda Meir, then Israeli Foreign Minister, gave a eulogy at the United Nations praising the man for his valiant work on behalf of her people.

The attacks on the Pope only really began in the 1960s when a German playwright claimed that the Vatican had somehow done nothing to help the Jews. An anti-Catholic German intellectual full of guilt. Hardly a reliable source.

It is true that the Pope did not issue an outright attack on the Nazis but there were reasons for this.

The leaders of the Catholic Church in Holland did make a public statement, condemning Nazi anti-Semitism and protesting the deportation of the Jewish people. In response the German occupiers arrested and murdered every Jewish convert to Catholicism they could find in The Netherlands. The group included the brilliant Edith Stein, a nun who was dragged from her convent to the slaughterhouse of Auschwitz. She was gassed in August 1942. Stein was declared a saint by Pope John Paul II and is revered by him as one of the greatest minds and souls of the church.

Another witness who cries out to be heard is Titus Brandsma, a monk and scholar who helped smuggle Jews to safety. He worked with the underground and for his heroic stance was taken to Dachau. There he was the victim of human experiments and was finally given a lethal injection by a Nazi nurse. As he was dying he gave his rosary beads to the person who had killed him and forgave the crime. Brandsma's final letter, written while in physical agony, stated "Many greetings to the parish priest and curates at Bolsward, to Father Provincial and all the Confreres. Let us remain united, under the protection of Jesus, Mary and Joseph. Not too much worrying about me."

Brandsma was one of hundreds of thousands of Roman Catholic priests, monks, nuns, bishops and lay people who risked their lives and sometimes gave them to help the Jewish victims of the Nazi pagans. But the last word should go to a Jewish man.

In 1945 the Chief Rabbi of Rome, Israele Zolli, publicly embraced Roman Catholicism. This extraordinary conversion was partly due to Zolli's admiration for the Pope's sheltering and saving of Italian Jews. Since the conversion the former Chief Rabbi has been slandered because of his actions, but then so has Pope Pius XII. But the truth is still the truth, and heroism is still heroism.

Him

First He is interrogated, abused, threatened, both by the imperialist thugs who have raped His country and by the collaborators who have allowed the invaders to have their way. Then a group of soldiers throw Him to the ground, beat Him and spit in His face. They make fun of Him, push Him around, punch and shove Him. But the sport is just beginning.

He is tied to a post and whipped with a weapon so cruel that it often causes death. It's a multi-stringed whip, each strap weighted with lead balls that rip and tear lumps of flesh off the body. So bad are these thrashings that they expose the bowels and organs of the victim. If death doesn't occur at the time it usually takes place days later when infection sets in.

As part of the mockery one of the soldiers suggests that they make Him look like a king. After all, he shouts, He claimed to be a king. They all laugh loudly, enjoying what all bullies enjoy. A pretend crown is made, composed of the razor-sharp thorns that grow so readily in the area. They are around four inches long and so dangerous that the locals use them like knives.

The clumsy headpiece, consisting of dozens of thorns, resembles an upturned bowl. It is placed on top of His head and then pushed, hard, down onto and into His scalp. It lacerates and slices the skin, causing even more pain and loss of blood.

A crossbeam weighing more than a hundred pounds is slung across His shoulders and He is shoved into the public streets, forced to carry the weight to His place of execution. Already faint from agony and exhaustion He drops to the ground, where He is shouted at and kicked. People He considered friends and brothers turn away and hide. Old enemies laugh at the state He is in.

More soldiers scream at Him to stop. They push Him down to the ground and step over Him like He was dirt beneath their feet. Three of them hold Him down while another produces a set of thick, rusting nails six inches long, and a large, heavy mallet. The first nail is hammered into His wrist. The initial blow of the mallet pounds on the head of the nail, splitting flesh and ligament, splattering blood over His body and over the sandals and tunics of the guards.

Another nail, into the other wrist. And then the area around the ankles. Sometimes it takes several blows, sometimes the skin and muscle simply cave in, so weak have they become. The world spins, the people shout, the overwhelming pain washes with the confusion and the fear into an ocean of horror.

This is a form of judicial murder so evil that even the ruling authorities will abolish it soon afterwards as being too cruel. He has been treated with the very worst kind as well. Often wrongdoers are tied to the cross and left to die of thirst and exposure. But not Him. Every sinew of His body screams out for relief. So alone, so despised, so perfectly and utterly good.

Death will come when there is no strength left to lift the chest and breath. It is excruciating to breathe at all because it puts pressure on the wounds, but nothing can extinguish the lust for life. Finally, though, the muscles give way, the blanket of numbness smothers all else and it stops. It stops.

A soldier pushes his spear into His side and a mixture of blood and water gushes forth. The sure sign of death. They take Him down. But it is still not enough. Guard His body and tomb, the collaborators demand. So they do.

Then the world begins again. First a few, then more, then hundreds see Him alive. They feel His wounds, eat with Him, laugh with Him, weep with Him. So sure are they of His resurrection and truth that they themselves are prepared to face deaths as bad as His. They abandon selves so as to gain everything.

Today? He is still abused, beaten, mocked and spat upon. Crazed zealots run into His churches and try to destroy the sacred; the state television system runs a show depicting a woman feeding His body and blood to a dog. It hurts, very much indeed. But in the finally analysis it does not mater. Because He died, because He rose, because He is risen. For you and for me.

I Love My Bank

I love my bank, I really do. The people at the branch management level give me loans and mortgages when I desperately need then, they don't bounce my cheques when the things should really hit the ceiling, honestly seem to care about my finances. Sure I pay a great deal of money in interest and charges but it's worth it.

The staff who serve me behind the counter are friendly and warm. They take time to learn the names of the customers, to pass the time of day and to treat us like human beings. People aren't rushed too much, aren't treated like necessary but annoying cogs in the wheel of finance.

And then come the guys in dark suits who earn extravagant salaries and decide on major policy. With these individuals I am not particularly enamoured. The latest reason? A letter informing me that for my "convenience" they are closing down my local branch.

Think about it. For my convenience, in other words to make my life easier and more pleasant, they are terminating the place where I have banked for five years and where I feel known, liked and comfortable. For my convenience they are making me drive further and begin a relationship all over again. For my convenience they are making my life just a little more inconvenient.

Time to cut the nonsense. The banks have an agenda. Their vision is of a banking system where computers replace people and where banking is conducted by Internet and bank machine. People cost money and, as the banks have repeatedly shown, profits are far more important than personalities.

The bankers' brave new world envisages every person with a laptop and a bank account, no overheads caused by sick pay and pregnancy leave, no need to pay severance or deal with unions. Bank customers are mere dollar signs with names attached. The less faces we see the better for everyone.

This is why that instead of standing behind a counter and helping you, bank employees are told to walk up to customers and ask if they know how to use the teller machine in the room outside. Odd really. Like some financial kamikaze pilots these poor men and women urge people to force them out of a job.

"Use the machine to get your cash and pay your bills. Every ten people who use the machine makes it that much more possible for Joe Pinstripe on Bay Street to fire me."

Banking is not so different from any other profession in that it should be rooted in human decency. Personal contact is important because, well, because we are people. We crave the individual touch and, by our nature, despise the cold crassness of metal and buttons. If I, relatively young, healthy and educated, feel this, what of others less fortunate?

Every time I bank at my branch I see people whose English is poor and new, helped and coached by the staff. Their faces light up, their frowns of concern become smiles of confidence. I see old people, relishing that tiny slice of conversation with as they cash their pension cheques. A chore has become a pleasure.

For their "convenience" these people will now have to walk to a new branch, possibly a twenty minute trek, to be shown that the bank machines there are much nicer and cleaner than the ones back home.

Then we have the coffee and cookie approach. We're closing down your branch because our enormous profits are not enormous enough, but we giving you a plastic cup of bad coffee to make you feel loved. Take a tiny slice of cake too, all courtesy of a very powerful if anonymous man who earns more money in a week than you do in a year. Which is why he knows how to make your life more "convenient."

I do not fear change. A controlled progress is to be welcomed, even encouraged. But I do not trust bank propaganda and I do not believe for a moment that they have our interests at heart. They do, however, enjoy an effective monopoly on their business and it is impossible in the contemporary world to operate without a bank account. Which makes us a captive clientele.

And sometimes that just isn't very "convenient".

A Mother's Tale

Goodness knows what actually happened last weekend when the Emergency Task Force fired three bullets into Henry Musuka. The 26-year-old father was holding what turned out to be a pellet gun to the head of a doctor in the middle of St. Michael's hospital and was threatening to kill the man. Musuka had been demanding instant medical attention for his baby son and refused to put down his weapon in spite of repeated pleas.

I suppose we have to ask why it required three shots from expert marksman using high-powered rifles to bring down a man standing only a few feet away, but we also have to put ourselves in the position of those officers and of the terrified hostage. But gone are the days when I would immediately assume that the police were always in the right. The reason is that I have met the ghost of Faraz Suleman.

For those who don't remember, Faraz was 16-years-old when in 1996 he was shot dead by a policeman. A bullet smashed through the side window of his car, ripped into his spinal cord and killed him instantly.

What made the case particularly tragic was that the takedown had been planned with the cooperation of Faraz's mother, Shaheen Kamadia.

"I had no idea that my son was in any trouble until the police came to my door and said he was wanted for being involved in a car-jacking" she says, her large eyes dry now after so many tears. "Of course I knew that he had to be stopped, had to be saved. We arranged for him to be arrested and I played along all the way."

Unfortunately the police acted too quickly and what should have been a routine arrest became dangerous car chase. The car was eventually stopped and Detective Robert Wiche says that he took up a position in front of Faraz's vehicle, gun drawn. He told the boy to get out but instead the car rolled towards him. Frightened for his life, he fired in self-defence.

And this, in an odd way, is where I come in. I was asked to be an expert witness in the coroner's trial last month. I visited a recreation of the shooting and gave my opinion of where the officer might have been and if, indeed, his life was actually in danger. You see, there was an eyewitness watching from the window of his house and while he could see the front of Faraz Suleman's car, he could not see Detective Wiche.

This is vitally important. Because if the officer was not at the front of the car but at the side, his life was not in danger and there was no need to fire. If he was at the front, as he says, lying across the bonnet, he was acting foolishly and against training, but at least he might have had reason to shoot. Yet the eyewitness saw no man at the front of the car and believes he heard orders shouted from the car's side. Something does not quite add up, especially when we remember that the bullet smashed through a side window and into the side of Faraz's neck.

There is more. The police knew that the guns involved in the car-jackings were air-pistols.

Shaheen Kamadia wasn't informed of her son's death until the following morning. She had been led to believe that everything had gone smoothly and that her son was in custody. As I stood on the spot where Faraz took his last breath I asked this woman who refuses to give up her struggle if the pain had become any easier. She paused, began to speak, and then turned away.

At no time has Detective Wiche apologised for killing Faraz and he is currently suing the Special Investigation Unit for $30 million for malicious prosecution. As for Shaheen Kamadia, she still wants to know what she did wrong and how the police can expect the cooperation of a parent in the future.

As for me, I still think our cops are tremendous. I just want to make sure that they stay that way, and that nobody thinks that he is above the law. Because just like you, Shaheen Kamadia thought that terrible things only happened to other people. And she meets her son's ghost every day of her life.

Selling Body Parts

Oh brave new world, what wonders you contain. The web site for the United States government's National Institutes of Health is advertising aborted baby parts for research purposes. The commercial, worth quoting at some length, states the following.

"Human embryonic and fetal tissues are available from the Central Laboratory for Human Embryology at the University of Washington. The laboratory, which is supported by the National Institutes of Health, can supply tissue from normal or abnormal embryos and fetuses of desired gestational ages between 40 days and term. Specimens are obtained within minutes of passage and tissues are aseptically identified, staged, and immediately processed according to the requirements of individual investigators.

"Presently, processing methods include immediate fixation, snap fixation, snap freezing in liquid nitrogen and placement in balanced salt solutions or media designated and/or supplied by investigators. Specimens are shipped by overnight express, arriving the day following procurement."

The advert is chilling in the inhuman way it speaks of human life. "Normal" embryos mean unborn children that are perfect; "abnormal" means babies with disabilities. When the piece refers to "term" it means unborn children that could survive outside the womb, possibly as late as nine months gestation. But business being what it is, even the large babes are guaranteed to arrive far quicker than the mail.

The laboratory will also provide only what is needed for any purchaser and will kindly cut up and dissect as required. It's more lucrative that way because one aborted child can provide a leg here, an arm there, a brain somewhere else, an internal organ in yet another location. Goodness me, this is a capitalist dream. Very few overheads and a product that is increasingly available.

Grotesque as all this sounds, it is not entirely new. A company in Illinois, Opening Lines, offers $999 for brains eight weeks old or less, $400 for an intact embryo eight weeks or less, $600 for an unborn child more than eight weeks old and $550 for gonads. All prices, of course, in US currency.

The outfit publishes a brochure for abortion facilities in which it states that now "you can turn your patients' decision into something wonderful." The document goes on to say "We know your patient's decision to have an abortion was carefully considered and we also know it was a very difficult one to make à we can train your staff to harvest and process fetal tissue. Based on your volume we will reimburse part or all of your employee's salary, thereby reducing your overhead."

Or to put it another way, there's a lot of money to be made here. Hey, nothing new. Henry Morgentaler has become a wealthy man through his work in the abortion industry. But the good doctor is a pauper compared to some of his comrades south of the border.

Although it is technically illegal to sell body parts in the United States those involved get around the law by "donating" organs and then receiving what is known as a site fee. So abortion is, as we have long known, a big business, yet we are still thought foolish enough to believe that it is all about choice. Desperate women who go to abortuaries are told that this might not be the right thing and that they should consider all the possibilities. Sure, and I've got a full head of hair.

One of the most poignant, and sickening, ironies of all this is that much of the macabre crop is used for research into HIV/AIDS. While everything human must be done to find a cure for this plague, it is hard to deny that the majority of sufferers in North America contracted the disease through perverse sex. 95% of the world's AIDS population is in the developing world and lack even basic health care. Nobody cared very much about these men and women before AIDS was brought to North America and, frankly, nobody cares very much now. They're poor and they're black and don't know Elizabeth Taylor or Barbara Streisand.

If experimentation must take place it should take place on animals. But I forgot. That would mean hurting little kittens and puppies and it just wouldn't be right. After all, we're human beings and cruelty is unacceptable.

Evolution

Prepare to see Kansas ridiculed in smart circles from Toronto to Texas. The reason? The state's Board of Education has voted to remove the subject of evolution from the list of compulsory course requirements for students to pass mandatory tests. Evolution can be taught, probably will be taught, but unlike English and math it will no longer be essential. And a good thing too.

You see, evolution is at best a theory and at worst a hoax. We do not have any concrete scientific evidence proving how we arrived at our present state, only ideas. The beliefs of the creationists, those who follow the literal truth of Genesis, held ground for centuries. Then, in the 1850s, Charles Darwin came along and wrote of evolution. Darwin was a great man but he was not a particularly great scientist.

I am not a great man at all and I am a useless scientist. But I am rather good at being skeptical, especially concerning the wisdom of the establishment. Let me throw a few thoughts into the pot.

Even with all of our scientific knowledge and with the millions of examples of living things, we are no closer to creating independent life than were our ancestors. Even the most basic organism, the prokaryote bacterial cell, is so detailed and sophisticated as to baffle the greatest minds. Each human being is filed with literally trillions of cells as complex as this little critter.

Those who believe in evolution and the Big Bang theory of how we arrived here believe in chance. They claim that primitive organisms developed by need and environment into men and women. Yet in the entire history of biological research we have seen no change of species. There have been tiny changes within species but this is to be expected. It's common sense. A blind man might develop a special sense of smell, but no blind man has ever grown a new set of eyes.

Until very recently school science textbooks often contained photographs of something called the Peppered Moth, resting on a tree-trunk. With its colour and behaviour the moth was supposed to be one of the best examples of natural selection. Last year, however, quite a scandal was caused when it was discovered that such creatures do not actually rest of trees and that 40 years ago a Dr. Kettlewell had glued two moths to a tree to take his famous photograph and prove his point.

If creationists had done such a thing they would, rightly, be condemned as frauds and their place in the school system would come into question. Not so with evolution and its followers.

Then there is the alleged development of the horse. We all remember pictures of a tiny horse, getting progressive larger as time went by. This, again, was apparently proven fact. Not so. A fox-like skull fossil was discovered in 1841 but it took 40 years for anybody to suggest that it was a prehistoric horse. Nor did they mention that the fossil, and others like it, are found not deep in the earth but quite near the surface, indicating that they are the results of relatively recent burials. They are also sometimes found next to the fossils of full-size horses, proving that this was not evolution at all.

More than this, even today we have horses ranging from mammoths like the Clydesdale to the 17inch Fallabella. "I admit that an awful lot of that has gotten into the textbooks as though it were true," says Dr. Niles Eldredge, curator of the American Museum of Natural History. "That is lamentable."

Finally comes the "Big Bang." The term was coined by English astronomer Sir Fred Hoyle, who came to doubt his own theory. Advanced telescopes have recorded more than 2000 so-called big bangs in the last thirty years, and none of them have resulted in very much at all, and certainly not in the creation of a new world. Even opponents of creation are admitting that they have to find another alternative explanation.

I don't really know the answer to all this but I do know that conventional science does not provide many truths. And that people who might one day have very red faces should not accuse other people of having very red necks.

Merry Christmas

A suburban Toronto school. A young women teacher with obvious liberal tendencies explains to her class of small children that she is an atheist. She asks her class if they are atheists too. Not really knowing what atheism is but wanting to be like teacher most of the hands of the eager young students punch the air like fleshy fireworks.

There is, however, one exception. A beautiful girl named Lucy has not gone along with the crowd. Teacher asks her why she has decided to be different.

"Because I'm not an atheist." Then, asks teacher, what are you? "I'm a Christian." Teacher is a little perturbed now, her face slightly red. She asks Lucy why she is a Christian.

"Well, my mum is a Christian and my dad is a Christian, so I am a Christian." Teacher is now angry. "That's no reason," she says loudly. "What about if your mum was a moron and your dad was a moron. What would you be then?"

A pause, and a smile. "Then", says Lucy, "I'd be an atheist."

Many miles away a Roman Catholic priest is on a walking holiday in rural Canada. As he sits down in an isolated area to eat his packed lunch he sees a flock of sheep suddenly fill the horizon before him, an ever-increasing smudge of wool and legs. A boy is at their side, an actual shepherd boy, like some charming anachronism suddenly strayed into the late twentieth-century.

Boy and priest begin to chat and share food, and it soon becomes clear that the young fellow is illiterate. He has heard of churches and Christianity, he says, but he doesn't really know what they mean. The priest proceeds to teach him "The Lord is my shepherd", using the fingers of his right hand to emphasise the words – little finger for "The", next finger for "Lord" and so on.

The following year the priest returns to the deepest countryside for a vacation. While sitting in a restaurant in the town he sees a familiar picture hanging on the wall, a newspaper photograph of, yes, of that same shepherd boy. He asks why the young man was in a newspaper. The owner of the restaurant looks saddened.

"Poor soul. He was out working last winter, Christmas Eve it was. The snow came in bad and he spent too long trying to save the sheep. He managed to get them all in shelter but it was too late for him. He fell, exhausted, and froze to death." A deep sigh.

"Odd thing was that instead of him looking frightened, he had a smile on his face. And although he froze to death, his little body was quite warm when they found him. Except for his right hand. He was holding, gripping, one of his fingers, the second one after his little finger. Don't know why. Suppose we never will."

The priest feels a shiver sizzle through his body. "The Lord is my shepherd. The LORD is my shepherd." The he drops to his knees and begins to pray.

Lastly to an unnecessary war, fought by young men who didn't even know this particular country existed before they were sent there to defend its questionable integrity. Bullets whistle around heads, like deadly stings from some hellish wasp. He has heard them a thousand times and knows how to keep low. Until, that is, he forgot. The breath is leaving fast now and although there is little pain he knows he won't survive. "Go to Mr. Thomas, my old teacher, go there and tell him that everything he told me now makes sense" he tells his friend. "Go there, please, please" and he stops, as still as stillness can be.

The friend returns home, goes to his comrade's old school and searches for Mr. Thomas. He finds an old man, growing small with age. He tells him what was said in that sandy slaughter-house.

"I was his Sunday-school teacher," says Mr. Thomas, tears bisecting his cheek. "I thought that he ignored every word I said. I thought I was wasting my time. Oh my God, I thought it was all for nothing."

Merry Christmas, and please remember the reason for the season.

Valentine's Day

I didn't like last Monday. It was Valentine's Day, giving yet another opportunity for people to claim that they remembered love, so that they could forget for the rest of the year. Because we love everything don't we. We love the show we just saw, love the pop group we just heard, love the flavour we just tried, love the person we just had sex with. What the hell has love got to do with it?

Love, romantic love, the love between a man and a woman must be put right. Because too many people have been trying to put it wrong. A few basics. No sex before marriage, fidelity to your partner after marriage, no divorce and a commitment to raising a family.

And what is extraordinary, what is truly extraordinary, is that many people who have just read that paragraph are incredulous, even angry. "I don't believe he could have written such a thing, I mean, is this guy for real? Why doesn't he change with the times?"

Yes I'm for real, and as for changing for the times, no. How could anyone want to change with the times when we have just exited the most murderous century in history. Would we ask a German in 1939 to change with the times?

First, the sex before marriage myth. A line as tired as a sleepwalker on a treadmill. We've all heard it. Unless you experiment with one another and find out if you're sexually compatible the marriage will never work. You might not click.

Horse feathers. Pre-marital sex became common only in the last forty years and all experts agree that its rate of occurrence multiplied enormously after the 1960s. Which, strangely enough, is precisely when divorce became so common. Far from guaranteeing that we were happy together, sex before marriage made it far more likely that marriages would fail. So much for the compatibility argument.

In fact all promiscuity achieves is a need for more promiscuity. Which is pretty much common sense. The really important factors in keeping a marriage together involve time spent outside of the bed, and these are precisely the factors that we jettisoned in the glorious rush towards so-called sexual liberation.

Actually sexual incompatibility is incredibly rare. When physical attraction and love are combined the result is sexual pleasure. Add to this the dignity of saving yourself for the person you love and joy is certain. All the arguments about the desperate need to behave like rabbits in rebellion are based not on logic but on lust. "I don't want to wait, why should I." The Me Generation.

Which brings me to the rate of sexually transmitted diseases and so-called unwanted pregnancies. They have risen every year since the universal availability of contraceptives and the advent of that great feminist pharmaceutical, The Pill. It would all be okay now, we were told, the sexual revolution will save our souls. Not quite. As some pointed out at the time, rather than save our souls it would sink our ship.

Look for yourself. Not only in North America but in every country where contraceptives are introduced the rate of sexual diseases and abortions are multiplied. Replace love with latex and we encourage irresponsibility. You might not like to hear the truth but that does not make the truth any less truthful. And you won't hear such truth very often.

Then we have divorce. Without doubt past marriages sometimes stayed together when they should have broken up. But these were relatively few. Ignore the social revisionists who have an axe to grind, the fact is that divorce is never positive. In fact divorce equals failure. If you have divorced, you have failed.

I heard a man say just the other day that his parents' divorce was the best thing that happened to him because mum and dad argued so much. No, no, no. The best thing that could have happened to you would have been if your parents had stopped arguing! Because divorce hurts kids and even sociological liberals now admit that single-parent families are never ideal.

We're not animals, we're not beyond self-control, there is glory in commitment, love involves sacrifice. And I'm tired of the sordid thinking they're the clever ones. Because they're not.

Trendy Criminals

Very few people had heard of Stephen Reid before this summer when he robbed a bank and tried to kill a policeman. Even less had ever heard of Susan Musgrave. The former is a serial criminal, the latter a poet from British Columbia. They met and fell in love, just as bank robbers and poets do. They then became one of the model couples of the literary elite, the centre of attention at dinner parties where boring people like police officers and men and women who do real jobs and do not break the law are mocked and laughed at.

I can still remember the comments. "Oh, Steve and Susan are such a lovely couple. So different, so new." Or "How refreshing to meet a couple who refuse to conform, just delightful." Quite so.

Reid was such a nice man that earlier this year he took up heroin again and returned to holding up banks and aiming guns at police officers. Which is just what he used to do before he originally went to prison and then married Susan Musgrave, being part of a gang that conducted 140 robberies and made the FBI's most wanted list.

But if we are to believe various newspaper columnists and pundits who have passed judgement on Reid's trial and conviction it is the gangster who is the wronged party in all this. They have described him as "charming" and "unfortunate", "An addict who needs help", "a fine man" and so on. Various west-coast types laid it on so thick that some in the courtroom were in tears. Remember, this is a man who pumped himself up with heroin so to obtain false courage and then robbed a bank and tried to kill a cop.

One writer went on, and on, about how Reid's supposed addiction to drugs made sense of it all. Really? For an addict he spent many years not taking drugs, which does not fit the pattern of addiction at all. Even if it did, so what? There are hundreds of thousands of addicts in Canada and they do not try to rob banks and kill people.

There is more though. Every day people are sent to prison for very long periods of time for committing various crimes. Their lawyers argue that they come from abusive, impoverished families and that they turned to drugs and alcohol as an escape. Often their defenders are right.

Guess what. We hear hardly a peep from the columnists and the poets and the commentators. Because these people, unlike the criminal Reid, are genuine victims. But Reid is superficially attractive, he is known by the elite, he is married to "one of us", he is now middle-class. And, forgive me, but he is white. Just like, well, just like the poets and the columnists. And people "like us" don't do bad things do we. Well, yes we do.

The same people who routinely ignore, or scream for blood, when the disadvantaged go wrong simply can't stand it when one of their own turns to crime. Good God, there is no hypocrisy so sickening as that of the chattering classes.

If the cop in this case would have been killed you can bet your bottom dollar that his name would have been forgotten in moments by the assembled publicly funded types who are currently screaming the virtues of Stephen Reid. A young woman might have spent Christmas looking into the fire and shaking as the thoughts of her dead husband punched and kicked their way through her mind. The tears have dried up by now but the pain only gets worse. The children are still too small to come to terms with daddy being gone forever, so they run around the house looking for him.

His friends and fellow officers are always there for her but it doesn't really make it easier. She asks them why his murderer is being painted as such a great guy in the newspapers and why her dead hero of a life-partner is so soon forgotten. They just look at the floor and say nothing.

As for Stephen Reid, your sentencing hearing begins next week and may you spend the rest of your life in prison, where you can write as many poems as you like.

Do We Care?

Last week I met Sharon. She's an attractive 27-year-old from New Brunswick who came to Toronto for a better life. She has two children, both under nine, and their father, her common-law husband, ran off three years ago. "I suppose I should have known what he was like really," she says, smoothing her skirt with her hand. "Love is blind right, and I should be wearing binoculars."

Sharon is on welfare. She had a succession of jobs but it was costing her more to put her children into daycare than she was earning pumping gas and delivering newspapers. "They're right when they say there's work out there. Particularly for someone like me. A lot of people in my situation have a mental illness or have had a drink or drug habit. I'm clean, not dumb, so they want me. But I can't afford to work."

This is why, I say, many people agreed with the government when it lowered the welfare rates, and others believe they should be lower still. "Yeah, then I can starve, let my kids sell drugs. Christ, what are we talking about here. It's a few dollars. If the low paying jobs gave just a little more I'd be off welfare like a shot. D'you think I enjoy the humiliation? D'you think if you take welfare suddenly you're an animal with no feelings?

"My mum and dad worked all their lives. Never broke a law, never put their hands out for help. I was brought up to be the same. I'm not lazy," and her eyes shine with intensity.

I tell her that the Premier implied that people on welfare might be spending the money on drink. "And he's not all wrong. Some do. Suddenly it's a crime to have a drink once in a while. You see guys coming out of restaurants who've spent two hundred bucks on a meal, on wine and stuff. If I buy a six-pack I'm a bad person. I'm just as human as they are you know.

"Look, I sit looking at four walls all day, living next door to hookers and pushers and down-and-outs. I can't buy the kids toys, I can't buy myself anything new, so yes I sometimes have a drink. Don't get drunk, have a drink. I don't understand why that makes me one of the scum of society."

She mentioned hookers. She young and pretty. Has she ever? "No. No. But I've thought about it. I know girls who do, girls who've never done a thing wrong in their lives. They get desperate. Just once and they can get fifty bucks. Trouble is, the once becomes a lot. Can't go down that road. Can't." She looks at her two small children, playing with a handful of old toys in the corner.

"You know, we still joke about that Tory politician who was caught in a police sting for guys using hookers. Funny, eh. They cut welfare, that puts more girls on the streets, more chance for those boys to find some business." Lots of laughter.

"I'm not looking for sympathy here. I should have chosen a better guy, I should have never left school so early, I should be able to find a job that lets me afford daycare for the kids. But I didn't and I can't. I'm not asking for very much, don't want to ask for anything at all. I just need to be able to live. That's all."

I tell her that there are people who have been in circumstances like hers, even worse, and that they have managed to drag themselves out of the pit. "I suppose there are. I know there are. I see guys from other countries who can hardly speak English. They work like crazy, do okay. But they have people around them, big families, supports and stuff. I haven't, and there are a lot like me.

"I'd like to see all these people who look down on me and judge me", gulping back emotion, "I'd like them to be me jut for a week, see how long they survive. I would." Pause. "I really would."

And for the time since I have met her Sharon cries. And cries for a very long time indeed.

A Patriot!

The year is 1776. Enter Mel Gibson, an Australian pretending to be an American pretending to be an actor pretending to be a patriot. "Okay boys. The British have eaten all the babies in New York and if we don't stop them here they'll take away our DVD machines. It's time to make our stand, brothers all. Except for the brothers who are black, of course, who we'll use as slaves. Oh, and the brothers who are Indians, and them we'll just kill.

"As that great American once said, once more unto the breech thing dear friends, or something like that. Or was that the big chicken with the American accent in Chicken Run? Not sure."

He is interrupted by a young soldier, one arm hanging by a thread, the other gripping the head of the British President, Adolf Stalin III. "There were only five of us sir, but we managed to kill 180,000 British soldiers, all of them with really bad teeth. The ones we didn't kill are setting fire to school-teachers and torturing old ladies."

The Patriot takes a deep breath. A tear bisects his perfect cheek. "Never in the field of human conflict was so much owed by so many to so few, and it's time to get off the island. You might want to be a millionaire my friend but I want to save the United States of America for freedom. Yes, freedom!" Crowds roar, dogs bark, a young Bill Clinton talks about a town called Hope.

An actor from U-571 comes into shot pulling an enormous plastic submarine, followed by George Washington, played by Sylvester Stallone. He begins to give a speech, accompanied by a choir led by Brittany Spears and The Artist Formerly Known As Prince.

"We just want our country to love us as much we love it, ya know. Communism is a filthy thing, like a cancer. And just like cancer it can seem popular and good to people who have nothing. So for the people who have nothing, well we'll have to give them something. And then they won't be people who have nothing any more."

Thousands of extras chant "Rocky, Rocky, Rocky" over and over again. Stallone pats the heads of young black children and tells them that in a thousand years everybody will be equal because of the work of a man called Martin Luther King who, aided by the US Marines, the FBI and Al Gore, will convince all Americans that racism is not only immoral but makes for very bad movies.

Suddenly an explosion sends people scattering. Intestines cover the floor, limbs revolve through the air. Striding through the smoke is a figure dressed all in black and breathing through a huge respirator. He wears a cape and carries a light-sabre. He is accompanied by men in red coats who routinely say, "Hello mate, fancy a cup of tea and a game of cricket?" and then bayonet pretty young virgins to death.

"Not so fast General Vader" says The Patriot. "There comes a time when a man has to do what a man has to do what a man had to do. I may be a mere American, or at least someone pretending to be an American, but I'm fighting for something you just don't understand. For sequel rights, for royalties, for television spin-offs. Fight me, if you dare."

One of General Vader's men fires a sub-machine gun at our hero. Hundreds of bullets tear into his flesh and he falls to the ground. But only for a moment. "You'll have to do better than that," he says, a smile flashing across his tanned cheeks. At this he fires a tactical nuclear weapon at Vader, who explodes into a thousand pieces and turns out to be have made of metal all the time.

The movie ends with the British swearing to become soccer hooligans because of the defeat, and The Patriot explaining to Congress that true freedom will have only been achieved when every man and woman, black and white, Jew and gentile, Catholic and Protestant, transgendered and bi-curious, can buy a Big Mac and own a second car.

The screen dissolves into a huge American flag and Mel Gibson walks into the dusk, holding a very large cheque indeed.

Spanking

Gavin was having a bad day. A very bad day indeed. And when 5-year-old boys have bad days everybody gets to know about it. He began to kick the cat. His father told him to stop it. Gavin refused, and gave the creature another few kicks. At which point Joe Cleary did what many parents might do. He gave his son a spanking. End of story.

But no. The spanking on the bum left a very slight mark and this was noticed by a teacher at Gavin's swimming lesson. The teacher reported it to her supervisor, who in turn reported it to the Durham Children's Aid Society.

The first thing that happened was a telephone call from a young social worker to Joe's wife, Perry, the mother of their six children. The social worker wanted clarification of the incident and requested an interview with little Gavin. "I'll have to speak to my husband first", said the heavily pregnant Perry. The social worker was incredulous, even annoyed. Why on earth did she have to speak to her husband?

"Because" replied Perry, "he is my husband, because he is Gavin's father and because he is the head of the house."

There is an expression concerning a bull and a red rag that comes to mind. The social worker seemed extremely angry now, almost beyond reason.

It was a month later when the police came to arrest Joe Cleary. They came to where he worked, handcuffed him in front of his workmates and employers and took him away like some rapist or murderer. He was charged with assault and was told by the police that he really should make a statement before his lawyer arrived because if he didn't it would look bad in court. Joe had nothing at all to hide and so he made a statement.

This good, honest, hard-working man was now incarcerated for two days in a holding cell and then in Whitby Jail, where prisoners are kept for up to two years. He had to fend off sexual advances from other men, had to watch out for the men around him charged with unspeakable crimes of violence and sadism.

After a brief court appearance the Crown asked for $1000 bail. His wife managed to get the money and offered it to the court. She was turned down, because of a statement she had made to the 22-year-old social worker on the phone. She had referred to her husband as being "the head of the house" and this was to be used in court by the prosecution, the accusation being that the couple had a "slave-master" relationship.

So the money had to be found elsewhere, and this wasn't easy for a large family who put their children first and have limited personal savings. But they managed. The bail conditions initially prevented Joe from having any contact with minors, effectively stopping him from seeing his family. Perry, now with a 10-day-old baby in her arms, protested so loudly that eventually her husband was allowed to return home.

The couple had to go to court a further seven times, with the crown demanding continuances and further investigations. "It was almost as if they were trying to punish us," say the Clearys. The couple's legal bills eventually totaled $10,000 but their lawyers were so outraged by what was going on that they halved the cost.

Finally the judge dismissed the charges under Section 43 of the Criminal Code, which allows parents to, well, to be parents and to spank their children with reasonable force if they see fit to do so.

The whole family was and is still in shock and Joe is hardly confident of promotion at work after he was seen being arrested and his bosses read about his court appearances. If it hadn't been for the strength of his union Joe Cleary may well have been fired.

As for young Gavin, none of the people behind this persecution seemed to care very much about him one way or the other. It seemed to be his parents they were after. He is, by the way, an extraordinarily happy and content little boy. The only thing that worries him these days is the idea of social workers and policemen coming to take his daddy away.

His parents are more concerned about those people who want to remove the right of mothers and fathers to chastise their children and expunge Section 43 from the Criminal Code. Such zealots quote the United Nations Charter forbidding spanking, a document that also says that if little Johnny or Jenny run to their room and slams their door shut no parent has the right to enter. It would be an "infringement" on the child's personal space and could even be "emotional abuse".

Do look behind the gentle façade of the so-called children's rights activists and do question their agenda. If you have any doubts, just have a talk with Joe and Perry Cleary. If you can still find them, because they are so upset and disillusioned that they are considering leaving the country.

The Morality of Movies

So much dogma about Dogma. The latter is a movie saying the usual nasty things about God, Jesus, Christianity. It was rejected by various American distributors but has been picked up by a Canadian company. The former is the attitude demonstrated by some Roman Catholic groups towards the film, particularly the Catholic Civil Right League.

The movie first. It features Alanis Morissette as God. This hilariously pretentious woman has little to say about anything, let alone the timeless mystery of the creator. Might as well ask the cat about nuclear physics. The plot includes trash-talking fallen angels, abortions, mockery of Catholic and Christian beliefs and the usual stuff that we've now seen on television show after television show, movie after movie.

Does it matter? Not really. The eternal truth of God, Jesus, the Trinity and salvation will not be changed or challenged in any way by a bunch of people making a movie. For some time now particularly cowardly and artistically immature people have gone for the easiest targets, more often than not being family life, traditional values and Christianity. They know that they can get away with it because unlike, say, the Jewish or homosexual lobby, resistance is weak and largely toothless. They will also be congratulated by the men and women who populate award organisations and trendy parties. People who wear black all the time, smoke furiously and contemplate how "bloody awful" the world is and why suicide is probably the best option.

Once again, it doesn't really matter. This movie will receive most of its publicity because of the activities of its opponents and will thus make a few more dollars for the people who made it and acted in it. Enabling them all to buy even more wardrobes full of black clothing. Best to ignore the whole thing. Remember, the incredibly bad Last Temptation of Christ was savaged by the critics and did badly at the box-office. The only thing that did it any good were protests by Christians, inspiring people to see what they thought would be a provocative film.

Christians would do well to remember that they are not the only targets. Empathise with people of colour, or Arabs. They are routinely portrayed as salivating terrorists and ignorant peasants. Mere objects to be killed by all-American heroes as they dash their handsome way towards the cheers of the audience, grateful that the United States has been made safe for, well, for the production of movies such as Dogma.

Seldom do I see campaigns launched by Christian groups against such racism, seldom do I see letters pages full of righteous anger from God-fearing North Americans about such a wicked stereotyping. I honestly and sincerely believe that the Biblical evidence suggests that Jesus Christ would today have been more concerned about the poor, the incarcerated, the abused and the oppressed than about some fatuous movie taking cheap shots at Him and His followers. Ignore films like this one and spend your valuable time doing His work.

Remember that the company that picked up Dogma in Canada, Lions Gate, is the same outfit that is producing American Psycho. The film in question is based on a book that glorifies the sexual torture and murder of young women and was the favoured reading of Paul Bernardo. The families of victims begged that the movie not be made but some people obviously thought that freedom of expression (or the size of a bank account) mattered more than the ripped feelings of the parents of young girls slaughtered by a serial killer.

So let's put it in context and let's treat it with the derision and contempt it deserves. But there is something else, and something that people are not going to like. It has been much trumpeted that the person who made Dogma, and several of its stars, were raised as Roman Catholics. Surely the Roman church has got to ask itself how its schools and churches produced waves of people who seem to hate the church and all for which it stands.

So many of the people I know who were born and raised as Roman Catholics are angry and full of hate. Somewhere something went terribly wrong. Instead of campaigning against the result, perhaps activists should ask why all this happened and wonder what can be done in the future to prevent it reoccurring.

As for Alanis Morissette as God, I shall react just as I do when my five-year-old tells me he is leaving home because I won't give him what he wants. Smile, pat him on the head and say "There, there, it will all be better soon."

Funding Religious Schools

So the United Nations has declared the Canadian public funding of Roman Catholic schools to be a violation of human rights unless other religious schools are given similar financing. Loath as I am to support to an extreme and self-serving club like the UN, in this case they're correct. It is incredibly unfair that the mothers and father of evangelical, Jewish and Moslem children have to pay twice for their kids' education.

The answer is a voucher system, so that parents and teachers rather than school boards and politicians may decide how and where children are taught. In other words, the proportion of a person's tax-bill that routinely goes towards education would now be given to that person in the form of a voucher and could be directed to any school of that person's choosing.

There would be some direction from above, making sure that health and educational level requirements were satisfied, but otherwise the school would be left to itself to do its job. Get the state as far as possible out of the lives of families. In the United States this has been tried in some areas and has worked very well. Religious schools have been established that cut across class and race lines, raising young people with a much higher moral and intellectual attainment than in the public system.

After all, surely nobody seriously believes that the public system works anymore.

The voucher scheme is fair and it is practical. The teachers' unions oppose such an approach because they fear a loss of power, many education experts oppose it because they are invariably on the liberal left and support state power, incompetent teachers oppose it because they know that parental choice reduces the ability of lazy or inefficient teachers to hide away somewhere.

Vouchers would enable us to scrap the Roman Catholic school system as we know it and see hundreds of authentically Catholic schools set up. Thus genuinely faithful Catholicism could be taught rather than the trendy, secular, anti-intellectual nonsense that currently dominates in those Canadian schools that have the audacity and arrogance to call themselves Roman Catholic.

If parents wanted a watered down, liberal Catholic education for their kids they could choose to give their voucher to such a place. If it just so happens that very few parents opt for such a choice, so be it. As for the public system, there would still be such schools and parents can send their kids there. But let's not kid ourselves that the secular schools are neutral.

State education in this country is secular and routinely atheistic. To assume that a refusal or failure to believe in God is moderate and the norm and that any other philosophy is extreme is just silly. In fact most Canadians still believe in a moral code based on The Ten Commandments and The Golden Rule, ideals taught in Christian rather than public schools. Lack of belief is just as much a religion as belief, and secular humanism is these days a far more aggressive creed than Christianity.

The Roman Catholic schools of Ontario, for example, have been largely raped by this dogma. I guarantee that any thorough survey of such schools would find a high number of teachers who are not practicing Catholics, lessons based on political rather religious precepts, contempt towards Papal teaching and secular attitudes towards faith and morals.

Legion are the examples of orthodox teachers being marginalised, conservative priests being excluded and members of staff living together outside of marriage. Trusting Catholic parents send their children off to be indoctrinated in moral relativism and wooly thinking about their Church and then are surprised when junior drops out of the Church. There are still, of course, many teachers in the Catholic system that are doing a fine job and are serious Roman Catholics. But they are invariably under siege. The public funding of Roman Catholic education largely destroyed Roman Catholic education. I say again, the giving hand of the state in fact slapped Catholic education into semi-consciousness.

The same would happen if government or bureaucracy got its hands on other religious schools, which is why a voucher system is the only guarantee of freedom of religion and freedom of money. After all, they're our kids, and it's out taxes.

God Bless the Big Mac

This week we celebrate the world being made safe for the Big Mac. That is, we throw a party to commemorate ten years since the Berlin Wall came crumbling down and Soviet Communism melted away like the icy monolith it always was. Let me make it clear that Marxism is a detestable ideology and that Moscow's empire was oppressive and stale. But before we all give ourselves a collective slap on the back we really should look at what we have now.

Russia itself is a shambles. Mafia gangs control the economy and Russian children sell their bodies on the streets so as to provide food for their families. The wonderful world of pornography, AIDS and crack cocaine has swept over this defiant country's major cities. Poverty, unemployment, national humiliation.

The battle against communism was not the war to end wars but the war to start them. In the former Soviet Union alone there have been almost a dozen armed conflicts as nationalistic poisons are suddenly pumped into the blood stream of Russia and its republics.

In the nearby Balkans, Serbia was bombed into the stone ages, ethnic cleansing became a household phrase and arms dealers made a fortune selling their products while the tax-payers of Canada and its allies watched in impotence. Rumania is a virtual third world nation, the Czech Republic has become the playground of hippies and Ukraine isn't quite sure where some of its nuclear weapons went.

In the former East Germany the level on unemployment and social unrest is far higher than in the west and Germany is in reality still a divided country. There are some success stories, such as Poland and Hungary, but then both countries were progressing long before Moscow let go its grip.

The Americans boasted that once they were the sole super power they would bring about world peace because the Soviets would stop beating the war drum. What nonsense. International conflict is still uncontrolled and the developing world is left to stew in its own misery. The difference now is that the United States can destroy entire cities, such as in Iraq, without anyone uttering a word of protest.

Big business applauds the changes because entirely new markets have been opened up and millions of dollars can be made in even less time than it takes a make a fortune on the stock exchange. More than this, American tourists can now eat the same food, buy the same clothes and watch the same television as at home almost anywhere in the world. And if that isn't progress I don't know what is!

As for freedom, certainly freedom of speech, assembly, religion and publication are far greater now than they were before the wall came down and that is a glorious thing. But freedom is a relative term. A third generation welfare kid from Detroit sometimes fails to appreciate the nuances of liberty when he sees mum gunned down before his eyes or turns to drugs because reality is just too hard to contemplate.

He is joined by a new underclass of people in Eastern Europe, by new depths of suffering. Far from the world being a safer place, nuclear proliferation is terrifying and terrorist groups have access to weapons that were previously restricted. The free market has enabled not just stereos and cars to be imported into Russia and its satellites but a whole carnival of examples of western materialism, from cyber sex to racist videos.

The very spiritual beauty that gave eastern Europe its meaning has been undermined by such a rapid and reckless charge towards western values, and powerful men in New York, London, Paris and Toronto don't seem to mind a bit.

Am I glad the wall came down? I suppose so. Dictatorship has to end, just as night must become day. But what a dawn it has been, and how dark are still the clouds. True freedom will be achieved when everybody, everywhere, can look forward to a full belly, a roof over their heads, a job, an education, a doctor and the right to live in peace and at liberty. The Russians are arguably further from that morn than they were twenty years ago, and we Canadians are probably right alongside them.

Chiropracty

Kim Barton was a working mother. A probation officer, she had also just given birth to her second child. All was well. Apart from a headache that wouldn't submit to medication. She went to see a chiropractor.

The usual manipulations took place. Lower back, upper back, neck. But when Kim left the office she felt dizzy, uncomfortable. She drove home, made it to the bottom of the stairs in her house and then collapsed. Her husband carried her upstairs and called the chiropractor. "If she doesn't improve, bring her back in" he said.

Kim didn't improve so she was taken back in. "I've allowed just a little too much blood to flow to her head, that's all."

The following day things were so bad that instead of driving to the original chiropractor Kim went to see someone closer. She explained what had happened. The new chiropractor manipulated her back, then gave her neck the usual sharp turns, resulting as they do in audible cracks.

"It was as if this wasn't happening to someone else," says Kim. "I could no longer speak, I couldn't see, the entire left side of my body had no feeling." The woman chiropractor then did the unthinkable. She lifted Kim into a sitting position. "I was totally powerless, and this woman was moving me when I had assumed my neck was broken. I thought I was going to die."

Eventually an ambulance was called. Kim had had a stroke. Her doctors thought she would not make it but she did. Three years later her left leg drags a little, she sometimes drools and she must never turn her neck too quickly or, for example, take her kids on the roller-coaster.

She also suffers mood swings, possibly leading to anger. So the job of probation officer is out of the question. "What else could I do but sue. I thought that even if just the house was paid for I could stop worrying about having to work to pay the mortgage. I could look after my children."

It was not to be. After a long and often humiliating process of mediation Kim and her husband were tired, poor and were willing, in their words, "to make a deal with the devil." They walked away with a fraction of what they had asked for and were told that the name of the chiropractor could not be revealed. She is, by the way, still practicing.

Is this typical? No. Chiropractors do some tremendous work, changing lives as they eliminate pain from people who have suffered for years, sometimes decades. My mother thought that she would have to tolerate back problems for the rest of her life. Until a chiropractor said otherwise. He was right, and my mother will be forever in his debt.

Lower back problems, shoulder pain, stiffness and much else can be healed by the skill of the chiropractor. But know this. The largest chiropractic college in Canada estimates that one stroke can occur every million neck manipulations. There are approximately 25million such procedures performed in this country each year. Doctors who work with stroke victims estimate the number of chiropractic caused strokes to be much higher.

People have also died from neck manipulations, and the real number is only now beginning to surface.

Then we have those chiropractors that believe that babies should be treated and that the spine deteriorates from birth. I have met several such people. There are those who claim that they can cure asthma. I have met several of these as well. Further still, there are chiropractors that believe that Multiple Sclerosis and other such profound problems can be cured by the manipulation of the spine.

These people are quacks. As are those who make instant judgements for almost everything. Three chiropractors I myself saw gave radically different diagnoses to my problem, which turned out to have nothing at all to do with my spine. One of them tried to sell me a special cushion, another a set of neck weights. Both were totally unnecessary and potentially harmful.

Conclusion. Chiropractic treatment is a small but important part of any medical amoury. It claims far too much and must be strictly monitored. As for Kim Barton, she used to think that there was justice in the world.

The Right to Say No

By now most of you have heard of Scott Brockie, the Christian printer who refused the work of a homosexual organisation and was fined for his actions. Two points. First, I broke the story originally. Second, it's profoundly important. Thus it's worth repeating.

It is vital to understand what actually happened. Brockie declined the printing work not because the customer was homosexual but because the material to be printed was, he thought, contrary to his religious views. "I have Gay clients," said Scott. "That's not the issue. The issue is the nature of the material."

This, indeed, was Scott defence when, after years of stress and legal fees, he appeared before the Ontario Human Rights Commission. No matter. He was still fined $5000 and ordered to print the material. Scott Brockie intends to take the matter to the courts, but this is not as straightforward as it sounds. No public funding for him, no groups giving money and time. There are also major companies out there who will run for cover if they think the financially powerful homosexual community is offended. Scott Brockie has problems.

Imagine. We have reached a point in society where the beliefs of those who hold the founding faith of Canada, Christianity, are given less status than the sexual preference of people who prefer to have intercourse with people of their own gender.

Consider the consequences. Let's say that the head of the Ontario Human Rights Commission, for example, Keith Norton, himself a homosexual, became a printer. A Christian organisation comes to him and asks for some material to be printed. Within that material are some of the many Biblical references to the sinfulness of homosexuality. Should Norton be obliged to print such literature?

I say no. He should be able to say that he is personally offended by the work and that there are other printers who would eagerly accept the commission. Should a Jewish printer be obliged to produce material from, say, Jews For Jesus? No, no, no.

A civil and tolerant society is based on compromise and give-and-take. Scott Brockie has been told that he is allowed to be a Christian and hold Christian beliefs, but only if he keeps them private and out of the workplace.

Homosexual zealots, on the other hand, have been told that their sexual preference can inform everything they do and MUST be part of their working experience and environment. Those who scream for tolerance appear to be becoming some of the least tolerant people in North America.

If Svend Robinson is anything to go by this is certainly the case. The homosexual MP has been accused of harassing an elderly priest outside Ottawa's parliament buildings. The cleric regularly stands there with signs commenting on moral issues, including homosexuality. He is absolutely peaceful. Robinson apparently took offence, grabbed the sign and tried to destroy it. He seems to assume that his moral authority is such that in his case the use of violence is justified. Pretty dangerous stuff.

Then there is Dr. Laura Schlessinger in the United States. Her proposed television is under siege by homosexual activists. Comic Ellen DeGeneres has called for Dr. Laura to be censored and her comrades have been told to make sure that ten protest calls are made to Paramount Television. Remember that this is the same Ellen De Generes who claimed that she was not political and only wanted to be tolerated.

Quite right. And in return we certainly did tolerate her, probably allowing this woman to continue with her television series when most people would have been told that it was time to move on. But the good lady has shown her true colours, and they do so clash with the bright hues of democracy and freedom of speech.

Which leads me to believe that we should invent a special word to describe this new wave of hatred and intolerance sweeping the continent. Heterophobia perhaps. And remember, if you bury your head in the sand the world does not go away. You do.

On the homosexual issue I say, no compromise on truth and no compromise on love. Take that to a printer. But you'll be lucky if one is brave enough to take your work in the current climate.

The Lord's Prayer

Sir Cliff Richard is known in Britain as "the nice man of pop." The 59-year-old began his career as rock singer and actor almost forty years ago and was knighted by the Queen recently for his services to the music industry. He became a Christian as a young man and since that time there has been not one ugly rumour or a nasty comment about the man or his reputation. Simply, he is one of the good guys. And one of the good guys who has recorded a staggering 132 hits, even more than The Beatles, and topped the charts in every decade since the 1950s.

What a surprise, then, when his last song, Millennium Prayer, was effectively banned from almost all of Britain's radio stations, both public and private. The official explanation was that Cliff was too old, too conservative, not sufficiently progressive. The real reason is that the extremely secular people who control the record business in Britain, just like in Canada, cannot stand the moral and ethical stand taken by people like Cliff Richard.

"The words may well be offensive to people out there in our new society", explained one radio executive, "and they're certainly offensive to me."

Not only was Cliff Richard boycotted by British radio stations but so were numerous charities. Because Millennium Prayer was produced to raise cash for a number of worthy causes, with none of the money going to Cliff Richard or his people.

But miracles do happen. Suddenly the usual fluff that dominates the airwaves, little ditties about sexual perversion, drug-taking and the joys of killing cops, was replaced by Sir Cliff. Boyzone and something called The Wamdue Project lost their number one spots to a well-known collection of words sang to the tune of Auld Lang Syne.

So what are the lyrics that have caused so much distress? I have printed them in full here, but I must inform readers that the following may disturb and shock. Be warned.

"Our father who art in heaven, hallowed be thy name. Thy kingdom come, thy will be done, on earth as it is in heaven. Give us this day our daily bread, and forgive us our trespasses as we forgive those who trespass against us. And lead us not into temptation, but deliver us from evil. For the kingdom, the power and the glory and yours, now and forever."

Yes, The Lord's Prayer. It has come to this. That the most beautiful set of words in the history of humanity is considered offensive by people who routinely condone and normalise the most dreadful and dehumanising of acts.

"I will be celebrating with friends with a couple of glasses of champagne and pinching myself to believe that this is really happening," said Richard, incredulous at the sale of hundreds of thousands of CDs of his song. He continued that he was "astounded at the knives that have come out on a personal level" and that "I find myself hated, with people in television telling the public 'Don't buy it'. And I'm thinking 'Gosh, this is for charity' – I'm just a pop singer and this is just a charity record."

Cliff Richard is being kind. He knows exactly why the knives are out, as does any genuine member of a faith community who dares to raise head or hand. Well, it's too late for me, so here goes. I invite people to suggest a piece of music to accompany the following, which will also be horribly offensive to some.

"Hail Mary, full of grace, the Lord is with you. Blessed art thou amongst women, and blessed is the fruit of thy womb, Jesus. Holy Mary, mother of God, pray for us sinners now and at the hour of death." Or, perhaps, John 3:16, or a psalm or two, or the Ten Commandments.

No apologies, no excuses, no cowering. I am proud to say that I respect every person's faith, and I expect the same of all Christians. But in turn I expect similar respect to be given to me and my beliefs.

So did Sir Cliff Richard, so does Sir Cliff Richard. Bless him for that, and bless you as well. The band will play on, in spite of the few in the audience who scream for silence.

The Evils of Communism

We in Canada are reluctant to wave the flag. We cringe a little when people speak of our victories, as though somehow they don't matter. But they do. In reading Loung Ung's "First They Killed My Father" I realised just how important it is that Canadians and their allies build monuments and museums to commemorate our greatest triumph of them all. The defeat of Communism.

You see Loung Ung is a young Cambodian woman who was a child in 1975 when the Marxist Khmer Rouge took over her country. Her father, a policeman, was the first to be exterminated, followed by most of her family and friends. They were not alone. Millions of Cambodians, including women and children, were murdered in the name of Lenin and Mao, and many liberal and socialist opinion-shapers in the west said that the Khmer Rouge was simply being misunderstood. If only they could have spent some time on the blood red, communist-red killing fields of Pol Pot.

No surprise there. The same sort of people who thought the regime in Cambodia deserved understanding also proclaimed that Stalin was misunderstood and that he was one of the greatest men of all time. So much so, in fact, that when British journalist Malcolm Muggeridge came back from the Soviet Union and wrote of the regime's brutality, he was effectively banned from appearing in print.

We go on, and on, these days about poor little screenwriters and directors who lost their comfortable jobs because of McCarthyism. Well I'm sorry, but remember that many of them did agree with Uncle Joe and wanted a Soviet system in the west. And those on the left were just as harsh, if not more so, in snuffing out opposition as was the Senator from Wisconsin. The difference is, the left is still at it.

But history does not always favour the brave. Muggeridge spoke out against the communist holocaust and was abused as a result.

So were other writers and thinkers, men and women who dared to oppose the establishment wisdom of newspapers as powerful as, for example, The New York Times.

Yet Stalin was only one communist dictator. True he wiped out tens of millions of his own people, raped and slaughtered Poles, Hungarians, Slovaks, Czechs, Rumanians, Germans, Bulgarians, Christians and so many more. But he was not alone.

Mao exterminated entire regions and classes. He fired his simple and bloody followers with the sort of hatred that even Hitler failed to achieve. Mobs ran through towns and cities ripping their opponents apart. Unlike the monster in Berlin, the communist dictators did not have the means of mass killing. They used whatever was at hand.

Beyond Russia and China there were puppet regimes in Asia and Africa, repugnant little quagmires of darkness where, according to one eye-witness, "the smell of blood drenched your clothing." But, again, whilst during the war against Nazism the press condemned Hitlerism, so many people of influence not only refused to criticise communism but even praised it. There are still political parties in Canada that praise Lenin and Marx.

When Lenin launched his campaign against the Kulaks, wealthy peasants, he and his people said that there were "sub-humans who stank and lived like animals. Even their children are scum and no mercy must be shown them. Like flies they must be exterminated."

The communists said this because they wanted the Kulaks' land and property, and they got it. You'll be pushed to find a memorial to those poor souls anywhere in the world. As you will to many other such victims. Which is particularly distressing. Because while the Nazi holocaust, which must never be forgotten, ended more than half-a-century ago, the embers of the Communist one are still alight. Witness North Korea and China. And if you doubt me, ask a refugee from Tibet.

Canadian streets bulge with people who fled communism, people whose parents, children, husbands and wives were expunged from the earth simply for being who they were. Loung Ung knows this, and Loung Ung will never forget it.

Which is why I would be more than willing to give a contribution to erect a statue in every Canadian city to the victims of communism and our victory over that evil creed. Why, I wonder, are our leaders so reluctant to do the same?

Holocaust Deniers and Other Insanity

His defenders refer to it as the court-case of the century. It isn't. But David Irving's libel suit against Deborah Lipstadt is certainly significant. British historian Irving is the darling of the extreme right and has written a series of books condemning Churchill and Roosevelt and defending Hitler. He has also made speeches denying the Holocaust.

He is suing Lipstadt because in her seminal book on Holocaust denial she refers to Irving's views and, according to the plaintiff, this led to a whole series of publishers rejecting Irving's work and preventing him from making a living.

Our friend Irving will likely lose the case, but whatever happens all this says a great about the hypocrisy, let alone the immorality, of the writer and his followers.

It's odd to say the least that people who go on interminably about a Jewish conspiracy launch a legal war against their Jewish opponents over what they claim is a conspiracy to silence them. Actually it is not a conspiracy at all and not Jewish, simply a consensus of opinion by intelligent professionals that books containing lies ought not to be published. The freedom to say no.

Irving claims to be the champion of free speech but he is attacking a fellow author because in her expression of free speech she said negative things about David Irving. Remember, nobody here has stopped Irving being published, it is just that major publishers have dismissed his work. Big deal. Self-publishing is increasingly favoured, particularly by people who sell their books at public speeches or on the Internet. Which is precisely what Irving does.

But consistency has never been one of Irving's strong points. A self-proclaimed mild fascist, he initially accepted the Holocaust but claimed that Hitler didn't know about it. Perhaps the Fuehrer slept in late that day. A few years later Irving changed his mind and said the Holocaust didn't happen, although some Jews did die because of British and American bombing raids and through disease and wartime starvation.

Actually I do not think that denial of the Holocaust, or of any other historical fact, should be illegal. Nor do I believe that it should be illegal for publishers to treat such denials with the contempt they deserve. What is good enough for the goose (step) is surely good enough for the gander.

Irving is merely the corpse of hatred with a few coats of make-up and oodles of formaldehyde Life-like at first glance but still rotting. A few years ago he made a video in which he said "I am not an anti-Semite." Long pause. "Yet." Well that's good to hear. Presumably our man in the expensive British suit has now made up his mind.

Doubly disgraceful about all of these types is their cowardice. If they would only say that they hate Jews, hate Israel because it is a Jewish state, think Hitler was a savior in spite of the moustache and, though they don't think the Holocaust happened, wished it would, I would at least respect their crude honesty.

Instead they claim to be interested only in historical accuracy, despise Israel because they love Arabs (when their skinhead followers in Europe spend a great deal of time beating them up), have no views on Hitler at all and even quite enjoyed Fiddler on the Roof.

Consider the irony. The vast majority of Holocaust deniers are Nazi sympathisers connected with people who publish violently anti-Semitic books and tapes, blame Jews for all the world's evils and call for a racial revolution. Yet they would never harm a Jewish person and know that their spiritual forbears in Germany would not have done so either. In the words of the Cookie Monster on Sesame Street, what is wrong with this picture?

The fact is Mr. Irving that there are 12 million reasons why your books should be rejected by serious publishers, and they speak Yiddish, Polish, Russian, German and most other languages. They are Jewish and gentile, male and female, adult and child. And the latter in particular, in their pure and perfect wisdom, cry out that you are a man who has well earned the disgust of the living.

Publish and be damned sir. But don't cry like a brat when the good guys tell you that they just aren't buying.

Voyeurism

What happened in Kitchener to four children and their mother is truly horrible. What happened to the man who killed them, and then himself, less so because of his crime. This, surely, is a self-evident truth and requires very little debate.

What happened after the event, however, is also quite sickening. A stinking mess of exploitation, neurosis and manipulation as journalists and neighbours of the slain family vied to outdo each other in their spasms of vicarious martyrdom and suffering.

Perhaps the worst scene of all was of silly parents dragging their children along to the crime scene to leave teddy bears and dolls for kids they never knew and never really cared about. Suddenly they were all brothers and sisters under the skin.

No parent worth the name would take a small child to a house of horror like that in Kitchener. Children cannot understand such violence, they will not be made any safer by such a visit and they may well have nightmares and develop irrational fears.

"I didn't know them or anything but I thought it might be good to, like, to come here and see what happened," explained one little girl to a desperate journalist. She then looked at her mum, and as if reminded of something she had forgotten said, "Oh yeah, and it was really bad what happened and, like, mustn't happen again."

People who lived miles away wept for the camera as they made their ghoulish procession to the latest place of interest. Wayne Gretzky's house this week, the house where those kids were killed the next.

It was almost as if we could hear these women, track-pants freshly ironed, telling little Brittany and Chelsea to "Put the toy Barney down there honey. That's right. Now look at the nice man with the microphone." Where did all these mothers and children come from, and didn't they have real mother and child things to do all day?

Neighbours paraded themselves for television, radio and newspaper reporters. Again and again and again. Legends in their own lunchtime, they were grist to the mill of journalists who swoop down on every sea of anguish and splash around until it's time to forget, move on and find another big puddle of pain.

What happened in Kitchener concerns the family, their friends, the police and the authorities. People readily admitted that they didn't know the Lufts or, if they did, hardly had any contact with them. Yet now their few moments of fame came because of indescribable suffering. I don't believe a word of it.

Those of us who have experienced genuine loss, and most of us have, know that what is desired and required is privacy and space. This was less a wake or a funeral than a sordid little thrill-ride.

Reporters suddenly became intimate friends of the community and employed every clich_ in their repertoire as they wrote of the secret world of suburban Kitchener. The "I understand, you don't" approach was used in nauseatingly large doses.

Following the journalists came the pop-psychology types, offering counseling and empathy. Not sympathy you notice, but empathy. Saying "I'm sorry for what you're feeling" is no longer sufficient. Now we have to lie, because that's what the whims of fashion require. Now we have to say "We sorry for what you feel, and we know how you feel."

Rubbish! We don't know how the relatives of that family feel, and the whole point about genuine compassion is that we offer love and support even though we haven't any idea what they're going through. I feel therefore I am, the justifying battle cry of the modern mourner. Framed by talk-show wisdom and plastic emotions, nothing will stop the modern from telling you just what everything feels like.

Professors of Psychiatry were dragged out from local universities to explain how children must be told they were not in any danger. Well, knock me down with a doctorate not worth the paper on which it's written. No child should be reading about such a crime in the first place and having the living daylights scared out of them.

I have little but contempt for those who made the deaths of the Lufts an exercise in personal satisfaction and greed. God forgive them.

A Miracle in Parkdale

If it were made into a movie they would call it "A Miracle in Parkdale". Audiences would weep, the critics would praise and the cynics would argue that this just doesn't happen in real life. Well it does. I refer to the rebuilding of Holy Family Roman Catholic Church in an area of west-end Toronto, Parkdale, that is known more for its problems than for its piety.

But rising up in the middle of the inner-city decay is the new Church of the Holy Family, the old one having been destroyed by an all-consuming fire in the summer of 1997. There is still a great deal of work to be done and completion is not expected before December. But since the foundations were laid this building has become a symbol of hope, a glorious icon of faith. And it is a product of the hard work and financial selflessness of the priests who staff it and of the people who live here.

The insurance payment for the fire provided only a fraction of what was needed to build a larger church in the classical style to cater to the needs of the community. The priests at the church donated half a million dollars themselves and then went out into the parish to find out if a financial commitment was there. It was. More than $2.5million was raised by donations from individual parishioners, local supporters, hard-working families. At a time when so many organisations run to the government and the tax-payer, Holy Family rested on its record, and its record played well.

This is because the priests at this church had become the centre of an authentic community, the hub of a spiritual and human wheel. Holy Family is the home of a group of priests and brothers known as the Oratorians, after the Oratory founded in the six-teenth-century by St. Philip Neri. This intensely humble and gifted man was renowned not just for his spirituality but also for his sense of humour and for his work with the poor.

The Oratory has since numbered amongst its ranks some of the world's greatest minds and souls, including John Henry Cardinal Newman, perhaps the most astute and influential Christian thinker of modern times and founder of the first English-speaking Oratory in the last century.

In Toronto people from all classes and races, men and women seeking the finest of worship, orthodox preaching and outstanding music travel to Holy Family in ever-greater numbers. The Oratorians also administer nearby St. Vincent de Paul, a church undergoing a similar growth and transformation.

Although the residents of Parkdale are working hard to improve the area, it is still soaked with prostitution, drugs and, because of the location policies of hospitals and the number of available rooming houses, mental illness. The church deals with these challenges on a daily basis but, unlike some Christians concerned with the poor and needy, combines this with a traditional, some would argue conservative, theology. The informed, however, would simply call it genuine Roman Catholic belief. The extraordinary within the ordinary.

Such devotion is familiar to locals. Which is why they offered the money they did and why the church is such a living, vibrant place of worship and fellowship. In simple terms, it not only talks the talk but walks the walk.

There is something truly inspiring here. An entirely natural mingling of all of the human varieties that make up the sparkling carnival that is modern Toronto. Not forced, not legislated, not publicly funded. Real, as it should be. Nor will anyone here settle for second best. Why should they? Why should we accept badly played guitars and fatuous pop hymns when we can have choirs and Mozart? It is not only the financial elite and the privileged that can appreciate the best things. True equality, surely, involves raising people up, not bringing them down.

Unlike some, the Oratorians do not make a huge fuss about their work and because of that they go largely unnoticed. There is much that is fine and sensible in that. But sometimes it is right to be celebrated. And one cannot escape the feeling that the Church invisible is partying tonight.

Daycare

Earlier this year a young Montreal couple sued a local photographer. They had decided to pose for him for a group of "erotic photographs" as some perverse sort of gift to themselves, but had expected the pictures to be kept private. While casually browsing in a pornographic magazine store, however, the woman found that she and her husband were actually featured on large posters.

My conclusion is that it served them right. If you live by the smut you may well die by the smut. There is something else though. And that is nature of the good lady's profession. She works in a daycare.

I am not for one moment implying that everyone who works in a daycare is a consumer of porn, but I am questioning the underlying premises behind the phenomenon.

CFRB radio more than a year ago. A woman explains that daycare is better for children than being at home. She should know, she said, because she worked in a large day-care centre. I disagree, arguing that she could not be objective because she was part of the highly lucrative day-care industry. But at least, I continue, your children are under your supervision in their mum's daycare. No, she says. They go to another day-care facility.

"So you go out to work in a day-care so that you can earn enough money to send your kids out to another day-care. You look after other people's children so as to be able to afford to have other people look after your own." Yes, she shouts. And I don't care, because it makes me more fulfilled. "What about your children" I ask. "Don't you see the irony and the absurdity of all this?" She does not, and angrily ends the conversation

This dialogue from the dark-side came back to me recently after going to see an acquaintance with whom I'd lost contact. I write this, by the way, because I care for him very much indeed.

He and his wife are wealthy and come from wealthy families. Their house is huge and highly decorated. But where is the new baby? Sleeping apparently. Mum is at work but the nanny is here, and here is her bedroom, because sometimes she sleeps over. We go out for lunch, come back and begin to watch a video. Baby wakes. She is beautiful. But after just a few moments of inspection she is given back to nanny and removed from our sight. Dad knows I love kids and would welcome this little one in our presence but still the new life is put aside.

Dad isn't working at the moment and probably doesn't even have to. Goodness me, the house could hold three large families and not even know it. When dad discusses mum going back to work and stopping breast-feeding he explains that "she had to." He then quickly corrects it to "she wanted to." I leave feeling rotten inside, almost in pain.

Now let me immediately distinguish between those who cannot avoid using day-care and those who can. Single mothers, couples who genuinely need two incomes to put a roof over their heads, these people have to use day-care because of the dictates of our cruel economy. But let's be honest here. What about the others who simply prefer the fantasy of being parents to the reality of the job. So much easier to employ a woman from a developing country to be a mother for you, and maybe you can even pay her cash and get her at a cheaper rate.

I was raised without very much and it could well be that in the modern world my mum would have had to go out to work. Instead my dad worked seven days a week and my sister and I knew that mum was always there, that there was tea on the table, that there was our own flesh-and-blood to listen to us, talk to us, be there. Be there.

Cut the nonsense. If there's really no economic option, use day-care. If there is, do the job you're supposed to do and raise your kids yourself. If dad can do it, fine. If mum, better. But a stranger should be the last resort and no amount of lies and revisionism will turn what is unnatural into what is natural. One day you might be asked what you did in the war to preserve family. Don't let your answer be that you decided to put up your hands and surrender.

Sex Ed for the Confused

The people of Guelph like to call their city "Ontario's best kept secret." By that they mean that their hometown is surprisingly picturesque and pleasant. Yes it is. But dig a little deeper and there is another little surprise. For the past two decades Guelph has hosted the Annual Conference and Training Institute on Sexuality, where teachers and lecturers go to learn how to educate you and your children about sex. This year's jamboree runs for ten days, beginning June 12th.

And what a stew it is. Large helpings of perversion, ample chunks of homosexuality and cross-dressing, spices of transsexual nonsense and chunks of indoctrination. All stirred with oodles of public money.

The tone is set by a one day workshop on "Sexual Education in the Classroom", explaining how to teach sexuality to kids. Sounds relatively harmless. But what sort of sexuality? The following day we meet Marshal McLernon, "a 26 year old mid-transitional transsexual man" who is "an activist, trainer/educator, writer/poet and a graphic designer by nature."

He is joined by Rupert Raj, who "is a Man and a Male – transsexual and bisexual, identifying more as a gay man right now and has been living as a man for close to 30 years. Rupert came out in the queer community in 1971 and was hormonally and surgically reassigned the following year, from female to male." Oh, I see.

If these gentlemen/ladies are not to your taste you could drop in on "Getting together: How and why bisexual women form communities." I would have thought the answer was obvious really. To apply for government grants, share each other's journey and have buddy hugs.

Then there are workshops on "The Joy of Cybersex", "HIV and Lesbian, Gay and Bisexual Youth" and "Awakening your sexual self: A women's workshop series on orgasm and sexual fulfillment." As for the last one, how many conferences does it take before these silly people have mastered the obvious. If you haven't "awoken" yourself yet then buy a bloody alarm clock.

June 20th sees a seemingly useful discussion of "Teachers' Perspectives on Sexual Health Education", but followed the next morning by 'The women's bathhouse experience", where the session "will bring together a group of women who organised attended The Pussy Palace, Toronto's first women's bathhouse."

The final day of the conference should be a joy to behold. "Tribes of Adornment: Piercing, tattooing and other forms of body art." The sessions also explores "scarification and branding" and is led by someone from the "Toronto Raver Information Project." Nice to hear that an "ice cream farewell" will follow. Flavours? Don't ask!

The theme is clear. There are no sessions on normal, healthy sexuality, no affirmation of, God help us, kids who might want to date teenagers of the opposite gender, enjoy themselves, get married when they grow up, have kids. There is no support offered for teenagers who might actually want to remain celibate until marriage. Nothing, in fact, for anyone who is not into body piercing, homosexuality, dressing up in someone else' clothes or running around like chickens with their heads cut off.

Individual teachers are given financial support to attend the conference and many of them have the entire fee, and it's $325 plus expenses for the full conference, paid by schools and school boards. The conference itself is held and partly financed by the University of Guelph, which means from your tax-dollars.

I find it difficult, genuinely difficult, to understand how at a time when student fees are being increased and schools are unable to buy books for their children, neurotics anonymous can gather together to gaze at their own navels (and pierce them) with so much of the cost being paid for by poor, boring old people like us.

This attempt to normalise the abnormal and give an intellectual veneer to the anti-intellectual is bound to fail. But what is so very dangerous is that this conference is supposed to give teachers an education in how to shape and mould the young. Sure it will cost us financially. More important, however, it will cost us morally. Young people desire protection, not demand promiscuity. The organisers of this circus might be forgiven for wasting our cash, they might not be let off for wasting our kids.

I Like Teachers

I better say this very quietly. I've been told, in fact, that it's most unwise to utter such remarks at all. But here goes. Okay, deep breath. Right, too late to stop. Here it is.

I like teachers. There. I've said it. I think they do a great job. I think they work very hard and deserve all the pay and vacations they can get. I think the Ontario government has made them out to be pariahs and scapegoats, almost inciting public opinion against those who practice the profession.

I think that teachers are generally the sort of people you would like to live next door to you. Intelligent, sensitive, thoughtful about the community, patient with children, prepared to sacrifice their private time and money to help the kids in their class.

Thus I must have gone completely mad. Because I keep reading editorials and columns marginalising them as lazy, parasitic, extreme, incompetent and stupid. Yes of course their union leadership can be annoying and intransigent, and of course there are some teachers who are pains in the blackboard. But in my experience as a parent and a writer the overwhelming majority of teachers I have met have been much better people than, say, the politicians and journalists, that I have met.

So why the contempt? Partly we are jealous. We all want long holidays and the teachers do themselves no favours when they try to disguise their generous time off. "It's not as long as you'd think"; "we always work during the vacation" or "without it we would burn out."

Don't be so defensive. Take the high road here. Kids have to have long breaks and if kids have them, you have them too. Don't spin the truth simply because all the rest of us envy you. There is nothing worse than hearing a teacher say that the public somehow over-estimates the length of school holidays.

I'm wrong. There is something worse. Hearing teachers explaining to know-nothings that they work longer than the basic school hours. Anyone with a mind knows this to be true, and the ones who don't never will. Don't waste your time.

"Hey, they arrive at nine in the morning, stand in front of the class giving out papers and doing what they've done thousands of times before, ya know. They leave right at four in the afternoon and then they have holidays all the time. Some job."

Yes, it really is some job. We shouldn't care about such bigotry. There is a line in that remarkable play and movie A Man For All Seasons when an ambitious young man is advised by the great Thomas More to be a teacher. He is told he would be a great one. But if I was, he says, who would know it? "You, your friends, your students, God. Not a bad audience that." No, not a bad audience at all.

Then we have the usual accusation that the children are caught in the middle of any dispute and that they are being used as political pawns. To a degree this is true, but there is not much else you can do when the Kings and the Queens are abusing the chessboard.

Certainly any teacher who uses valuable teaching time to introduce political indoctrination into a class is a thug. But most don't. The withdrawal of their labour is something different, simply their final show of defiance towards a government they believe to be indifferent if not hostile both to them and to public education. Ironic that those who preach the free market dispute a worker's right to go on strike.

Whether the teachers are right or not I don't know, though I have an idea or two. What I do understand is that the constant barrage of insults thrown at them will do nothing but create a dark and dreadful atmosphere in which neither children nor teachers can blossom.

Responsible politicians, just like responsible journalists and responsible parents, have a duty to search for truth and balance and to seek a common, middle ground upon which the majority of people can reach a workable compromise. There aren't many teachers who believe that this is happening at the moment, and shouting at them will solve absolutely nothing at all.

Children's Aid

It's hard to know what to make of the Children's Aid Society. On the one hand there are some fine, dedicated people working for the organisation. On the other, we here too many tales of inexperienced and radical CAS workers intervening where they shouldn't and causing pain past baring.

This is not to say that the removal of nine children from an apparently upstanding family in Ontario by the Children's Aid Society earlier this month was wrong, but there are certainly more than a few questions that have to be answered.

Two CAS workers arrived at the home of a man while he was at work and expressed concern about one of his daughters who had shown up at school some weeks earlier with a black eye. The girl and her parents explained that it had been due to a fight with a sibling.

Not good enough. The children were taken away and split up amongst five different foster families. The youngest, a two-year-old, was separated from all his brothers and sisters. According to the family the CAS workers told the children that they were there "because we heard such wonderful things about you that we just had to come and meet you."

The family also claims that the older children were asked to accompany the younger ones "to help them keep calm" and under the impression that they would be allowed to return almost immediately. They weren't. In fact the father in question alleges that initially he had problems communicating with his children and that the promised telephone-calls on the first evening did not come.

He further claims that the person taking charge of his two-year-old would not allow him to speak to the boy at all. She is reported to have said that since she did not know the family she would not let them speak to the child and they would have to trust that she was looking after their baby adequately.

The CAS concerns seem based on this couple's children spending too much time in the hospital. The emergency department clocked up a certain number of apparently play-related injuries in too short a time and were obliged to call the CAS. The parents say that with a total of 13 children it is not surprising that they spend a fair amount of time dealing with cuts and bruises.

The CAS now claim that they also have problems with the cleanliness of the family home, but this seems to be an after thought in that they only entered the home on the premise the father was abusive.

The children claim that CAS workers have given them written reports about their parents and why it made so much sense for them to be removed from the home. "In other words", says the father, "the CAS can tell our children whatever they want but we can't tell them anything."

The children have said that they have been taken to the stores by the CAS and told that they can buy anything they want. Perhaps an effort to make them feel better but, if so, more than crass and also far from being good parenting.

The parents have now had some contact with their children, when they were united for a church service – with two CAS workers present. Perhaps significantly, both the father and an elder of the church noticed a sudden lack of discipline on the part of the children. When the two-year-old began to cry during the service his mother, naturally, left the sanctuary. She was immediately followed by a CAS worker.

When this same child was removed from the family again after the evening service he gripped his father in an attempt to stay. As he was belted into the CAS car he screamed, "Home, home, home". The doors were closed and the vehicle drove away.

The future? The CAS have explained that if the family is to be allowed to resume it will take months and that the parents and children will be monitored for years, meaning random and surprise visits. The parents of the clan are already looking for another home but it is difficult to see how they can restore their family after all this.

Perhaps this had to happen. But if it didn't, the injustice of it all is quite, quite horrible.

The Police and Racism

Okay, let's get the niceties out of the way. The police do a great job; they're the last line of defence; our cops are tops; I wouldn't do the job, whatever you paid me; there are only a few bad apples; it's dangerous; we take them for granted, etc., etc.

The point is, however, that 99 times out of 100 you can praise the police, but if you once criticize you become a police-basher. A great shame.

Two weeks ago a fine man was shot in the face by bad guys. He was protecting private property and keeping the rule of law. My heart goes out to him and his family. One of the wanted men was described as being white, the other dark skinned. Yet by the afternoon the police had pulled a black man from a subway train and even before this happened talk-radio stations were discussing the problem of "black crime."

Bear in mind this was the day after a white man was sent to jail for the brutal murder of a young black woman in Toronto, and only days after it was revealed the extremely Caucasian Karla Homolka had been indulging in little trips out of prison. Some people have reason to be rather angry.

Let's be candid here. It is extremely rare to meet a black person, particularly a young black man, who has not had some unfortunate experience with the police. Being stopped in the car for no apparent reason, being asked what you are doing when you are simply walking home, asked for identification because you're not in the right area.

If I, white and middle class, have heard this from the black guys I have met, we can only imagine what those in the middle of the black community experience.

This is not to say the police service is racist. I don't know a racist cop. I know cops who do their jobs. Perhaps unquestioningly but seldom with malice. Yet somewhere something has gone wrong.

Ignore the zealots and the professional complainers, just ask the black men and women you know if they have ever felt intimidated or wrongly treated by the cops. If, of course, you know any people of colour. And therein lies a great deal of the problem.

The police service has to mirror and reflect society in general, otherwise it is at risk of becoming something separate and detached. Difficult to achieve, though, especially when the greater society has its own problems.

I was in St.Jacobs recently with the kids. My 9-year-old daughter and her cousin went into a store to buy some candy. As they walked in the crowded place the owner followed them, only a yard behind all the time and always staring at them. They bought some gum. Then they tried on a hat in the corner.

"No trying on!" barked the woman, and grabbed the hat from them.

We tried an experiment. My wife went into the store five minutes later. She was not followed, she tried on some hats and everything was roses. Conclusion? The storeowner didn't like and didn't trust kids.

Find out how often black people are followed in stores, watched as if they were all potential thieves. Treated, in fact, like naughty and dishonest children.

It's not the cops who are to blame but all of us. We ignore the big-time criminals in our rush to condemn. We ignore the arms-dealers, the people who actually control the drug trade, the serial killers, the sex criminals, the people who start wars and colonize, the people who commit enormous fraud and tax evasion. Loath as I am to appear racist, they tend to be as white as the snow from above.

Perhaps we should start to investigate the phenomenon of "white crime." Or perhaps we should simply address the issue of crime itself.

Blame the '60s radicals who said single-parent families and the drug culture were cool, blame the urban planners who put people in sky-high monstrosities, blame an economy that forces both parents to work and blame our own obsession with discriminating against those who are not only our equals but our brothers and sisters.

And for goodness sake do it quickly, before it's too late.

JFK Jr.

I am not particularly sorry that John F. Kennedy Jr., his wife and her sister died last weekend.

I am sorry, of course, in that I am sorry when anybody dies, particularly people who are relatively young and have not fully lived out their lives. But not "particularly" sorry.

You see, I didn't know them, didn't have any links to them, didn't feel anything for them. And I do not understand those people who act as if the did.

Nor do I understand, or approve of, the ridiculous amount of publicity given by Canadian media outlets to the death of an extremely ordinary American and his wife and sister-in-law.

Again, I'm sorry and all that, but in the final analysis, why all the fuss?

This latest Kennedy was in fact little more than a rich kid with too much time on his hands. He had money, power, good looks and charm. He could have used these free gifts to do so much. In fact he had an obligation to do something constructive but instead his major contribution was a rather tepid and somewhat self-indulgent political magazine.

He owed the world more than this, because the world had given him so much.

What I mean is that merely because this man was born the son of a famous American president he was awarded a mythological stature, an almost spiritual status as the heir of a mighty clan. After his death people who knew him testified to how wonderfully "ordinary" he would make himself.

"He used the subway, just like everyone else," commented one fawning editor at Kennedy's George magazine, as if this choice of transport denoted some sort of unique inner goodness.

But then his dad was treated in the same way.

President Kennedy was a liar, an adulterer, an abuser and a

fraud. He lied about his war record, he had someone write his books for him and then claimed they were his own. He used women as pieces of meat and passed them onto other men for use as living toys, including members of his family.

His own father was a criminal who bribed voters, ran a corrupt political machine and at one time thought that it might be a good thing if Hitler defeated Great Britain.

Kennedy the president led his country into the Vietnam War and then the little sycophants around his so-called "court of Camelot" rewrote history so as to blame anyone and everyone but their King Arthur. He was a vacuous playboy who knew neither hard work nor integrity. Naturally, he became Bill Clinton's hero.

As for young John's uncle, Sen. Ted Kennedy, it is a mystery and a scandal that this man has been able to continue with his political career. His infamous abandonment of "date" Mary Jo Kopechne after good old Teddy drove their car into a lake at Chappaquiddick would have destroyed, if not incarcerated, most other people.

The senator's well-known drinking and womanizing make both himself and his office a laughing stock, yet his name guarantees him a place within the higher reaches of America's political elite.

The cult of John F. Kennedy Jr. has already begun. The pundits ask what would he have achieved and how great would he have been, as if he was a young sports figure who had broken all records but had not yet reached his prime. Hold on a minute, this was a spoiled brat in a spoiled country.

As for his death, he was flying his own plane to his ludicrously expensive family compound, when he was not really sufficiently experienced to do so.

It seems that on this occasion his almost saintly penchant for public transport did not emerge. Bad luck. Once again, I am sorry the three people are dead. But give me a break. This is Princess Diana all over again, but at least she had been forced to put up with an inbred husband and had managed to do many good works.

Little Johnny had done little, and is now absurdly celebrated by people who every day look right through heroes and heroines. Heroes and heroines because they do what most people do – work, save and sacrifice.

Goodbye, JFK Jr. I didn't know you, and I'm not sure that I really care.

"Woody" is 17 years old and has been living on the street and in shelters for three years. He left home because there was no home. "I'd never seen my mom and dad together." His mother lived with an abusive boyfriend who would regularly beat up Woody and his sisters. Even now not a big guy, as a child he would face up to the thug living with his mum and say, "Leave my sisters alone, hit me instead."

One night Woody's mom got drunk and ended up going to jail for manslaughter. Shortly after this, Woody's natural father died of a heart attack. A Children's Aid Society home followed, but Woody ran away. "I suppose I couldn't come to grips with my parents being gone and with me being split up from my sisters." Then came the streets of Toronto. "Sometimes I wake up in the park with the blanket over my head and I think that when I take the blanket off that my family are going to be there and everything is going to be okay." A pause. "But they're not. And it isn't."

Leah, like "Woody" a fictitious name, is 16 and has a bright and beautiful little son who is approaching his second birthday. Her mother was never on the scene and her father was only slightly better. "He was very young when he had me. I didn't know him, he didn't know me."

She lived with her grandparents, in the midst of constant arguing and fights. At the age of 12 she ran away. "It couldn't be worse on the streets than it was back there," she says. "I just wanted some affection, somewhere to belong." Drugs, violence, pimps and pushers smashed into this articulate, intelligent girl's life. But she found commitment. Sure she is a teenage mother, but her child means the world to her and is pulling her towards salvation.

Her boyfriend is very much there for her and she is dedicated to building a new life. I saw her with her son. Saw her bursting with warmth and care towards this tiny light in a dark world. She seemed a better mom than many extremely wealthy parents I have seen.

I mention all this because for the first time in my life I walked not past but through the doors of Toronto's Yonge St. Mission. The facade of this place of help for young people in trouble can be disquieting. Street kids. Doing what kids, on the street or not, tend to do. Pushing, shouting, dressing in a way that is designed to cause unease amongst older people. So what.

Inside I found a relaxed discipline, a respect for other people and a comfortable order. More important than this, I found ordinary teenagers who just hadn't received a break.

"When I'm on the subway I'm one of the regular people, just like everyone else" says one boy, holding an enormous ham sandwich. "Then I get to the doors of the shelter and I'm scum again." A girl nods her head. "Sure there are a few people who play at it, but for most of us the last place we want to be is on the street or in a shelter. We know how you live, we know about family and love. We want that too. But it doesn't just come. You ignore us as though we were animals. We're not animals. We're not."

Between them these kids have done it all. They've squeeged and panhandled, even committed crimes and sometimes been in prison. The latter they regret and know was wrong. The former? "It's not fun y'know," they explain. "We do it because we need money for food. If we had homes we could go to we'd be in them. But try finding a job when you haven't got an address, try keeping yourself presentable when you're sleeping on a park bench."

Conclusions? I demand proof before I take a position. But this time I'm convinced. These kids need help and, most of all, need love. "Are you going to forget us as soon as you leave?" asked one kid. I said I'd try not.

They broke my heart and they would break yours. If any politician tells you otherwise, tell them to stop condemning and start repairing.

Will Power

Another trip to Stratford last Saturday, with my 10-year-old son Daniel. A cathedral of taste and beauty in the middle of the Ontario heartland, the theatre festival is an essential journey for anybody within reach. We saw The Alchemist by Shakespeare's lesser-known contemporary Ben Johnson.

The cockney genius of the early 1600s was a superlative satirist. In other words, he made fun of the powerful and the pretentious. He held a mirror up to their foolishness, and by so doing burst their bubbles of reputation and grandeur.

Which sort of got me to thinking about some of the other productions that we might have seen run at glorious Stratford.

Romeo and Juliet. A play about two families with much in common but who fight one another with dreadful results. Specifically, the story concerns the attempts by a group of Reformers who used to be Tories to form a new party with Tories who are still Tories. Often seen in tandem with A Midsummer Night's Dream, except that the role of the Queen of the Fairies is apparently highly unpopular with the audience, some of whom think that the person in question should "get to the back of the store."

The Comedy of Errors, a drama that deals with the attempt by Svend Robinson to have himself taken seriously by the national electorate. In this piece Svend is mistakenly taken for a responsible politician, but all ends well when a mighty princess turns him into a frog.

Which leads me to Jane Austen's Pride and Prejudice, currently running to rave reviews. Searching for a separate identity, poor Mr. Parizeau realizes that labeling people and accusing them of doing naughty things is just not cricket. While all this is going on brave Mr. Bouchard struggles with his inability to listen to anyone other than himself.

All is settled, however, when everybody realizes that they are a bunch of privileged brats who should have better things to do with their time.

King Lear, in which a man becomes strangely complacent in his rule and increasingly detached from the realities of life and his people. He finally goes mad and wanders around the country searching for answers. A stellar performance here from a man who rehearsed hard for this part by throttling protesters and throwing pepper spray at students. He was apparently allowed to take on this role and leave his soap opera career only with the permission of the Prime Minister's Office.

The Taming of the Shrew, where a feisty wench by the name of Sheila Copps loses all hope of becoming leader of the Liberal Party and instead takes up a lucrative position at the United Nations as commissioner for telling the truth about taxation. Unfortunately, she does not last very long.

A Man for all Seasons, a play specially written for Jean Charest, who as a Progressive Conservative condemned the Liberals for being a threat to Canada's way of life and now as a Liberal condemns the Parti Quebecois as being a threat to Canada's way of life. Nobody is condemning Mr. Charest as being a threat to Canada's way of life because most people have forgotten who he is.

The Merchant of Venice, in a new version written by the authors of Mike Harris' Common Sense Revolution. In this witty adaptation, severely cut back from the original, Shylock's demand for a pound of flesh is praised as sensible obedience to the laws of the free market, while the compassionate Portia is dismissed as a puppet of various special interest groups.

The Merry Wives of Windsor. Such an obvious title for double-meaning that I will not even attempt to make fun of those Canadians who zealously defend or purport to represent a severely dysfunctional family living in a set of castles 3,000 miles away.

Then comes Much Ado About Nothing, a riveting spectacle about confusion, hidden identities and clowns who get their words mixed up. Definitively portrayed by one Dalton McGuinty during the 1999 Ontario Election. Oddly enough most other members of the ensemble prefer Richard III, in which people pretend to be loyal to the monarch while he has power, but desert him immediately another leader comes into view.

Finally, as the Bard of Avon had it, All's Well That Ends Well. Not.

Hatred for All

So Rev. Fred Phelps didn't quite make it to Canada to provoke people with his offensive and hateful remarks about homosexuality.

How sad. I interviewed the man over the telephone last week and asked him to justify his calling homosexuals "faggots" and thanking God for AIDS.

He distorted Scripture, shouted and ranted. He called me a "perverted talk-show host" and then slammed the phone down on me. I was quite flattered, actually.

What is conveniently forgotten when this lunatic is discussed in the media is that he does not confine his hateful remarks to homosexuals.

He refers to Billy Graham as a "coward and a heretic," to Southern Baptists as being "pro-homosexual" and to the Roman Catholic, Lutheran and Presbyterian churches as being part of a huge "pro-fag" conspiracy.

Phelps described Elizabeth Taylor as "a Jew whore," dismissed the world's Jewish population as not being Jewish at all but being sinners who are "pro-faggot" and slandered the mass of evangelical Christians as being liars and blasphemers.

This information is important, because it positions Phelps squarely as someone who is about as representative of Bible-believing Christianity as Ernst Zundel is of Canadians. He is a nut who has nothing to do with the debate about homosexuality and its place in contemporary North American society.

He calls himself a Baptist but fits none of the fundamental principles of Baptist theology.

In fact, his church consists of a couple of hundred people, many of whom seem to be members of his family.

Indeed, it was this issue that made Phelps hang up on me.

Apparently, he didn't like it when I asked him why so many members of his congregation had the same surname as their pastor.

But there were other disturbing events surrounding this sad and bad man's proposed trip north to chastise Canadians.

Sgt. Pat Callaghan, head of the Ottawa-Carleton hate-crimes unit, was reported as saying, "If this was done against a Catholic or a Jew or a black person, charges could be laid. If we had that legislation, we wouldn't have to put up with this nonsense. We could have told him, 'If you show up and start spreading this hate, we'll arrest you.'"

Well, wait a minute. Roman Catholics are frequently attacked in the media.

CBC Radio's Michael Enright described the Catholic Church as the "greatest criminal organization in the world outside of the Mafia."

To be sure, this is less egregious than Phelps' rantings.

Then again, Enright, far from being censured, received a job as the CBC's leading radio personality, paid a six-figure sum in public tax dollars.

Gay newspapers frequently make dreadful remarks about Catholics and evangelicals and no action is taken.

I myself have been threatened with physical violence and with being stabbed.

This latter remark was made at a public conference and repeated in print. Again, no action was taken.

On a more general note, aren't public servants meant to implement the law without favour?

Should they be speaking publicly about why our Parliament, the voice of democracy and the people, should change the law?

Whether liberal or conservative, left or right, their politics should be kept private.

There is something else, something for which I suppose I might get into some trouble.

The religions of Judaism and Roman Catholicism and the noble heritage and honour that is being a person of colour are very different phenomena from a mere sexual preference, particularly one that is considered sinful by all of the world's great faiths and most of the world's cultures.

One day our whole society – police, civil servants, politicians, all of us – are going to have to struggle with where the rights of genuine Christians, not to mention followers of Islam, clash with those of homosexuals.

Truth is exclusive. Christians should not tolerate what they know to be wrong, even if is at the expense of sounding politically incorrect.

The answer must come not from cultists in Kansas, pressure groups or even the police.

It must come from a referendum on the legal place and privileges of homosexuals in Canada and it should be binding.

If both sides believe in their cause, what do they have to lose?

The Jews of Iran

I have just heard a story about a ghost. Had the misfortune to learn about a spectre that once haunted the world but, I thought, had been put to death long ago, buried in some stinking hole of darkness.

Of course, I knew the corpse grumbled occasionally and that a handful of zealots felt those tremors and danced to the vibrations. But no state would do such a thing, no government.

The ghost I speak of is anti-Semitism, and the arrest of 13 innocent Jewish people in the Iranian towns of Isfahan and Shiraz. The alleged crime of these teachers, rabbis and storekeepers is international espionage and support for "the Zionist entity." In other words, they are accused of being Israeli spies.

Their trial will be speedy and their punishment, if found guilty, will be just as swift. They will be executed.

That the charged are innocent is a self-evident truth. The Iranians, let alone the rest of the world, know that spies do not spend all of their time working in mid-level jobs in provincial towns. Israel's Mossad has a long and successful history of infiltrating the governments of hostile nations but has not devoted too much time and money to positioning operatives in the history departments of tiny schools in the middle of nowhere.

The official statement that "The elements, who were identified and arrested, played a vital role in the espionage network" and "were arrested with the help of the noble people of the province" is not taken at all seriously. Interestingly enough its wording is similar to that of releases issued by Eastern Bloc governments when they organized their show trials.

What all this is about is the power struggle between the Teheran government, intent on building bridges with the West and easing internal restrictions, and a judiciary still controlled by Islamic fundamentalists. In fact, Iranian Jews have been treated quite well in recent times – as they have been for centuries.

Genuine Islam guarantees freedom of worship for "People of the Book" – Jews and Christians – and in Iran there are 40 synagogues, 10 Jewish schools and relative security and freedom for the country's 30,000 Jews. These people could have left years ago. They didn't because they consider themselves Iranian and love their country.

So this entire mess is about politics. There are three possible motives.

The first is that the hardliners want to provoke Israel and the United States into taking action against Iran, thus pushing Iran into reacting with a tougher position toward the non-Muslim world and dragging it back into its former isolationism.

The second is that the extremists simply want to frighten the remaining Jews of Iran so they will leave the country of their birth and ancestry and go elsewhere, possibly Israel. At the moment any Iranian who visits Israel will not be allowed back into the country.

The third is that the captives will be used as bargaining tools, just as were the Jews of the former Soviet Union. In other words, we will release a certain number of Jews for a certain amount of money, supplies or concessions.

For those 13 people now in prison, however, the politics of the situation is largely irrelevant. They simply do not want to be hanged from a scaffold until their necks are broken, after being given a few moments of mock justice in what would be a kangaroo court.

Another grotesque consequence of this stupid and callous act could be more international hostility toward Islam, which would be unfair and unjust. The Muslim faith is one of peace and respect, as anyone would know if they had spent any time with any members of Canada's Muslim population. They feel as powerless and embarrassed as anybody else when they see their religion exploited and perverted for base political reasons. They also know that the bigotry that has endangered the lives of 13 Jews in Iran is the same sort of bigotry that has them called names on the streets and abused on the cinema screen.

For the sake of Canada's championing of right and wrong, as well as for the Iranian Jews and their families, we all should do our bit.

To help, call the Canadian Jewish Congress at (416) 635-2883, extension 186.

A rally to protest these wrongful arrests will be held on Sunday at 7:30 p.m. in the Leah Posluns Theatre, 4588 Bathurst St.

In Praise of the Welfare State

I have just received a letter from a Mr. Morgan in Mississauga. He wrote the following: "When you sacrifice to send your kids to get a good education they might end up rich. Why should anyone, including the government, have the right to take more of their earnings away than anyone else? A lot of people who complain about the health care system are suffering from alcohol consumption and smoking cigarettes. They want the government to look after them.

"How many people were abusing the welfare system before Mike Harris came along? When they got their welfare cheques they went to the beer store in a taxi.

"Children were leaving home because they did not want to listen to their parents, they knew they could get welfare. Liberals and NDP support a welfare state. Mike Harris' policy makes you accountable."

I am sure Mr. Morgan is a good man. But he is wrong and he has surrendered to malicious gossip and urban mythology.

Let me emphasize that I am not inexperienced in the ways of the world, not someone who has been handed anything on a plate. My dad drove a London taxi; my mum comes from the same place as the notorious east-end gangsters the Kray twins.

My four grandparents never owned property. One set lived in an apartment in Hackney, the other in Stepney Green. Believe me, you wouldn't have liked it. My dad, Jewish, was an amateur boxer and then took his fists to the streets in the 1930s to deal with local fascists. He was in the RAF at 17. My grandfather spent the entire Second World War in the army. They made him a sergeant, even offered him a commission. He turned it down. Either way, he was doing to fascists in North Africa and Italy what my dad had been doing to a lesser extent on the cobbles of Mile End.

Tough. Poor. Don't take nonsense from anyone. Work hard, do what you have to do. But sometimes you just can't make it. There were people even back then who fell through the cracks. Fell, fell and fell. Died young and alone, mere meat in a corner. Because the government in those days, in Britain as well as Canada, believed that the people who couldn't find a job or a home were lazy and worthless.

I was lucky. The welfare state. Until I was five we lived in a little apartment. But then my dad managed to get the down payment for a three-bedroom semi. Which is where I lived, and loved, for most of my life. Where my parents still live. I remember the day my dad announced he had paid off the mortgage.

So proud. It took him 30 years.

I had free education, free health care, free milk at school. The dentist, the libraries, the museums were all free. Those who needed help? They got it. And in the name of the living God, they deserved it. It was good. It was fine. It was worth fighting for. It was worth dying for. Worth it then, worth it now. In Britain and in Canada.

Mr. Morgan, you are so wrong. Of course there are frauds and parasites. But they are rich as well as poor. For every drunk who takes a cab to a beer store there are thousands of people who are humiliated beyond belief because they have to go to the state, cap in hand. Single mothers, people who have a mental illness, those without families, those who just don't fit in.

Sure there are kids playing the game of being poor. But they're the few. Meet the teenagers who fled abuse and indifference, who scream out for love. Know the poor who are told to do what they're told and to shut up.

Yes, Mr. Morgan, there are people who made money out of their own labour. But there are also many who inherited the cash or simply got lucky. Or made money through the efforts of the very men and women you now marginalize. Either way, we live in community, and we're all a pay cheque away from trouble.

Hear this from a man who is not a liberal bleeding heart or a champagne socialist. You do not understand, my friend. Pray you're never forced to at first hand.

Tell NAC
the Well's Run Dry

Give us your money or we'll attack you. This seems to be the attitude of the women who lead the National Action Committee on the Status of Women. They're meeting in Ottawa, threatening to protest and picket unless the government gives them what they refer to as "one enormous cheque."

That cheque, of course, will come from your tax dollars.

NAC has been given millions of dollars by the federal government over the years and just recently was given another $281,000. The organization employs seven people, and manages to spend the lion's share of its budget on salaries and staff. The bulk of NAC's money, as always, comes not from donations by concerned supporters but from the largesse of civil servants and ministers.

NAC's story is rather like that of the emperor's new clothes. The women at NAC claim to be well dressed but in fact they're completely naked.

The increasingly isolated organization has boasted a membership of hundreds of thousands. Not true. Because some organizations affiliate en masse it means that people suddenly became NAC members when they might despise everything NAC represents.

The YWCA has been a member, meaning that if a woman goes for a swim a couple of times a week she is suddenly a committed supporter of abortion on demand, lesbian adoption and the compulsory wearing of Birkenstocks.

Unions join as single lumps. So a woman who perhaps votes Tory and thinks men are usually nice guys helps to finance NAC's silly and often hateful vision of a gender war. Ridiculous as it might seem, this matters.

Because of NAC's ability to pretend it speaks for Canadian women, various governments have directed legislation and money along paths dictated by a handful of zealots. The lives of Canadian women and Ottawa's responses have been based on a vision seen through the smeared prism of a radical feminist ideology that is no longer backed even by mainstream feminists, let alone mainstream women.

That is changing because fiscal conservatism is in fashion, and because there are no longer any vocal supporters of NAC in cabinet. Thus the squeals from the ranks of the apparently dispossessed.

NAC wants your money. And it wants it now. Why? Well, to continue what it calls "a major political struggle and revolution" against "racism, sexism, homophobia, ableism, ageism and classism." It also wants it to help the struggle of Marxist terrorists in Colombia and to help bring "about a just and peaceful resolution to world conflicts."

Okay. You can also fight for the rights of UFO aliens stranded in Nevada and universal health care for hamsters for all I care, but do it with your own cash. The neurosis of government dependency has to be cured. It's time to cut the apron strings and make it in the big world. Organizations such as REAL Women, a conservative pro-life and pro-family group, have survived and prospered without enormous injections of government money.

NAC has also suffered from the rule of diminishing leaders. Today's leader, Joan Grant-Cummings, has little profile and has not managed to win many friends in high places. Her somewhat strident predecessor was similarly deficient. The most successful leader of NAC was Judy Rebick, a politician who has since demonstrated her abilities on television and radio. Though, it has to be said, mainly on publicly funded television and radio.

Judy, however, was able to present a veneer of importance for NAC and also managed to convince at least some women the organization was relevant to them. Those attempts seem to have been abandoned by more recent leaders, who at times appear almost contemptuous of women who do not accept "the line."

NAC leaders just don't seem to understand, for example, that the plight of what they call "sex-trade workers" is not the major priority of a woman working in an office or a stay-at-home mother. They have failed to grasp the fact that gender is only one issue in a highly complex equation. They still fight wars won long ago or launch battles for imaginary or unworthy causes.

Women of the world unite. You have nothing to lose but your grant applications. Move on, comrades, and get a job.

Same-Sex Spousal Rights

Just like M & M's candies, M and H have such a lot in common. Or at least they did until these two lesbians went their separate ways. A court battle followed, with M wanting spousal support.

Eventually the Supreme Court agreed and hundreds of laws will have to be changed to make sure no Canadian homosexual feels in any way slighted. The act that various democratic legislatures have said no to homosexuals being spouses is irrelevant. A handful of unelected judges in Ottawa knows best.

And so does the lawyer for M, one Martha McCarthy. She was too busy to speak to me on the day of the judgment but her legal assistant was more forthcoming. I asked if we should continue with our battle against discrimination and allow brothers and sisters to marry. A long pause.

"I'm not really sure."

Be sure.

"Well, it would depend if there was a power relationship. I mean males have power in a family."

What about brother and brother?

"Well, I don't know. I suppose it could be okay. But it's against (the) law isn't it?"

Yes, but the law can be changed. After all, homosexuality was against the law not so long ago.

"Yes, I don't really know."

Shouldn't we have an absolute answer to such a deeply moral question? Why are you discriminating? Are you intolerant? If men having sex with other men is now considered normal and approved behaviour, why not incest?

"Look, I'm really not comfortable with this conversation."

Another supporter of the ruling was more confident.

"I would be very careful about brother and sister relationships because of the power dynamic, but brother and brother or sister and sister would be acceptable."

Before you talk about the possibility of genetic defects from an incestuous union, in the sexual quagmire of the late 20th century two siblings could always practise what is known as "safe sex." Or if not, just have a publicly funded abortion. No problem there.

The point is this, if discriminating is wrong, it is wrong. We cannot decide to validate one "alternative" form of relationship between consenting adults and refuse to accept another. After all, we're not bigots. Either there is a moral law or there isn't. I opt for the former.

What the ruling has done is to equate the ultimate sexual act between a man and a woman, with its innate grace and the possibility of procreation, with the ultimate sexual act of two male homosexuals: sodomy. As for lesbians, best to use your imagination.

Logic, truth and common sense cry out to be heard. The mere fact our bodies are designed to function in one way and not another is enough to show the absurdity of this ruling.

Nor is this about tolerance, it is about forced praise. Homosexual activists won the fight for tolerance long ago, they now demand that we approve of what they do. I for one – and I believe I speak for the majority – do not approve of homosexuality. But nor would I pass a law making it illegal or prevent people from indulging in it in the privacy of their own homes. If only gay activists were so broad-minded.

One of them, at a media conference attended by several newspaper editors and television producers, asked why nobody "has stuck a skewer down Michael Coren's throat."

Homosexuals have long been able to adopt children but will now be virtually encouraged. If you smoke or have particularly strong religious views you will not be allowed to adopt. Yet homosexuality is no barrier.

Indeed, if homosexuals are turned down they can run off to the courts and make sure justice is done.

We play with children's lives. Do we really believe a child will blossom fully and normally with two parents of the same gender? Do we seriously believe two lesbians will have no objection if their son is heterosexual?

The lesbian mothers I have spoken to, all good women, have told me that while they will try not to consciously influence their children, they would be heartbroken if they were "straight."

The doors have been opened. And what comes in will not be as sweet as a packet of candies.

Shed No Tears for Salman

Salman Rushdie is in Toronto this week and tonight he will be speaking at a university gathering of "his" people. I am proud to say I will not be in that number and that, while I do not support any threat against his life, I believe Salman Rushdie is a blasphemer who should pay dearly.

Stop! Horror! What has that crazy man said? Let me repeat: Rushdie is a blasphemer who deserves to pay a price. Let me also explain that I am not a Muslim and that I also know Salman Rushdie, having written a chapter about him in my first book as well as having produced and written a documentary about him for British television. I have always found him to be a highly intelligent man.

Let's get back to the blasphemy statement for a moment. We take offence at people's actions every day. The thief, the thug, the fraud and the hate-monger may all go to prison or be fined. The person who libels and slanders is subject to a lawsuit. So society agrees that words, like actions, can cause harm and even break the law.

Society also agrees, surely, that words are often more harmful than actions. One speech by Hitler, for example, did far more damage than the fists of one Nazi hoodlum. The pen, runs the saying, is more powerful than the sword.

Now blasphemy, the profane abuse of a religious person or faith, is likely to offend not just a few but a multitude. We in the post-Christian West no longer understand this because for the most part we have given up worshipping God and instead bow down to the dollar, to television and to our own gratification. Because of this we call ourselves civilized and dismiss Islam as being uncouth and extreme.

Salman Rushdie abused and mocked Mohammed in his book The Satanic Verses. He was told long before its publication that the book would deeply insult every faithful Muslim. In his arrogance he concluded he knew better. People have died because of that arrogance.

If the Anglo-Indian writer had told malicious lies about a wealthy or powerful man, he likely would have been sued and his book would have been scrapped. Instead, he told malicious lies about a great world faith and he was lauded by the launch lizards and the chattering classes.

Such people, of course, make a great deal of money out of shouting down people's religious beliefs. Because of the Rushdie case and the fear it produced they tend now to throw their mud at Christianity, but their hatred has the same root. Full of invincible ignorance, they never seem to learn.

Salman Rushdie did learn, however. He learned how to change his ways. From comparing the British government of Margaret Thatcher to that of Adolf Hitler, he then asked for and received the enormously expensive protection of the British police, paid for by the British taxpayer. And the British taxpayer, just like the Canadian taxpayer, really doesn't care about Salman Rushdie and his buddies.

You see, it is also a question of class. The patricians around Salman Rushdie see the Islamic world as dark, dangerous and demented. "Not our sort of people at all." In the same way they despise Christianity. "All nasty little types in the deep south and in Alberta. How utterly wretched." For this they call themselves liberal.

There is another issue here. Hundreds of good and great men and women have been imprisoned, tortured or even killed because of their writings in the past few years but none of them, not one, has received anything like the attention given to Rushdie. That's largely because many of them are black, most of them not famous and none of them had the connections in fashionable London and New York enjoyed by the Cambridge-educated author of The Satanic Verses.

It appears that self-appointed martyrdom discriminates as well.

I sincerely hope Rushdie is allowed to walk around freely and feels entirely comfortable doing so. But I also hope he and others like him have realized that liberty is the child of responsibility, and that sometimes the underdog bites back.

Cruelty Doesn't Discriminate

A letter concerning the recent massacre in Colorado is circulating within the Toronto District School Board. Naturally, it expresses its horror at that terrible event. It then explains how vital it is for the teenagers in Toronto to "talk openly and honestly about their feelings" and adds that "of particular concern to us are the racial aspects that surround this tragedy."

The rest of the letter covers an extensive list of actions under the headings of "Do" and "Don't," just in case any of the teachers concerned would like to actually think for themselves. Under the latter section are "Don't be afraid to show your emotions, don't be judgmental, don't lecture and don't moralize."

Goodness me, where do I begin? First of all, part of the underlying problem of youth culture, and North American culture in general, is the recently established cult of the feeling. I feel, therefore I am.

Before children can read and write they have to be conscious of their feelings. Kids are no longer asked what they know but what they feel. The little monsters in Colorado did what they did because they "felt" they wanted to, instead of "knowing" it was wrong.

Feelings are by their nature transitory and unreliable. We might feel like stealing something we want, kissing a person we desire, hitting someone who angers us. We don't because a higher moral law submerges our often negative feelings. Simply, feelings can be wrong.

American talk shows splash around all day in feelings, where the dysfunctional poor to the famous rich weep on call and share their journeys of pain. They then do it again on another talk show. And then on another and so on and so on.

It's odd that the truly hurting people, those in the developing world, are never asked how they feel. Perhaps because we don't care or perhaps because we already know. A white middle-class teen in Denver with rich parents, a full belly, good health care and an expensive education has no right to feel anything but contentment and good fortune. Especially when just an airplane ride away his contemporaries watch as their flesh rots away from malnutrition and see their parents die of diseases routinely cured in the west.

As for teachers showing their feelings, I would fire any teacher who cried in a classroom. Teachers are supposed to show maturity, learning, responsibility and strength. Not to wallow in the "please like me, I'm just like you" nonsense currently pushed at them. They are paid to teach, not to be Oprah Winfrey.

As for the so-called racial aspect of the Colorado murders, yes, a young man of colour was singled out by the miniature satanists. So were human beings in general. We should also remember that the gruesome pair searched for Christians and asked them if they believed in God. They then killed them.

Surely the lesson of this bloody quagmire is that evil people are full of hate. For themselves, for other people, for God. They tend not to discriminate in their cruelty.

Then we have the gem of teachers being told not to moralize, not to lecture and not to be judgmental. You couldn't make this stuff up. Judging and making moral statements are precisely what teachers should be doing. It is exactly the absence of moral absolutes and judgments of right and wrong that led to the mass murder in Colorado.

It is wrong to kill, wrong to hate, wrong to disobey your parents, wrong to be jealous, wrong to despair, wrong to lust, wrong to steal, wrong to use foul language, wrong to treat your teachers with disrespect, wrong for teenagers to have cell phones, wrong for children to be given anything and everything they want, wrong for people with so little life experience to be treated like adults. This should be taught every day in our schools.

It is also wrong for teachers to be emasculated in the classroom, wrong for parents to be told not to chastise their children if they are bad, wrong for us to constantly obsess about a child's self-esteem, wrong for 16-year-olds to drive a car, wrong for there not to be school uniforms. Wrong.

Shame on you, Toronto District School Board. Sorry if I sound judgmental, but I just felt like it.

The Law Doesn't Know Best

There are so many things that can be said about the Francis Roy trial. So much that can be pleaded and screamed about the slaughter of the innocent.

We drag our tired and blunted emotions through pools of tears knee-deep, but we seem to get no further towards answers and closings. Children should come first, but so often today they come last.

One man has been convicted. He should be declared a dangerous offender and never see freedom again. Should we kill him by state decree or let the prison population take their savage revenge? No. We are better than that, we are better than him. The young and perfect Alison Parrott was better than that, better than him.

I say again, one man has been convicted. But evil has suffered merely a flesh wound. The greater picture is about how we perceive justice, how we draw that seemingly ever-shadier line between right and wrong.

Before we give ourselves a collective pat on the back and cheer that a bad guy has been caught, we ought to remember that pedophilia is even now being "reconsidered" by some of North America's leading psychologists with a view, as one member of the American Psychological Association had it, "to questioning the old values and considering the place of inter-generational sex in our society."

As we all know, in "beautiful" British Columbia a judge has said it is not a crime to possess child pornography. The law thinks it knows best. The law frequently knows nothing.

The jury took a great deal of time to decide the fate of Francis Roy, a man who seemed so obviously guilty. Because of this some critics are arguing the jury system is in need of fundamental reform, even of obliteration. Perhaps so. Yet the notion of 12 ordinary men and women deciding the future of a fellow citizen is still a noble ideal and any alternative would probably centre on an even more powerful judge or panel of judges.

Lawyers with increased powers and a judicial elite with still more clout. Lord save us from that.

It was a judge and not a jury that ruled that in this trial Roy's previous convictions for rape could not be mentioned, even though they were directly pertinent to the case. He also thought the jury should not know of the defendant's photography experience, even though Alison's murderer had posed as a photographer. That iceberg looks almost harmless when you can only see its tip.

Good has to come out of all this bad. Parole boards should be restructured and there must be a greater degree of accountability.

Roy committed this hellish act after serving less than half his prison sentence for two other gruesome crimes. A group of allegedly qualified people thought him fit to go free.

If a police officer makes a mistake with his gun and shoots someone he will be held accountable. If parole board members make a mistake with their equally dangerous weapons they should also be held responsible.

Sentencing must be increased and must be served. The sadistic rape of two teenagers cannot be punished with five years in prison. It makes a mockery of a victims' suffering.

There has to be an overhaul of what is admissible in a trial and what is not. A sexual assault victim's past can be dragged through a court and her name be darkened with tales of past incidents that in fact have little to do with the case in question. Francis Roy's history, however, remained hidden in a cloud of unknowing.

This is all about the balance between the victim and the culprit, a balance that has swung too far toward the latter. The law is merely a means to and end, and that end is justice. Yet many people in the legal profession seem to have forgotten that fact, more interested in winning and losing than in what's moral and immoral. Of course all people deserve a legal defence, but all victims and all victims' families deserve fairness. And all of society deserves protection.

As for lovely, gentle, clean, immaculate and good, yes, good, little Alison, she is in a place where no more harm can come to her. The same cannot be said for Francis Roy. Sleep well, sweet child, sleep peacefully now.

Not all Jews Oppose HLI

I seldom devote two columns to the same subject but sometimes events demand a change in policy. The propaganda campaign against the anti-abortion group Human Life International (HLI), currently holding its annual conference in Toronto, has become so intense and so absurd that a response is essential. To summarize the arguments of HLI's opponents, the organization's leaders, and by extension its membership of more than 70,000, are hateful, violent and, most significant of all it seems, anti-Semitic.

There are also rumours that the chief of HLI tried to murder the Easter bunny and wouldn't let Rudolph join in the other reindeers' games.

Last week's column dealt with the allegedly racist remarks made by HLI's founder Father Paul Marx by simply quoting them properly and in context, thus showing that the priest in question is perhaps more concerned about unborn Jewish children than many Jewish leaders seem to be. It listed just a few of the Jewish people who support HLI and then demonstrated from video evidence that any violence at HLI's Montreal conference in 1995 came from protesters, who were throwing used condoms at children and wrecking a police car.

Best now to let one of HLI's leaders speak for himself.

Yehuda Levin is from Brooklyn, New York and is an orthodox rabbi and the father of nine children. He has met with presidents Reagan and Bush and with Pope John Paul II. In other words, a highly respected man.

"For 20 years I've been an occasional spokesman for the Union of Orthodox Rabbis of the USA and Canada and the Rabbinical Alliance of America, on issues of abortion and family values. Those groups have a combined membership of a thousand rabbis, many with congregations or schools. That's a lot of people," Levin explains. "The problem in Canada is that most rabbis, even most

Jews, don't even know what HLI is. They get a line from the Canadian Jewish Congress or B'nai Brith and that's it." A pause.

"I, however, do know HLI. I've worked with them for ten years now. If thought there were Jew-haters here I'd be out so quickly you wouldn't even see me. These people have spent tens of thousands of dollars helping Jewish pro-life groups. They're in the process of setting up a crisis pregnancy centre in Israel, to save Jewish babies. This is anti-Semitism? If it is, give us some more anti-Semites," and he almost laughs.

"Look, their enemies constantly quote one article written by Father Marx 12 years ago, and then forget to say that he begins by thanking many of the leaders of the pro-life movement who are Jewish. He then calls on Jews to take back their organizations from people promoting abortion and homosexuality. I find it interesting that the likes of former Austrian Chancellor Bruno Kreisky, feminist leader Betty Freidan and Henry Morgentaler up here can scream for abortion and proclaim their Jewishness, but take offence when they're identified as being Jewish (in this context). There are groups who throw the appellation 'anti-Semite' around so loosely that it becomes meaningless. And these same people won't debate the issue."

He's got a point. In attempting to prepare a show on CTS's Michael Coren Live on this issue my producer, researcher and myself made the best part of 50 telephone calls and spoke to every Jewish or pro-abortion group we could find, asking them to participate in a discussion. All refused. Nor would any of the militants preparing to demonstrate outside of HLI's Toronto conference stop shouting for a few moments and speak with an orthodox rabbi on the subject of Judaism and its foes. So much for freedom of speech.

The Canadian Jewish Congress explained that none of its officers would appear in a discussion with a member of a group whose leader is an anti-Semite. Pretty ironic stuff. Decide who is an anti-Semite and then refuse to speak to that person and let him defend himself against charges of anti-Semitism. Understandable with a holocaust denier or a thug, but surely not appropriate in this case.

As one critic had it, "This is the type of nonsense that was exposed by brilliant Jewish minds such as Kafka and Koestler." And as Rabbi Yehuda Levin has it, "a terrible waste of time and opportunity while unborn Jewish babies are being slaughtered."

Pro-Life but not Anti-Semitic

So the knives are out for Human Life International or HLI, preparing to hold its 18th annual conference in Toronto in early April.

No surprise there. The pro-life movement has been routinely slandered and smeared in the media for more than 30 years. But the attacks upon this particular organization have taken misinformation to new heights. HLI is being condemned as "dangerous," "virulently anti-Semitic" and "hateful."

A pause while I stop laughing and realize that in fact this is no amusing matter. Let me make it clear this is not about, or should not be about, whether you are pro-life or pro-abortion. It is about the freedom to express your views without fear of violent attack or ugly propaganda.

When HLI met in Montreal in 1995 there were many scenes of violence. Not one came from supporters of HLI.

There is video evidence of demonstrators, bused in from all over North America, destroying a police car, throwing used condoms at children, pelting pro-life delegates with prophylactics containing broken glass. Children leaving a church were spat at and attacked by members of various anarchist and extreme homosexual groups, young families were abused and threatened.

One CBC reporter present, hardly a supporter of HLI, told me it was as if "the inhabitants of hell had come up for the day to say hello."

Even now an extremist group known as Anti-Racist Action is organizing a demonstration for the Toronto gathering.

"Fascism and neo-Nazis are not an isolated phenomenon" explains the group on its website. "They are supported in many ways by racist police and government policies." It then goes on to say a great deal about the apparently rampant "Nazism" and "homophobia" in Canada and calls for a "sexually diverse society."

Seldom has such a noble term as anti-racism been applied to such an undeserving gang. These naive zealots should also ask black leaders why so many abortuaries in the U.S. are built in areas containing large numbers of people of colour. Abortion has long been a racist tool.

Then we have the big lie: HLI is anti-Semitic. Give me a break. One of its leaders, Father Paul Marx, has been quoted by his opponents as singling out Jewish abortionists and attacking Jewish leaders for supporting abortion.

What these critics conveniently omit from the quotation is where Marx says these people are being "disloyal to the teachings of Judaism" and asks Jewish people "to form specifically Jewish pro-life organizations, and to take back the leadership of the Jewish community from the pro-abortionists. By doing this, you will not only help save millions of non-Jewish babies, you may well help save the Jewish nation from the truly 'final solution' of abortion."

Goodness, the man is worse than Hitler.

Marx has never, for example, said anything as extreme as "even if the butcher of Jewish babies is a Jewish doctor, he's still a butcher." According to Western Report, that was uttered by a national director of the Jewish Defence League of Canada. The JDL, of course, is hardly known for its conciliatory nature. But Rabbis Mayer Schiller, Yehuda Levin, Isaac Levy, Zalman Zell, Eliyahu Scheinberg, Yosef Friedman and Michael Weinberg are. As are doctors Monte Liebman, David Harris, Solomon Rendler, Avrohom Katz, Eliyahu Rothkpf and Melech Gilbert. They are just a handful of the leading Jewish men and women who signed a letter of support for Human Life International.

How odd they all managed to get it so terribly wrong.

The facts. There is a growing split between orthodox and liberal Jews over many issues, and abortion is one of them. A growing alliance has been formed between evangelical Christians, conservative Roman Catholics and orthodox Jews to fight what is seen as an extreme anti-God, anti-family and anti-life agenda. This angers and frightens liberal people of all religious backgrounds. Good. I long for the day when practising Muslims will be fully included in this new coalition as well.

Unfortunately, there may well be violence at the HLI conference but it will not come from the delegates. It will come from people who are truly hateful. And it will have been partly fuelled by those who really should know better and have resorted to name-calling when they have lost the arguments.

Kids' Theatre Hung Up on Homophobia

If you go down to the Young People's Theatre today you're sure of a big surprise. Or maybe not, depending on what you expect from the Toronto venue, where the slogan is "Plays for a Better World."

I have seen many productions at YPT, some of them good and some of them bad. My main complaint has been that too often the company refuses to let children be children and the pieces are too elaborate and over-staged.

One or two productions have also been somewhat political, but not to a worrying degree. All that has changed now, however, with something called The Other Side of the Closet, starting its second run at the theatre in a few weeks time.

Predictably from the title, this work is about homosexuality. Just as predictably, it is about that great propaganda vehicle known as homophobia and, also predictably, the blurb for the piece drips with clichés.

"The play deals with one teenager's attempts to understand his sexuality and the impact that his struggle has on his family and friends." Yeah, right.

A play about the derision faced by students who are handicapped, students who reject permissive ideas and pursue chastity, students who are deeply religious, students who wear Islamic headdress, students who are of colour – all this would be valid. But with the homosexual population at under 3% this is nothing more, and nothing less, than an attempt at indoctrination.

"There was a great demand for it, we just had to bring it back," said Lorraine Bell Weisdorf, the chair of the theatre. I can just imagine thousands of schoolchildren rising as one person to demand that they be taken to this little thriller and then complaining when the run ended. The reality, as we all know, is that teachers choose what plays their classes will see and in this case vari-

138

ous teachers decided their charges should hear about the great sin of homophobia.

Just in case they don't get the message, there will a talkback session at the end of each performance led by a social worker from the Human Sexuality Program at the Toronto District School Board. Comforting to know that whatever cuts the education system might face, we still have brave souls to help our little ones with their human sexuality.

I can't help thinking that the individual in question might not be an advocate of traditional values and might not inform the class that Christianity, Islam and orthodox Judaism, as well as most of the world's cultures, condemn homosexuality.

Nor will these messages be heard on The Lesbian Gay Bi Youth Line, which will be the recipient of money raised by a special fund-raising production of The Other Side of the Closet at YPT.

In fact, the issue of teenage homosexuality is a minor one, horribly magnified and then exploited by extremist groups trying to make their case appear stronger.

They claim the suicide rate among teenagers is highest for those who are "unsure of their sexual preference." Teenagers are unsure of many things, and their years of maturing sexuality can be difficult and sometimes painful. But homosexuality seldom has anything to do with it.

Be warned. Figures that link attempted suicides with homosexuality come from organizations that have condemned as "unethical" any attempt to cure homosexuals or to treat homosexuality as a pathology. In other words, the psychiatric profession is now acutely political.

Then we come to the old regular of public funding. The Young People's Theatre receives more than $750,000 a year from the taxpayer.

When I asked theatre chair Lorraine Bell Weisdorf about this she replied it "was not a lot of money at all."

Really. Many of us would think it was, in fact, an awful lot of money, particularly at such a time as this and particularly if tendentious dramas are to be force-fed to impressionable school children.

One last thing. In this era of cutbacks and belt-tightening I wondered if The Other Side of the Closet made any money when it was first at the theatre.

Reply? It broke even.

Next question. Have any plays made a profit recently?

Yes, Treasure Island.

Last question. Are you going to bring the Stevenson classic back for another run as well?

Still waiting for a response.

CBC Strike:
Food for Thought

Think CBC. Think strikes by people who are already well paid and have more job security than most of us. Think bias. Think a fortune in public money.

Think enormous wastes of cash on patronizing and terribly acted soap-operas. Think greedily taking yet another FM radio spot, this time away from a black station, and then claiming to be caring and fair-minded.

Think pretentious newsroom comedy shows that are nothing more than watered down versions of American products. Think hosts who are paid $150,000 a year with long holidays and large support staffs and then complain they work too hard. Think revising Canadian history and belittling the achievements of millions of fine Canadians.

Think Friday Night With Ralph Benmergui. Think about miserable failures being ignored. Think about the same people, who all seem to know one another, coming back year after year. Think of people who don't even know what their show's ratings are because there is no chance of them being cancelled.

Think of people with famous mums and dads. Think of quite a lot of people with famous mums and dads. Think of weekly shows with four researchers when nightly shows on private stations have one or two. Think of people constantly complaining about how hard it is and about how the cutbacks are intolerable.

Think of people whose main job is to pour water for talking heads. Think of hosts complaining privately that they are held to ransom by lazy and petulant technicians and then stating publicly that they support the claims of their technicians.

Think of journalists who are obsessively committed to public broadcasting pretending to have any semblance of objectivity when they are interviewing politicians who oppose public broadcasting.

Think of self-indulgence. Think of mediocrity. Think of so many critics who watch only the CBC and who count as their personal friends men and women who appear on the CBC every night. Think unfair advantages against any competition. Think of a sterile and pompous environment where ideas contrary to the liberal mind-set are marginalized and trashed.

Think former heads of radical organizations walking into jobs. Think endless panels that reflect not the beliefs of the country but the beliefs of the producers, who so often have tangible agendas. Think preferring Quebec to Alberta, because the former seems exotic and the latter is apparently so right wing. Think constantly meeting people who affirm your views at the same dinner parties and book launches. Think seldom meeting real Canadians. Think despising private broadcasting. Think gruesome insularity.

Think of a publicist who defended a CBC legal drama and its colossal expense because "it teaches people that Canadian lawyers wear wigs in court." Think of the absurd statement that you're the only "truly Canadian" broadcaster, somehow implying that all of the others are not genuinely patriotic.

Think of a producer who took down a photograph of his family from his office door because a colleague complained about its patriarchal tendencies. Think that the producer was yet another American draft-dodger. Think that these draft-dodgers have to scream their anti-American and extreme views otherwise they would have to admit they simply ran away and left their poor, black and Hispanic buddies to do the fighting for them.

Think hockey being the one thing we really watch. Think how well any other station might package the hockey, and without the public having to pay taxes for it. Think of hockey's advertising making the rest of the CBC's advertising profile look much better than it really is. Think of silly, neurotic women simulating masturbation on radio and their actions being defended by CBC producers. Think of endless attacks upon the family.

Think hypocrisy, think privilege, think sheer nonsense. Think yet more shows about body piercing, homosexual singing groups, single mothers defending whales, juggling pacifists, the need for Quebec to be given more language rights and the sheer joy of having an abortion.

Think CBC. Think we don't need it, at least not in its present form. Think of what you watch beyond hockey and The National. Think. For goodness sake, think.

What's Ted's Real Message

So Ted Turner has done it again. In 1990 the founder of CNN and vice-chairman of Time-Warner, said Christianity was "for losers." Now he has made a racial joke about the Pope.

Addressing a meeting of the National Family Planning and Reproductive Centre in Washington, Turner was asked what he would say if he met the pontiff. In reply he commented, "Ever seen a Polish mine detector?" Then he held out his foot and showed it to the audience.

In other words, all Poles are stupid.

Poland has produced Chopin, Joseph Conrad, Copernicus and some of the greatest minds in history. It has suffered brutal invasion and domination by Russia and Germany, been wiped off the face of the map and still blossomed as a vibrant and fertile nation. The United States has known little but privilege and has given us Madonna, Norman Mailer and the Big Mac.

All this aside, what would have happened if Turner had made such a joke about Jewish or black people, or homosexuals? The question is rhetorical, the answer is obvious.

But Turner did not have to resign. He made some sort of apology and that was that. Not quite. He also suggested the ban on adultery should be removed from the Ten Commandments, that the world is grossly overpopulated and that there should be a one-child-only policy in force.

On the adultery issue, Turner might just ask himself what the encouragement of the betrayal of a spouse has to do with responsible parenting.

He might also question his research. Because the world is not overpopulated. Repeat, the world is not overpopulated. In Europe and North America we are not even reproducing ourselves numerically and in the developing world families are often quite small – but food is scare and money is like water in the desert.

Where, then, does the money go? Let's say hello again to Ted Turner and his good old buddies. These lifestyle liberals seem unaware the West is so greedy, so over-fed, so exploitative and so consumer-obsessed that the Third World suffers as a direct consequence.

What Turner is in fact saying is that if you are black or brown you shouldn't have children. For such a statement he is described by his friends as a visionary.

Yet by a slight adjustment of the world's resources we could feed the hungry and, in so doing, silence the nasty shouts of the likes of Ted Turner. That, however, would take a small sacrifice. So much easier to tell the poor to do what they're told.

If Turner wants a few cases of North American indulgence I can help him out. Just by chance the new catalogue by the Dundurn Group of publishers arrived today. It devotes a full page to a new book entitled Fits Like A Rubber Dress.

"At 29, three things occur to Indigo Blackwell: she hates her job in public relations, her life is decidedly unremarkable, and death is inevitable.

"Indigo is married to Sam, a self-absorbed wannabe novelist, who nonetheless supports her decision to forfeit her career in favour of film school. No sooner has she made the leap from financial security than she walks in the back door of her house to find another man's head between her husband's thighs.

"Alone for the first time, Indigo finds herself propelled into the kind of intense, urban life she'd always wanted. She begins an affair with Jon, a toxic young artist who treats his own life and the people in it like he would a sculpture – as things to manipulate. Through him she experiences the underground world of drugs, fetish parties and sadomasochistic sex."

The blurb is accompanied by a photograph of a woman in erotic underwear lying on her back. Oh, and by a nearby statement acknowledging the support of the Canada Council for the Arts, the Ontario Arts Council and the Department of Canadian Heritage. In other words by you and by your tax dollars.

Look, if you want to write a stream of embarrassing clichés, if you want to indulge your sexual and personal fantasies, if you want to produce a novel based on strikingly unoriginal banalities, fine. But do it with your own cash. Or ask Ted Turner for a loan.

My Wife's Run-In with the Law

Valentine's Day began beautifully.

Sunny, crisp, a day full of optimism. My wife, Bernadette, set off for church at her regular time. Because I attend a different church I caught a few more minutes in bed.

I always meet Bernie and the family for the last part of their service and the children run into my arms and Bernie smiles. But not this time. Indeed, they all looked to be on the edge of tears.

"We were stopped by the police. Oh, darling, I'm so sorry."

"What happened, are you okay?"

"Yes, but they want $400 from us, and they made me out as some sort of criminal."

The story went like this. Bernadette, a high-school teacher and mother who has never broken any law, was suddenly stopped by a police car as she was about to park the minivan. A policewoman approached and stated: "You went through a red light."

"I didn't, my wife replied. "I only even took my foot off the brakes when it began to change. I would never endanger the children in such a way."

"You went through a red light," insisted the policewoman, her voice louder.

Suddenly another officer, a heavily moustached man, approached and asked if this mini-van, filled with four children aged between one and 10 years, belonged to my wife.

Nervous now, Bernadette said that it did.

"Where are you going?" demanded the policeman.

My wife explained that she was going to church, only yards away.

"Well," said the boy in blue, "you're going to be late."

And Bernadette was. It took more than 40 minutes for these two heavily armed officers to write my terrorist spouse her tickets. Our new insurance papers were sent late by our agent, and Bernadette tried to explain this.

The female police officer, seemed indifferent and became rather aggressive.

This officer, a short, plump woman who in spite of her loud make-up could not be long out of college, took my wife's wallet and tried to get the documents out.

Unfortunately, her painted nails could not complete the task. My wife had to do it.

Thank goodness Bernie wasn't armed with an Uzi.

At this point one of the children, Lucy, began to cry.

"You've got at least four kids back there and you're driving without up-to-date insurance papers," said our brave crime-fighter. What the number of children we have had to do with all this was beyond Bernadette.

"If you'd do that," continued the cop courageous, "what else would you do?"

My wife, admittedly inexperienced in all this, wanted to ask why she was being treated in such a manner but told me: "Mike, I was frightened of saying a word. It was like she was enjoying all this."

The officer then explained that Bernie had not come to a halt at a stop sign as well.

"But I did, and then edged forward slowly because of the parked cars blocking my view. I was driving sensibly."

None of it mattered. The female officer went back to the car with a smile on her face to join her male colleague, who was sitting back with his arms behind his head. They held a long conversation, interspersed with bouts of laughter and the writing of tickets – all witnessed by my entire family.

Four tickets in all, possibly thousands of dollars in insurance penalties, at least two trips to court. All this in Parkdale, only yards away from where drug deals are going down and AIDS-infected prostitutes are selling their bodies. But the police got their man. Or, should I say, their woman – and her four little ones as well.

What do I tell my children? That not all the police are like this, that most would be polite and fair. But it's hard to make that story stick, particularly with the 10-year-old who is in a grade higher than his years and knows a thing or two.

What do I think? That the next time the police complain about understaffing and pay conditions I will have a good chuckle.

Happy Valentine's Day.

Now the Christians Feel Rushdie's Lash

So he's done it again. Salman Rushdie that is, the Anglo-Indian author who outraged Muslims and was threatened with death because of his book The Satanic Verses.

Believe it or not the product of the most expensive and exclusive British private schools, the darling of the chattering classes, has now attacked another great world religion.

Writing in Indian Today Rushdie stated: "We're celebrating the 2000th anniversary of the birth of Christ, as Catholic cardinals and believers of all stripes constantly remind us. Never mind that this will put Jesus in the odd position of having two birthdays in the space of a week (Christmas Day as well as the Millennial Instant) or that all serious scholars and even Church leaders now agree that he wasn't actually born on either of them.

"Faux millennium or not, it's the only one we are going to get. But will the faux millennium turn out to be a dark sabbath of what one might call faux Christianity?"

It soon becomes clear that what Rushdie refers to as faux or false Christianity is in fact anyone with whom the author disagrees who happens to be a Christian.

On the Bill Clinton affair Rushdie says that "hardline but essentially counterfeit Christian values have been the driving force behind the rabidly partisan attack by U.S. Republicans."

Odd, this. There is nothing counterfeit about believing a man should be faithful to his wife and that lying under oath is wrong. Nothing counterfeit about criticizing a man who bombs Iraq as a way of distracting attention from his sordid little escapades with the office help.

Rushdie continues: "If the Senate now brings the sorry saga to a close, it will be because sober considerations of state have finally gained the ascendancy over mad-dog godliness: because

147

worldly-wise politicians have put the faux Christians back in their kennels at last."

He goes on to discuss an extremist Roman Catholic priest who performed a mass for Chilean dictator Gen. Augusto Pinochet and the British Prime Minister Tony Blair, who is known for holding some Christian beliefs, somehow linking them all to mainstream Christianity.

In all, the piece is rambling and angry, a stew of generalizations and stereotypes. It is sad to read. Sad because I knew Salman in London, went to his home, saw him at parties and remember him as a gifted writer who had things to say.

It is now almost as if he has been driven mad, not by power but by the lack of it. There appears to be hatred in him, perhaps for himself as well as for others.

Some of these feelings are understandable, because for many years Rushdie was forced to live an artificial, hidden life. But even that event was brought about by a similar disregard for the faith of millions.

Rushdie was told and warned that The Satanic Verses would distress believing Muslims. He thought he knew better.

I am a liberal, secular man, he seemed to be saying, comfortable and familiar with influential people, influential ideas, modern thought and the permissive society. If I want to mock your beliefs, I will. If I want to marginalize your religion, I will. I and my friends are more important than you.

For Salman there was a price to pay. But for less famous people, for editors and translators, the price was much higher. People were murdered because of The Satanic Verses, families were devastated, children were orphaned.

People might also be murdered because of the reaction to what Rushdie has now written about Christianity. Because Rushdie, who has just been granted a visa to visit India, was writing for an Indian audience and because that country is presently squirming through a gruesome period of Christian persecution, culminating in the recent slaughter of a missionary and his two sons.

Some people will never learn. Certainly not, it seems, Salman Rushdie. He once called Margaret Thatcher a Nazi and then ran to her for protection when his life was threatened.

That protection was given by countries founded on Christian principles and by taxpayers who were Christians.

If Rushdie's not careful, he soon won't have any friends left. And I'd hate for that to happen.

A Fateful Date with Dr. Death

Karen Shoffstall is dead. She was young, she was pretty, she had so much to live for. But she is dead.

At the age of 30 the Ontario native was diagnosed as suffering from multiple sclerosis. The illness is a terrible one, but there are numerous people who live with it for many years, enjoying a fine quality of life.

Such seemed to be the case with Karen Shoffstall.

She took vacations, had fun, relished the opportunities that life offered.

Yet she had been for some years what her mother describes as "not mentally ill but mentally unstable." She would sometimes fantasize, perhaps tells lies, concoct stories that were not true.

When MS smashed its ugly way into her life Karen would experience bouts of terrible doubt, convinced she was about to lose her job, her friends and her quality of life.

All of this is a far from untypical experience for someone with a profoundly serious medical condition and something with which a counsellor or therapist could deal.

But Karen made the terrible mistake of writing to Dr. Jack Kevorkian.

The man who has transformed the horror of suicide into a grotesque cult quickly responded. He met the confused Karen in a suburban Detroit hotel room with one of his aides. Shortly afterward the 34-year-old woman was dead, knocked unconscious by an enormous dose of barbiturates, and then killed by potassium chloride.

Kevorkian claims he has a long and extensive list of requirements before he will engage in his grisly trade and that assisted suicide can only occur when the person requesting such a thing is truly in agony and genuinely understand what she wants.

Karen was not, did not. She seldom used a wheelchair.

She did not even use a cane very often, and as a trained nurse knew that while MS is chronic, it needn't be disabling.

But she was so scared.

"Oh yes, oh yes, so very, very scared," explained her sister, Tina, who lives in Guelph.

"She was terrified of what might happen and this was taken as a sign that she didn't want to live any more." A pause for anger as well as grief. "Maybe she did claim that she wanted to die, but was this a decision made sanely and with thought? Not at all. And as for it being her decision and affecting only herself, I wish you could have some idea of what this has done to her family, to her mother." And she points to a quiet, obviously still shaken woman sitting in the corner of the room.

"I just know she did not realize what she was getting into, did not understand she was creating horrors in her mind that were not really there," says Karen's mum, a brave woman whose wounds are so deep as to be almost visible.

"We would always have been there for her."

Which poses the question of what we now sometimes refer to as "compassionate homicide" is all about. The last person who can make a clear, cogent decision about the future, about his or her very life, is a person in profound fear. Pain and the anticipation of pain produce such a fear.

Then there are the social pressures.

Karen was afraid of losing her lifestyle, an attractive Manhattan lifestyle that we see lionized on television and in the movies. She believed that anything else was simply not worth having.

Death provoked by a lowering of social expectations is almost too repugnant to contemplate.

We also have to consider the implicit beliefs of the old or sick. "I know it would be easier financially for the family if I wasn't here ... it's such a long way for them to come every week and the grandchildren don't like it ... I've had a good life and the insurance will be so helpful for them ... I just don't fit in."

I just don't fit in. The chilling death-rattle exploited by the social engineers. The plea of despair screamed by Karen Shoffstall that fell on the deaf ears of a doctor and his sidekick in Detroit, Mich.

Karen's case is not unique. But Karen was. And for her mother and sister there will never be another.

A Hypocritical Attack on Pornography

It has been quite a week for purveyors of obscene material. In British Columbia a judge ruled it is not illegal to possess child pornography.

For those who have never read of such stuff, it sometimes features children as young as 6 months and involves incomprehensible scenes of bestiality and sadism. It routinely depicts 5- and 6-year-olds being raped.

The judge in question was disturbed by the broadness of the laws governing such material and concluded they violated the Charter of Rights. But the mere production of this hellish stuff is illegal because it involves the abuse of children. It also normalizes the abnormal and allows pedophiles to emotionally legitimize their fantasies.

How bitterly ironic that in a country where people who smoke are seldom allowed to adopt children, men who possess pictures of tots having sex are protected by Canadian law.

The Americans, of course, go even further when it comes to the right to offend and nobody knows this so well as the prince of all darkness, Larry Flynt. The publisher of Hustler, however, did not reckon with Canadian hypocrisy. A recent Canadian edition of Hustler featured a photograph of Sheila Copps and asked readers to write in explaining why they would have sex with the federal heritage minister.

Before you could say "double standard," Silcorp Ltd. gave the order to more than 600 Beckers, Mac's and Mike's convenience stores for the magazine to be withdrawn. The same people who have been making money from selling a magazine that degrades women, debases sexuality and decays moral standards now decided to take the moral high ground and make a stand for decency. Corner stores that display Hustler within eye-shot of children pulled the magazine for a week or two because it included a picture of a Canadian politician.

Was Hustler not obscene before Sheila Copps was in it, and will it not be obscene afterwards?

Liberal MPP Dominic Agostino was furious at the incident, claiming, "It is at least sexual harassment; at worst an invitation to sexual assault." He urged the federal and provincial justice ministers to pursue criminal charges against Hustler.

Fair enough. But Hustler has long taken pornography to new depths of misogyny. All porn uses women as pieces of meat but Hustler goes further.

It showed a woman being forced into a grinder and quite literally coming out of the other end as offal.

I ask again, was Hustler not obscene before Sheila Copps was in it and will it not be obscene afterwards?

There have been accusations that the only people who complained about this infantile stunt were those who work for Sheila Copps. Her office denies it, claiming "citizens who were appalled by this absolute filth" made their anger known.

Hard to believe that the purchasers or perusers of Hustler suddenly developed a moral sense when they encountered the heritage minister instead of "Cindy" or "Brandy" in the pages of their favourite journal.

Whatever the source, the point remains that the repugnant comments made about Sheila Copps were mild compared to some of the trash in Hustler.

It is not the same as Playboy and Penthouse, whatever we might think of those publications. It jokes about rape, it depicts people of colour in a deeply racist manner.

In spite of the whitewash attempted by Oliver Stone in his movie about Larry Flynt, the pornographer is an angry, bitter man who seems to hate women with a frightening intensity. His daughter once wept in front of me as she alleged that her father systematically abused her (allegations he has publicly denied).

Nor is this the first time Hustler has made such attacks on well-known people, but it is the first time it has hit Sheila Copps. By a strange coincidence this is also the first time so many Liberal politicians have expressed their anger at the magazine. More than that, some of the people who are now so upset have in the past championed so-called freedom of publication for people like Flynt.

If Hustler continues to be distributed in Canada and if the friends of Sheila Copps fail to continue their attacks on the magazine, hypocrisy will have triumphed again.

In case you disagree, ask a possessor of child pornography in B.C.

*Your T*X Dollars at W*rk*

On Feb. 3 a new play opens in Toronto. It is called Shopping and F...ing. The third word is used in full in the actual title of the piece and by the work's supporters.

The play is hyped in promotional literature as a "controversial Canadian premiere" and makes no attempt to disguise the fact it is all about provocation. Genuine and constructive provocation, of course, consists of the presentation of truth in a challenging and mature manner. A press release says the following about this British import.

"In bedsit-land Mark, Robbie, Lulu and Gary struggle to define themselves in their world of junk food, junk culture, no jobs, phone sex, casual sex, rehab, shoplifting, club life and the temporary escape of designer jobs."

Fine. But can't they define their banal little lives without the support of tax dollars paid by people who are too busy making a living to waste their time on the above? You see, a full one-third of this play's costs have been paid for by you and me.

Both the Canada Council and the Toronto Arts Council fund Crow's Theatre, which is staging the play. So, in other words, while Ottawa cuts back on health care and Toronto experiences a crisis in homelessness both levels of government give money to a work such as this.

When I called the box office, where the title is again used in full, I was told "The play contains coarse language and graphic sexual imagery and may be offensive to some."

I'd like to meet the people who will not find it in any way offensive.

Because according to Jim Milan, the artistic director of the company and director of this particular play, "There's gay contact implied or shown by some characters. They'll be presented within the realms of the law but as we're not on the air or anything I can tell you that there will be a representation of anal sex and of one man kissing another man's bottom for his pleasure. And lots of swearing."

There are posters advertising the play on walls around the city and on many of these a single asterisk will replace the second letter of the f-word.

"Tens of thousands of pieces of literature are crossing the city as we speak," explained Milan. "There'll be posters up in restaurants. Children will be there so we thought we would use the single asterisk."

Won't children be able to figure out what the word is?

"I guess we'll have to see."

I guess we will.

The point is that people swore a great deal in the time of Sophocles, Shakespeare, Ibsen and George Bernard Shaw. But dramatists of the past possessed the ability to convey profound feelings without splashing around in the intellectual and moral gutter. Are we seriously going to believe King Lear would have been more effective if the old man's three daughters had taken their tops off?

The use of obscene language and gestures in such a manner is and has always been the preserve of the foolish. The teenager pretending to be an adult, the adult pretending to be a teenager. The drooping truncheon, if you'll excuse the phrase, of those who cannot express passion or anger in a more sophisticated way but are intent on beating us over the head.

"Yes but the f-word can still shock an audience," says Milan. "There are three flatmates who have an interchangeable sexual relationship. But you get the idea that it's a functioning unit. One of them is a recovering drug addict who takes up with a rent boy. It's about the lost boys and girls of our society surviving however they can. In a way it's like a fairy tale."

No comment.

He continues: "The play has some marvellous Chekhovian allusions."

Presumably a reference to all the shopping that goes on in The Cherry Orchard. "And, yes, we will confront people's boundaries and challenge convention and provoke an audience."

And is he at all guilty at taking public money for such a project?

"Not at all. In no way. I'm sure there's a much greater return on this than on all these grants to small businesses."

I'm sure there is. Just as I'm sure there are asterisks in the word garbage.

Another Feminist Idol with Feet of Clay

How often we praise those who so little merit our reverence.

There are plans to once again honour the founder of Planned Parenthood, a woman by the name of Margaret Sanger. She is lionized in many circles as a feminist pioneer who made it possible for women, and men, to have access to contraception and abortion.

Indeed she did. But what ideology underpinned her passion and her cause?

Margaret Sanger believed in the existence of so-called "dysgenic races" and "human weeds." These unfortunates were "blacks, Hispanics, Amerinds, fundamentalists and Catholics" as well as "Slavs, Latins and Jews."

Sanger thought such people were a "menace to civilization." They simply had to "stop breeding."

Her magazine, The Birth Control Review, favoured immigration restrictions based on race and published a glowing review of a book called The Rising Tide of Colour Against White World Supremacy, a fascist rant particularly popular with the later National Socialists in Germany.

Convinced of the need to do something about these groups, Sanger organized a 1925 meeting in New York of various "birth control leagues, race hygiene societies, family planning associations and social eugenics committees."

This would become International Planned Parenthood.

Sanger favoured the sterilization of "inferior races" and her intimate friend Ernst Rudin was to become Hitler's director of genetic sterilization. If members of the "human weed" groups refused to be thus treated, said Sanger, perhaps they should be forced.

She opened her first clinic in the ghettoes of Brooklyn and always targeted poor and minority areas.

"The mass of Negroes, particularly in the south, still breed carelessly and disastrously," she said, "with the result that the increase among Negroes, even more than among whites, is from that portion of the population least intelligent and fit."

She continued: "The most successful educational approach to the Negro is through a religious appeal. We do not want word to go out that we want to exterminate the Negro population." But a prominent clinic director wondered "if Southern Darkies can ever be entrusted with a clinic."

Sanger condemned marriage as a "degenerate institution" and fidelity to one's partner as "obscene prudery." She wrote that it was a woman's duty to "look the whole world in the face with a go-to-hell look in the eyes."

She argued that a woman had the right to "be lazy, the right to be an unmarried mother, the right to destroy." She once encouraged her 16-year-old granddaughter to lose her virginity and told her it was acceptable to have "sexual intercourse three times a day."

She also believed the only way for people to understand the merit of her ideas was for the state to impose universal sex education and to slowly increase the type of education and the explicitness of its nature.

She longed for the day when homosexuality and abortion would be taught in every school in North America.

How proud she would be of contemporary Canada.

On a personal level Sanger was deeply unhappy. She neglected her children terribly and was not even on the scene when her daughter contracted pneumonia and later died. So much for her care for women. She became absurdly promiscuous, sometimes seeing several sex partners a day, and she also dabbled in the occult.

This sad but dangerous person lived until 1966, dying shortly before her 87th birthday. The North America she saw in her final weeks was exploding into the vision for which she had so hoped: teenage and adult promiscuity, the normalization of the perverse, a massive breakdown in marriage and the family, enforced sex education by anyone other than parents and latex in place of love.

In a way, she has won the battle. Pray she does not win the war.

By the way, after several telephone calls to Planned Parenthood I did manage to speak to the national executive director, Bonnie Johnson.

"A feminist hero, no doubt. A model for all feminists," explained Johnson of Sanger. "As to her comments about race and eugenics, they have to be taken in context. But do remember, we also had such heroes in Canada."

Quite so.

Some Christians Still Persecuted for their Faith

Today she would be advised by doctors, social workers and even some friends to have an abortion – not yet married, very young, poor, no life experience.

"Miriam, don't be a fool. It would be kinder to the baby, kinder to you, kinder to Joe if you just got rid of it," they would say. "You can always have a kid later on, when you're ready. Have an abortion."

But Miriam didn't.

And today Joe would probably have been advised to make sure Miriam had some very deep therapy. After all, she had just told her fiancé that an angel had visited to explain what was about to happen to her, and to the world.

"Listen Joe," his buddy might say, "I can accept crystals, channelling, aliens, reincarnation and even Shirley MacLaine, but this is just ridiculous. Get her to a shrink. Now!"

But Joseph didn't.

The result, of course, is Jesus Christ. Tomorrow we celebrate His birthday. He had told His followers, Christians, that they would be treated badly, and indeed they are, perhaps worse now than at any time in history.

Yet governments, including our own, seem more interested in freedom of trade than in freedom of worship. We in Canada do business with people who are killing Christian families.

Some of our leaders will talk about peace and joy this week while ignoring the screams that ring out like a bell of death, so horribly piercing to those who will listen.

In the Middle East, in India and Pakistan, in China and much of the world, Christians have been – and are being — persecuted and murdered.

It is estimated that more than 200 million Christians are under constant threat of death, incarceration or profound discrimination

– the sort of discrimination unknown, thank goodness, to anybody in Canada.

China has a special method of torture for Christians. They force them to kneel in a praying position and then beat their stretched knees and thighs so that the bones shatter and the skin tears. Christian parents have been made to pay for the bullets that are used to execute their children.

In Iran, a Protestant minister was slaughtered by a mob. His children were taken in by another minister and his family. Only months afterwards this man was found hanging from a tree. The children became orphans. We no longer know where they are and even if they are still alive.

In Sudan, black Christians in the south are killed or raped or sold into slavery by Arab Muslims to the north. It breaks the heart. Canadian Christians have even gone to Sudan to buy back captured co-religionists, all this recorded on video.

In Kuwait, a businessman leaves Islam and embraces Christianity. He is threatened with death by a member of the Kuwaiti parliament, his wife is told to leave him, he is forced to hide and then to flee the country. He loses everything,

In Cuba, Christians have been imprisoned and beaten. Because so many churches are infiltrated by the secret police and are effectively state-controlled, Christians often hold their own services in their homes.

These are frequently raided and the participants put in prison.

In his outstanding book on the subject, Their Blood Cries Out, Paul Marshall quotes a report from the New Yorker about a young Christian girl in another country who had been raped all afternoon by soldiers. While she was being so vilely abused she "sang hymns, strange evangelical songs, and she had kept right on singing, too, even after they shot her in the chest.

"She had lain there with the blood flowing from her chest, and had kept on singing – a bit weaker than before, but still singing. And the soldiers, stupefied, had watched and pointed. Then they had grown tired of the game and shot her again, and she sang still, and their wonder began to turn to fear – until finally they had unsheathed their machetes and hacked through her neck, and at last the singing had stopped."

Have a wonderful and blessed Christmas, but do remember the reason for the season. And remember those men, women and children who are suffering as you read this column for that very reason. There will be no mistletoe for them.

A Burning Passion for Animal Rights

So he couldn't go through with it. Starve himself to death, that is, as a protest against the British government's refusal to launch a royal inquiry into vivisection.

I speak of an animal rights campaigner by the name of Barry Horne, who is serving an 18-year prison term for numerous firebombings and arson attacks.

For 68 days the 46-year-old grandfather was on a hunger strike, allegedly prepared to die for the sake of bunny rabbits. He became a hero to his comrades on both sides of the Atlantic.

Horne planted bombs in clothing stores, in high-street butchers and in pharmacies. Just like the Animal Rights Militia, the "military wing" of the Animal Liberation Front, he believed there was a war taking place. An armed struggle between the friends and the enemies of the animals.

Indeed, the Animal Liberation Front refers to people such as Horne as "prisoners of war," describes opponents as "scum" and frequently applauds acts of violence. The organization and its members are also deeply paranoid. Sections of the official website are devoted to "warning signs you are being watched" – perhaps by psychiatrists?

During one of Horne's arson attacks on the Isle of Wight, just off the southern English mainland, all of the island's fire trucks were called out.

This meant there was nobody to help with any other emergency for some hours.

On another occasion a young mother purchased a canvas carryall from a store for her holiday. She left it for a month and then asked her small children to fetch it for packing. Only then did she discover a cigarette box in the lining with wire and a battery attached. It was a bomb, hidden by Horne in a store that sold products made from animal skins. The device could have killed any number of people at any time but Horne has never shown any regrets.

Nor did he after planting a bomb in a Cancer Research Campaign store, where people buy and donate used goods to raise money to help find a cure for cancer. Or when one of his bombs almost killed a baby. The list goes on.

Horne's arresting officer, Chief Inspector Roy Lambert, said "This man was not going to let anything come in his way. He never gave a moment's thought about any loss of life that may have occurred."

Horne's wife Aileen had the right as next-of-kin to force her husband to be fed but she gave her legal position over to another person. She did so because she was frightened of the animal liberation movement's reaction if she gave the prison authorities permission to end Horne's hunger strike.

Horne is not alone. Some years ago in Britain a car-bomb injured and almost killed a cancer specialist working with animals. When arrested and questioned about the crime the culprits said the life of the rats in the laboratory were more important than that of the doctor they nearly murdered.

"The rats have done less damage to the planet," they said. "No rat and no animal has ever done to him what he does to them."

Anyone who knows a medical researcher in this country will be aware that security is now tight and that people who work in the field are advised to be extremely vigilant. In Britain, stores, laboratories and hospitals are on special alert, working closely with the police.

Horne and his violent allies – in Canada as well as in Britain – have turned a reasonable cause into a lunatic obsession. We should all agree that animal testing should only be carried out when it is acutely necessary. But we should also all agree that as human beings we have a right and a duty to use, though not abuse, animals.

We have to choose sides. We have to decide who is more worthy of compassion, because the needs of animals are sometimes in direct conflict with the needs of people. If a cure could be found for cancer tomorrow that would involve fatal experimentation on a million mice, for example, then it's time for Mickey to buy it big time.

I am not callous, I am realistic. And I am not uncaring, I am the contrary. It is just that I refuse to believe the animal kingdom is more deserving than the human democracy.

Cool Britannia?
Make that Fool Britannia

Two weeks in London, the city of my birth. Any events worth reporting? You bet.

In the same week that it was announced that Britain had the highest rate of AIDS infection in Europe, a statue of Oscar Wilde was unveiled in London to the delighted squeals of assorted actors and homosexual zealots.

Wilde was a man who left his wife and children at home, sometimes weeping, while he purchased 17-year-old boys and used them to satisfy his sexual appetites. These young men were unemployed and semi-literate and Wilde would pass them around as possessions to his friends. He had syphilis at the time.

If alive today, the Irish-born poet may well have been interested in the lucrative and prestigious Turner Prize for contemporary art. This year the award was given to a painter who makes collages involving elephant dung.

He originally imported the stuff from Zimbabwe, but in a spasm of national pride now buys directly from London Zoo. British is best.

Speaking of Zimbabwe, President Robert Mugabe flew into London in the middle of the controversy over the arrest of Gen. Augusto Pinochet. The former Chilean dictator is a monster and a murderer but then the same could be said of the dictator from Africa.

Mugabe has ordered the deaths of thousands of his people, yet he was treated by the British government as an honoured guest, staying in the best hotels and being wined and dined by the chattering classes. Not only is British dung best but British hypocrisy is pretty good as well.

And so is British political correctness. A popular series of learn-to-read books for children is being rewritten to make it "acceptable" in British schools.

There are to be no more references to "Dad's pipe," to anyone being spanked or to mum being in the kitchen.

Instead, dad (minus his nicotine fix) will make dinner and his wife will be the maintenance person around the home.

All this should appeal to the humourless and increasingly two-faced Tony Blair, who is now satirized on British television as a liberal and trendy vicar. The prime minister is, for example, intent on emasculating the House of Lords because he claims to be an enemy of privilege. Fair enough.

But he also sends his children to a school, which is a bastion of privilege and walks hand-in-hand with the rich and the famous. Indeed, he appointed to his government an inexperienced MP by the name of Glenda Jackson. Yes, Glenda Jackson. The actress who is best known for portraying Queen Elizabeth I on television and for winning Oscars is suddenly in charge of Britain's transport policy.

One imagines an important speech in the House of Commons: "I may have the body of a woman but I have the heart of a queen, and a queen of England too. We shall beat the Spanning Armada ... and also extend the central motorway system and make it easier for old people to cross the road."

Glenda might be daft, but she is also pugnacious and tough. Yet not as pugnacious and tough as Jane Couch, a woman boxer who won Britain's first professional female bout. The muscular and masculine lady knocked out a rather attractive German lass in a little over three minutes. She drew blood and sinew from the delicate features of a young woman who looked like she had never even seen a pair of boxing gloves before. Oh, the joy of equality.

Which is precisely what Barry Horne wants for his friends in the animal kingdom. The animal rights activist is, at the time of writing, very close to death as he continues his hunger strike in prison. His crime was to set off firebombs and lead a terror campaign, endangering the lives of many innocent people. One bomb he planted almost killed a young couple with a baby, another nearly smashed two children to pieces.

Like so many extremists in the animal liberation movement, Horne had come to believe that as people eat animals and experiment on them, they are the enemy. In an odd way he could probably identify with Oscar Wilde, who said he was more concerned with the beauty of a flower than with the pain of a beggar.

Perhaps one day they will erect a statue to Barry Horne.

Custody Playing Field is Far from Level

Last week the joint committee on custody and access met again in Ottawa. The intention was to level the playing field when it comes to divorce and subsequent custody issues.

First point: Any man who is able to pay child support but doesn't should go to prison. End of story.

But believe it or not it is not always men who are the baddies in all this.

In spite of what often bitter zealots say – one columnist wrote recently of "men's rights poison" and of "self-pitying" and "quite possibly fictional tales" by fathers – there is sometimes more to the story of custody disputes.

Although most men and women act like adults after divorce and work out a half-decent custody strategy, there are many cases where this does not occur. Cases where women, who invariably receive main custody, use their children as weapons and routinely break the law. This is the story of David, Stephanie and Tessa.

David is a man in his late 40s who was married to Stephanie for eight years. They had a daughter, Tessa. The marriage had its good moments but eventually fell apart. Neither partner was completely to blame, neither was completely free of it.

The court awarded joint custody. David would see Tessa every second weekend, one evening a week and half of the school holidays, and generous child-support payments were established. David never missed a payment date. He also gave extra money to Stephanie, when he could afford it, so Tessa could have those new shoes the other kids had, or go to the concert with her friends.

Stephanie remarried. She and her husband live in a fine house. David does not live in such a home, but he still pays for his Tessa. Then Stephanie decided David could not see Tessa any more.

"But the courts said that I can. For God's sake, she's my daughter!"

Tough, says Stephanie.

David goes to court for a second time. Once again, the judge orders joint custody. And, once again, whenever David arrives to pick up his child there is no answer to his knock on the door. This continues to happen.

It could cost David $10,000 or more to fight the case again, money he does not have. Even if he did, he is sick at the thought of money that could be going to his daughter's education being wasted on lawyers' fees.

If David went to Stephanie's house and demanded access, or submitted to the darker side of human nature and banged on the door and shouted, the police could be called and David would probably be arrested, maybe even losing his joint custody as a result and spending a night in prison. The chances are that he would be handcuffed in front of the house, so his daughter could witness the humiliation.

So instead he drives past Tessa's school and imagines her. And writes to her and keeps these returned, unopened letters in a file to show to his daughter when she grows up, to prove he did not abandon her. He will not deprive her of child support payments because he loves his child, just as most men, like most women, love theirs.

Recently David received a letter from his 7-year-old, explaining she never wanted to see her daddy again and that he was a very bad man. Experts agreed the vocabulary of the note was far too advanced for any child of Tessa's age. It had been dictated.

David's hope is that his daughter will eventually wonder about her father, go to see him for herself and decide what sort of man he is. This is the rallying cry of so many fathers raped of their fatherhood. It will be a long wait. As it is for so many men, who are not indifferent, uncaring reprobates.

David cries less now than in the past. The photographs he has are getting old and he'd love some new ones. He holds on to hope, as a drowning man holds a pathetic piece of soaking wood.

Is David unique? How I wish it were so. And how I wish people would understand that injustice is not the preserve of a single gender.

Poor Little April Didn't Have to Die

I had the privilege this week of meeting two truly authentic heroes.

Larry and Denise Evans are not famous, have not served in war zones and certainly do not regard themselves as being in any way special. But they are. And so was their tiny daughter, April, who died last week at the age of 1½ years.

This beautiful little girl succumbed in an ambulance on the way to hospital, after being on a waiting list for a heart transplant for six months. She could be alive today if there was greater awareness of the need for organ donations and if there was more money invested in the transplant program. We have the expertise in Canada, we simply lack public education.

"She was an incredibly courageous girl," explained Larry Evans, his eyes red with tears and sleeplessness. "She had to have needles every 12 hours or so. I gave them to her. That was hard." Pause. "Yeah, that was hard.

"But she knew she had to have them, knew they were doing her good. She would watch me preparing them, she was so brave. But she still cried. The same with the tube in her nose, she was so accepting and tolerant."

April suffered from restricted cardiomyopathy, which prevents the heart muscle from fully relaxing and thus filling with blood. Was April in pain?

"Near the end, yes, she was. Yes, she was," replies Denise, hesitating.

The Evans family videotaped April throughout her life. An angelic child toddles around, plays in a toy car, mumbles to the camera, smiles, laughs and waves. At the end of one particularly poignant clip she raises her hand and says goodbye. It would take a tougher man than me not to weep.

"She loved being outside and she loved being in the backpack," says Larry. "There was a game she had where she would point to her shoes when she wanted to go outside and then untie them as soon as we got out. She was just so ... " and his voice trails off.

The couple has two other young children. They have taken April's passing very hard indeed.

"One of them thinks we can go and get her out of the ground and everything will be okay again," says Denise. "It'll take time. It'll take forever."

It could have been so different. The donation of an organ at death is something we seldom even consider. And those people who have signed their driving licence or health card to allow a transplant should know this does not guarantee anything unless the next of kin have been informed and agree with the procedure.

In other words, if a spouse or parent decides the organs cannot be removed, the signature of the would-be donor is worth absolutely nothing. This has happened more times than doctors and sick people awaiting a transplant would like to count.

Most people, of course, simply never consider the issue. They believe they are immortal, they know that death is the great enemy and neurosis of the late 20th century and they've never met anyone who waits anxiously each day for the telephone to ring and a voice to announce that an organ has become available and the operation can take place.

So do it now. Make the appropriate arrangements and have a prolonged discussion with the people closest to you. Contrary to what some people believe, there is no major religion outside of Shintoism that refuses to allow organ transplant and most objections are based on a sorry mixture of ignorance and fear.

One possible policy is for hospitals to presume that organs have been donated unless the family specifies otherwise. This is now the approach in several European countries. In the United States there is far greater discussion of the subject in hospitals and often an approach for consent. In Canada we have some of the finest facilities for transplants and many of the best doctors, but we simply don't have the organs.

Denise and Larry Evans wish it could have been different. They are in no way bitter, but they are in every way committed to making it better for others. Bless them for that. And bless April.

Mercy Killing Whose Life is it, Anyway?

Earlier this week a woman was charged with the attempted murder of her 6-year-old daughter. The little girl has cerebral palsy and is severely handicapped. The near-lethal dose of medication given to the child did not quite kill her and at the time of writing she is in critical condition in hospital.

There is so much that can be written about euthanasia, assisted suicide and the obscene oxymoron of mercy killing or compassionate homicide.

There is the fact that in the Netherlands, where euthanasia is not actually legal but is accepted, 10,000 "Don't Kill Me" cards have been issued. These are like organ donor cards, but this time a person who might, for example, be hurt in an accident, is trying to make sure a doctor does not kill him. People are so frightened of eager medics that they fear for their lives in a place ostensibly devoted to the preservation of the same.

There is the fact that in Europe a Roman Catholic nun from a conservative order was killed in a hospital – even though she had given strict instructions that her beliefs were absolutely opposed to the premature ending of her life.

Or the fact that in Holland a third of all of the victims of euthanasia are thus treated by doctors without their permission having been given or that of their families.

There are, as I say, so many points to make.

- That the very last people who can make cogent, calm decisions about life and death issues are those who are frightened and are in pain.
- That often tired or just unscrupulous families will apply either direct or subconscious pressure on aging relatives to "make it easier" on everyone concerned.
- That almost all pain can now be controlled. Medicine is advancing so quickly that suffering which five years ago may

167

have led to "mercy killing" can today be alleviated and the causes cured.

But more important than this is one single letter, written by a young man from Vancouver shortly after the Tracy Latimer case in Saskatchewan. We must let him speak.

"My name is Teague. I am 11 years old, and have really severe cerebral palsy.

"I feel very strongly that all children are valuable, and deserve to live full and complete lives. No one should make the decision for another person on whether their life is worth living or not.

"I have a friend who had cerebral palsy, and he decided life was too hard and too painful. So he really let himself die. I knew he was leaving this world and letting himself dwell in the spiritual world. I told him that I understood that the spiritual world was really compelling, but that life was worth fighting for.

"I had to fight to live when I was very sick. The doctors said I wouldn't live long, but I knew I had so much to accomplish still.

"I had to fight pain all the time. When I was little, life was pain. I couldn't remember no pain. My foster mom, Cara, helped me learn to manage and control my pain. Now my life is so full of joy. There isn't enough time in the day for me to learn and experience all I wish to. I have a family and many friends who love me. I have a world of knowledge to discover. I have so much to give.

"I can't walk or talk or feed myself. But I am not 'suffering from cerebral palsy.' I use a wheelchair, but I am not 'confined to a wheelchair.' I have pain, but I do not need to be 'put out of my misery.'

"My body is not my enemy. It is that which allows me to enjoy Mozart, experience Shakespeare, savour a feast and cuddle my mom. Life is a precious gift. It belongs to the person to whom it was given. Not to her parents, nor to the state. Tracy's life was hers to make of it what she could. My life is going to be astounding."

It was. And when Teague died, naturally, in the early summer of 1995, with the flowers pushing their way into new life and the gentle rays of the sun replacing the harshness of the icy rain, he was surrounded by love.

He still is.

If this Nonsense is Art Then I'm in Hell

Art is, apparently, in the eye of the beholder. Such a concept does not, however, explain how we should deal with those people who claim to be artists but seem to be completely and hopelessly blind. Now, I am aware that as soon as I criticize modern art I will be labelled as a Philistine. It will not be the first time and I hope it will not be the last. And remember, contrary to popular belief, the Philistines boasted a particularly advanced culture.

The latest example of the genre comes from a fellow by the name of Arne Torneck. He is particularly proud of the fact that he has three so-called installations on display for the month of October in Toronto's Simcoe Gallery.

The first of these little masterpieces is entitled Pilgrim on The Way Of Return: The Stump Chronicles, the second is called The Unholy F... and the third Hooked. The three dots on the second piece, by the way, are my insertion. The word is spelled in full on the work itself.

In the accompanying material to the collection the Pilgrim exhibit is described as follows. "Fifteen hinged, double sided 4' X 8' collages which run in a zigzag configuration ... the toothed structure is a metaphor for the saw blade which produces stumps. Log sections scattered on the gallery floor suggest the lifeless slash of clear-cutting. These log sections are functional; they may be used to sit on while studying the work, and stood upon to read the material on the upper parts of the panels." Or sleep on if it all becomes too much to tolerate.

"The collages consist of three basic elements: the front pages of the Toronto Star for one full year, photos taken by the Chronicler of himself and the Stump during this period, and transcriptions of the Chronicler's concurrent meditations.

"Four blow-ups of the Stump, photographed during each of the seasons, line the gallery wall, while a blow-up of the Chronicler

169

and the Stump, cut off by the saw blade panel configuration, is mounted on the opposite wall."

Just in case this is unsatisfying, the next piece tries a little harder. The Unholy F... is a collection of mannequins and these "become metaphors for capitalistic intent." Naturally, because we can't have a proper art showing without an attack on good old capitalism, even though it is the only system that actually allows such nonsense to be shown to the public.

Irony aside, what of the poor dummies, who have harmed nobody and do not deserve such a fate as this? They have to "sit before, or point at a TV monitor which runs an endless loop of colour bars. One gallery wall supports a rectangular configuration of sixteen 18" X 24" photos, which suggest a giant TV monitor. Each of the 16 elements contains a photograph of the colour bars on top of which are black and white photos of the mannequins in various stages of being mass produced."

Arne Torneck explained to me that originally there were six figures in the piece, but one of them was accidentally smashed on the way to the gallery. "It doesn't matter," he said. "After all, five is a much more magical number than six." Did this not, I asked, destroy the integrity and balance of the piece?

"Ah, no," replied the artist. "At least I don't think so."

The last work, Hooked, is supposed to "convey the nature of addiction" and, surprise of surprises, the artist has used "pornographic images and fictional text" to make his point. He continues: "Each modular component of the visual element is a representation of a gram of cocaine. The relentless reverberation of this basic element, with its attendant sexual imagery, conveys..." Well, nobody really cares what it conveys. It does, however, apparently "provide an insight into the religious nature of its mistress, ritual." Oh, really.

Is this art? Is it hell! But at least it is not publicly funded, which in this day and age is something of a miracle.

As for the mannequins, as we go to press they have still made no comment on the pornography or the obscene language of the piece. But one of them thinks he might be able to bring a case before the Human Rights Commission.

An Arrogant Man, and a Bad Playwright to Boot

Last Saturday I took my 8-year-old daughter, Lucy, to see George Bernard Shaw's Major Barbara at Niagara-on-the-Lake. Now, the Shaw Festival and the town of Niagara represent two of this country's crowning achievements. Any Canadian who does not take advantage of their offerings on a regular basis is missing out on something uniquely exciting.

Having said that, George Bernard Shaw himself was a man with repugnant opinions, a self-conscious intellectual who was horribly wrong on almost every major issue of his day. His legacy is measly and monstrous and each time I see a bust, statue or portrait of the old wretch in the glorious Niagara I shudder just a little more than is comfortable.

The Irish writer was in fact a very bad dramatist. While he swam so well in a sea of extreme intelligence, he was also drenched in the dark lake of arrogance.

Like so many leftist revolutionaries, he knew that he was right. Just as importantly, he knew as a consequence that everybody else was wrong. Thus his plays have a clumsily didactic edge to them, full of artificial characters mouthing philosophy. The fact that some of the philosophy is funny and even challenging cannot alter the fact that it does not make for convincing drama.

Shaw was also a quintessentially modern man. He would have been acutely comfortable in the contemporary age, in that his ideology was inconsistent and based not on pure beliefs but on his own feelings. He was convinced that animals had rights and refused to eat their flesh. At the same time, however, he made abundantly flattering comments about Benito Mussolini and even about the early "achievements" of Adolf Hitler.

He refused to drink alcohol, because he was obsessed with his precious body and thought that beer and whisky might damage such a temple. Other people's bodies mattered less.

Shaw became a great supporter of Stalin's Soviet empire. He visited the hellish place in the middle of the forced starvation of the Ukrainian people. On returning to the West, he was asked by a reporter about what he knew was the extermination of hundreds of thousands of people, including women and children. In response Shaw laughed and threw a can of Russian meat at the journalist.

He preached equality of the sexes but treated women terribly, he wrote about the liberation of the poor but despised and misunderstood the working class, he supported Irish republicanism but was a bitter enemy of its Roman Catholic foundations, he sang of equality but practised snobbery.

The author G.K. Chesterton compared Shaw's opinions to a cup of coffee. They stimulated, he said, but did not inspire. Less like a cup of coffee, more like strychnine.

Nor was he alone in all this hypocrisy.

In the program for Major Barbara the British novelist and socialist H.G. Wells is referred to correctly as someone who irritated and provoked Shaw.

True, but Wells and Shaw also had much in common.

When Wells described Jewish people as termites, when he wrote that people of colour should be forced into eternal world slavery, when he recommended the killing of the "weak and sensual" and the extermination of "lesser races" who did not fit into "the needs of modern civilization," Shaw did little other than nod his approval.

This was the same Wells, in fact, who described himself as a feminist yet thought it most amusing to violate naive young women and then abandon them and who took a perverse joy in the public abuse of his wife and his legion of mistresses. The same Wells who had other people write some of his most important books and then refused to give them any credit.

Shaw, Wells, the patrician and patronizing Beatrice and Sidney Webb and their revolutionary friends differed on certain particularities, but not on the main thrust of killing God, killing family, killing traditional beliefs and values and replacing them all with a new utopia. As such they all have a great deal for which to answer.

Every dictator since has aped such fundamentalist nonsense.

The last word? "That man had some awful ideas, dad" from Lucy. Quite right, darling, quite right. But we'll both visit Niagara again next year.

The Pop Goddess and the Future Saint

It is, as they say, deja vu all over again.

One year ago large chunks of the western world rolled into an emotional ball. A mass spasm of grief was unleashed at the announcement of the death of Princess Diana.

A few days later a tiny woman who had grown into a giant, Mother Teresa, completed her journey on Earth. Though she had given her all to the poorest of the poor she was scarcely in her grave before the attacks on her character and achievements filled newspapers and television screens.

Princess Diana was celebrated in life and death as the queen of love and beauty. She was, of course, physically stunning and she certainly exhibited a warmth and an empathy toward the suffering. Yet it could be argued this was a facile love, a thin love, a love that could only lead to more suffering.

When Diana put her arms around a man dying of AIDS she was, yes, breaking a social taboo and restoring the poor wretch's humanity. She refused, however, to deal with the root causes of the problem.

Devotees of Diana described this as unconditional love. It could also be described as unconditional indifference.

Such an approach differed fundamentally from that of Mother Teresa. The bride of poverty put her arms around countless young men dying from the AIDS virus, held them close to her and whispered that she cared. She then told them they had been wrong. She dared to break the contemporary commandment of universal toleration, refuted the idea that on moral issues nothing is better or worse than anything else.

While Diana refused to pass any comment on the homosexual lifestyle that was responsible for most of the AIDS deaths in Europe and North America, Mother Teresa insisted on speaking out, and she was condemned for it. Yet it is surely the allegedly judgmental Teresa who exhibited the greatest love and the most meaningful compassion.

Those who disagree might want to consider the mother who will not take the carving knife away from her child because the tot has such fun playing with it.

Teresa criticized other modernist mainstays as well. She argued the pill and the condom had created far more problems than they had ever solved and that the rate of teenage pregnancies, sexually transmitted diseases, abortions and divorces had gone up every year since the provision of universal artificial contraception.

Many hated the message, and so despised the messenger.

Princess Diana encountered nothing but praise when she battled to bring about the end of land mines. Mother Teresa faced enormous opposition when she campaigned against the very evil, darkness and selfishness that leads to such violence and bloodshed.

The Albanian nun stated that land mines can disappear today, reappear tomorrow, whereas once a person's heart is changed it is transformed forever.

Which leads us back to the reason why so many people who had never met Princess Diana, had never even been in the same city as her, mourned as if a parent or child had died. It was not because of shared experience or vicarious pain, but because of the absence in their lives of the being to which Mother Teresa devoted her existence. It was and is all about God.

If we lose the real thing, we search for watery substitutes. It has always been thus. Diana took on the quality of the goddess, the higher entity who could do no wrong and be worshipped with a joyful ease. A divinity in a baseball cap and perfect make-up who teased the cameras, was cheated on by a cruel clown of a husband and then died an ostensible martyr's death speeding through the French capital with a drunk driver and a playboy lover.

This was designer exotica. The fantasy royal becomes the dying heroine, ambiguous and mysterious to the Parisian end. Bury her on an island, compose ludicrous conspiracy theories about her death and lionize her memory. The stuff of bad mythology.

Mother Teresa, on the other hand, was according to her influential enemies just a religious fanatic who insisted on pushing her own opinions on people and refused to change with the times.

Never mind.

Rest in peace, ladies. Both did their best. Only one was right.

Supermon Jodie:
She's Going it Alone

A quick flight around the world, with stops at some of the more troubling destinations. Not Washington, D.C., though, because of the dense clouds of hot air.

In the U.S., actress Jodie Foster gives birth to a baby boy whom she names Charles. Being very rich, very famous and very American, Foster immediately assumes she is now an expert on children, knowing far more about the subject than, say, a woman who has raised a dozen model citizens.

"I don't think a father is necessary to raise a healthy, happy baby," says the woman who made a fortune playing an FBI agent who hunts cannibals.

What this really is about is pride and social engineering. Pride, in that Foster is convinced she knows better than anyone else, even to the point of risking her child's well-being. Social engineering, in that Foster is playing the great vivisectionist, experimenting with ideas and theories.

Unfortunately, the subjects of her weird science are not rabbits or mice – that would be totally unacceptable these days – but human beings.

Of course, single mothers exist and often are outstanding parents. Their situation is the result of cowardly men who lack the courage to remain on the scene, or of abusive and dysfunctional relationships. But any woman who deliberately excludes a father from her child is committing a form of child abuse. The evidence that children require a balanced family and need a man on the scene is overwhelming, however much extremists like Foster lust for the contrary. Good luck, Charlie.

In Northern Ireland a breakaway group from the Irish Republican Army commits the most gruesome massacre in that troubled, yet glorious, country in 30 years. They are republican murderers, in the tradition of Gerry Adams and his gang. That Adams, leader of the political wing of the IRA, has condemned this bombing, the first time he has done such a thing, is good, but then he has no option. He knows the killers, may even have helped train them. His political future is at stake.

These men did more than merely kill people. Given one of their victims was a priest they tried to kill God. Given another was a pregnant woman they tried to kill the future. Given yet another was an 18-month-old child they tried to kill innocence. They failed.

In Kansas, a teenager was suspended from school for scrawling a Confederate flag on his notebook. A federal judge upheld the right of the school to remove the boy. The Confederate emblem is still incorporated in several state flags and, whilst capable of being used as a symbol of hate, is frequently employed otherwise. The brawny men and beautiful women in the silly television series The Dukes of Hazzard never struck me as being active Klan members, and those country and western fanatics I meet who wear the Stars and Bars have never once asked my opinion of Mein Kampf.

Could it just be this is yet another example of a politically correct over-reaction? If the boy in question is spreading racial hatred then he should be dealt with. Even then the answer is not to remove him, but to repair him. Show him the errors of his ways. But scribbling the flag of a former nation on a book, a nation that stood for a great deal more than slavery, is insufficient grounds for suspension. In the same manner I would feel uncomfortable if we expelled every teen who wore a Black Power T-shirt or a Malcolm X cap.

There were not many rebel flags on display at Woodstock 29 years ago, but then there were not really any genuine rebels. The festival represented nothing more than organized self-indulgence and mass hysteria. Ironically, it was the crowning moment of an age sorely lacking in majesty. The 1960s produced one of the most barren generational ideologies in history.

Last weekend a billionaire businessman organized a partial recreation of the jamboree, much to the chagrin of hippie diehards who have criticized what they see as exploitation. Big deal.

I do, however, wonder if Jodie Foster was there, and whether she allowed little Charles to scribble flags on his notebook.

Walk a Mile in a Terrorist's Shoes

Two terrorist bombs explode outside American embassies in Africa.

Slaughter.

U.S. President Bill Clinton, a man who has scrupulously avoided risking his safety on behalf of his country, condemns the atrocities as being cowardly.

Yes and no.

Either way, rhetoric is useless. Know the enemy, know why he is what he is and why he does what he does. Feel him, be him, understand him. Empathy is victory.

Imagine a letter home from an Islamic fundamentalist who has just planted a car bomb in a large concrete building. The explosion killed women and children as well as soldiers and diplomats:

"Clinton calls me a coward. A man whose fate depends on the possibility of his having left semen stains on the dress of a stupid young woman suddenly becomes a hero. He has never fired or risked a bullet, but he judges me. I killed my first soldier when I was 15 and saw my brother's head shattered by a mortar shell when I was 12. I risk death every day and the morning I delivered the bomb I could have been shot and killed at any moment. But Clinton calls me a coward. The cliché is wrong. Bullies can be brave, just as terrorists can be valiant.

"The people of the western world ape the words of their leaders. We are cowards, they say, and murderers. Yet these same people cheered when their bombs hit targets all over Iraq. Smart bombs fired by less than smart people. Canned death launched from total safety hundreds of miles away from the front line, killing innocent civilians whose president simply wanted oil and cash payment for having stood up to Iran in one of the bloodiest wars in history.

"I look around the world. In Israel Menachem Begin was given the Nobel Peace Prize and lauded as a world statesman. Only 30 years earlier he and his Irgun planted bombs and were hunted as terrorists. One of his successors as Prime Minister, Yitzhak Shamir, led the Stern Gang, who used hammers to beat people to death.

"Clinton invited Gerry Adams to the White House and embraced him as a brother. The pair made jokes about a well-known Protestant leader and laughed out loud. But Adams was personally responsible for murders and bombings and still controls one of the most successful terrorist organizations in the world. All active service unit members of the Irish Republican Army read The Revolt, a revered handbook on terrorism. The author is Menachem Begin.

"In South Africa, Nelson Mandela is loved and respected as a forgiving man, a peaceful man. This is the same Mandela who was arrested and imprisoned for terrorism. The same was true of the leaders of Zimbabwe, Kenya and so many other countries. Indeed, the early leaders of the United States were, in the eyes of the British, nothing but terrorists. Men operating outside the law who firebombed the homes of their opponents pushed Washington, Jefferson and Adams into power.

"In 1948 my people did not even know where Germany was, yet because of the brutalities of the Christian Europeans towards their neighbours of a different faith, part of the Arab homeland, Palestine, was given to the Jews from Poland and Russia, Hungary and Austria. We were not asked, we were merely told.

"Every time since then we have stood up as proud, self-reliant people we have been smashed down. We have been tied to foreign economies, tied to alien ideas, mocked and made monsters of the West's movies and their news. They deny us trade, they deny us the basics of life.

"I see a child bleeding and weeping, the result of what I did. I hate myself for it. I want another way of fighting back, of hitting back at the killers of my people. Give me another way, show me another way, come and fight me on the battlefield, man-to-man, rifle-to-rifle, on equal terms. Otherwise, I will strike as I can. And I will watch as you slide into the morals swamp and laugh at your drowning, and ignore it whenever one of your leaders calls me a coward."

I say again, avoid hyperbole and empty words and try to understand why people not different from us commit acts we find so repugnant.

The Stuff of Nonsense in Black Leather

Everybody is doin it. Or that is the opinion of supporters of Terri-Jean Bedford, the absurd woman known as Madame de Sade who is on trial in Toronto for keeping a common bawdy house. The dominatrix may well respond there is nothing comon about it. And considering her house of pain contains weapons of abuse, humiliation and bondage, she may well be right.

The defence testimony that such antics are common, therapeutic and not at all repugnant to community standards is the stuff of nonsense in black leather. One of the funniest moments in recent legal history, and a telling indictment of Canadian higher education, occurred when a professor from Toronto's York University explained at the trial how she enjoyed riding around on a man's back as if he were a horse and being carried to the toilet by a "slave."

Continuing with her thesis, the publicly funded academic explained that people like being whipped, degraded and tortured because "they are searching for their souls." She then gave a little lecture on the penile development of Socrates shortly before his death.

So we have established that certain professors in the country should be fired, but what of the merits of sado-masochism? Some years ago I wrote a long piece about all of this for a Canadian magazine. I spoke to people who were "into the scene" and each time I went to interview a dominatrix my wife said a bunch of Hail Marys.

There was no need. While some of these women were pleasant enough, there was a theme to their lives, a recurring flavor. They were sad and they were confused. In that they were selling services of sexual titillation to pathetic men, they were prostitutes, but most of them were obsessive in pointing out the differences between themselves and the average whore. "There is no sex, I would not lower myself," they would say.

They would, however, dress up in wild costumes, they would pretend to be an angry nanny to a middle-aged accountant dressed in a diaper, they would wear artificial male genitalia and do ridiculous things to men who probably should have received a good clip round the ear when they were children, not now that they are adults. Yet none of this, they protested, was degrading for them. I was also given a whole pile of essays that one woman's clients were forced to write, listing their fantasies and desires. Interestingly enough, the dominatrix in question had forgotten to remove the names and telephone numbers. Almost all were married. And in being intimate, sexually and otherwise, with a stranger they were being unfaithful to the women to whom they had sworn eternal truth. Adultery is and should always be "repugnant to community standards."

Sado-masochism is also a perversion. Part of the joy of normal human sexuality is that there are degrees of taste and preference within a specified wave-band that give a loving, married couple mutual joy and happiness. But when that wave-band is smashed all hell is let loose.

Men who pay for sado-masochism are aroused not by a woman, but by what that woman does to humiliate and hurt them. It is the act of masochism that gives them fulfillment and this, by any intelligent definition, is a perversion. One only has to actually look at the women who earn their cash in the dominatrix profession. At the risk of appearing rude, they do tend to be extremely unattractive in the traditional sense. Terri-Jean Bedford is a good example of this. As one of the men wrote in his little essay, "They can be as old and ugly as you like, as long as they hurt me good."

Which leads to the question of whether the police should have spent so much time and money on prosecuting this woman and whether the Crown should be indulging in such a costly prosecution. Of course not. There are rapists, drug-dealers, wife batterers and thieves to be caught. Madame de Sade is silly and her clients hilarious. But the only people really being humiliated by this case are the police and the public who pay their wages.

There is No Future in Despair for the Past

The World Cup is over and the only outcome that gives me any joy is the remarkable success of Croatia.

I have no Croatian blood, I am in no way anti-Serbian and as someone who lost Jewish relatives during the Holocaust I have no reason to be an admirer of the country's war record.

Yet I became an immediate fan of Croatia the day they were condemned by a French anti-racist organization for their red and white checkerboard soccer shirts.

"This was the symbol of the Croatian fascists during the Second World War," said the Parisian activists, "so we demand that they change it."

Demand is a strong word. So is fascist.

The Croatian flag goes back many centuries and has been used by groups and causes too numerous to mention.

Indeed, it was waved by the hideous Croatian fascists. It was also used by the repugnant Croatian communists. It would be like Canadian political parties adopting the Maple Leaf as their political symbol. As such it would be anachronistic and absurd to think of it as being exclusively fascistic.

Facts have seldom bothered extremists of any kind.

The alleged anti-fascist variety in Paris tried to soil the noble efforts of two dozen young men playing their hearts out for their troubled country, tried to inject politics into something far more pure. Tried, quite simply, to cause trouble and exploit misunderstanding.

So three cheers for Croatia.

Such attempts to rekindle the dying flames of hatred and fear are nothing new.

Growing up in England's Jewish community I saw organizations and individuals making anti-Semitic mountains of meaningless molehills in a sordid attempt to justify their existence. To actually admit the Nazi genocide was 50 years ago and Jew-hating was on the decline damaged their donor base and their status. It was in their interests to remind often frightened people of a terrible past.

Such behavior is little more than the manipulation of the dead.

While we must all be aware of historical injustice, I have had enough of what seem like constant reminders of Nazism, death camps and that stupid little man with the bad moustache. Forgive me, but it all happened a long time ago. Since then mass murder has occurred in Rwanda, Cambodia and even in Palestinian refugee camps in Lebanon.

The times have changed.

Historical monomania ties in directly to the troubles of Northern Ireland. Because of the polished propaganda machine of the Irish nationalists, naïve North American journalists tend to swallow the republican version hook, line and expense cheque. But in fact the absurd obsession with the past is as much a Roman Catholic trait in Ireland as it is a Protestant one.

Yes, there was a potato famine. Yes, Oliver Cromwell slaughtered Catholics in the 17th century. Yes, they were treated like second-class citizens for decades.

And, yes, Catholic rebels killed thousands of Protestants in the 1630s, many of them women and children. Yes, the Roman Catholic Church tortured people who wanted to read the Bible in their native language. Yes, the Irish Republic refused to take up arms against Nazi Germany.

But we cannot base the hope of the political future on the despair of the political past. Loyalist marches have to be rerouted just as republican terrorist fund-raising in Toronto and Ottawa has to be stopped. Today's children matter much more than yesterday's great-grandparents.

Some Irish Catholics reading this column will argue their case is different. So will some Irish Protestants. So will some Canadian Jews. And so will some people of Serbian, Ukrainian, native and every other heritage. No. The specifics become irrelevant in the wider scheme and the past must not be allowed to dominate the future.

Which is precisely what I remember whenever I see Israel's finest midfielder playing alongside one of Croatia's best strikers for the same soccer team in the English Premier League. When they embrace after yet another goal they do not discuss the events of 1942, but the excitement and pleasure of the present.

Oh, brave new world that does not dwell on the angst of old men.

The Promised Land: As Other See Us

Yesterday we remembered, so for the rest of the year we could forget.

Forget what Canada is, what being Canadian is, what this country means to so many people.

It is, of course, difficult to define, which is perhaps part of its greatness. Definitions can be simple, facile and ultimately meaningless. Let others define, let us be proud.

Canada Day is a joyous but passing moment, a glorious reminder of the noble quintessence of this nation. If only more people could be reminded every day.

For millions of those who live outside Canada the name of our country symbolizes freedom and liberation. For cynical citizens who would rather live in New York, London or Florida this all seems rather pathetic. But then they have probably not met Sean, Esther or Peter.

It was some years ago now but it still seems fresh in my mind. I had been a landed immigrant for four years and was to become a citizen. An ocean of people bathed in a sea of red and white. Entire families dressed in the national colors, from every corner of the world. Photographs, smiles, some tears and a great deal of patriotism. This meant something, this was something.

It meant a great deal to Esther but she was one of the people crying. A woman in her 20s whose dark loveliness was almost overwhelming, she was an Iranian Jew whose family had been fairly wealthy during the reign of the shah. Her father had lost his business during the revolution. That they could take. But they could not take the disappearance of Farri, Esther's 13-year-old brother. The boy was seen leaving school but was never seen arriving home. He had been bullied repeatedly for being Jewish in the new Islamic state but nobody had expected this. Not this. Esther and her family left shortly afterwards and came to Canada.

Where Esther was stunning, Sean was plain. Where she was dark, he was pale. He appeared to fade in with the background, looked like he didn't want to be noticed. He was twitchy, awkward, seemed almost apologetic to be in the room.

It was difficult to break through the barrier of silence but when he discovered some common ground with me he let loose. He was a Roman Catholic from Northern Ireland who, for some reason, had fallen out of favor with some local Irish Republican Army hoodlums. They had shot him in the leg and promised to aim higher next time. He came to Canada.

Peter was tall, black and Christian. From the Sudan, this elegant man took his new name when he came to Canada.

"After the leader of the early church," he told me. "And after a man who was prepared to be crucified upside down because he felt he wasn't good enough to die in the manner of Jesus Christ."

Peter was one of many black Christians in the south of the country who had been a victim of the Muslim Arabs to the north. The latter raid their neighbors, rape the women, kill many men and take others away to be forcibly converted to Islam and sold into slavery. Simon knew he had to leave. He came to Canada.

Esther will not be called a slut and a whore in Canada and her family will not be beaten up. Sean will not see sectarian murder on his doorstep in Canada and will not have to worry about his personal safety. Peter will not see his friends killed by brutal invaders in Canada and have his sister sold into slavery. Of course they will face problems, and of course they will have to adapt. But they are confident and brave, just like their new country.

And then there is me. An ordinary Englishman who meets a beautiful Canadian woman at an academic conference in Toronto, falls in love and leaves his home, job and family to come to a country he hardly knows.

He grows to love it, to care for it, to be grateful for it and to it. He will call it home. He will never take it for granted. And neither will Esther, Sean and Peter. In Canada.

Happy Birthday.

Soccer Violence Explained

I really am becoming rather tired of reading the views of instant experts about the world of soccer. It really takes more than a media pass to the World Cup and a copy of Football Made Simple to understand the game, its culture and its followers. This has been particularly true of the coverage of crowd violence involving English supporters. Some background first.

In Holland an organized battle between gangs supporting Ajax of Amsterdam and Feyenoord of Rotterdam resulted in deaths and a national investigation last year. This was merely the latest in a series of incidents involving these and other clubs, with regular hospitalization of injured fans. The Netherlands is plagued with football violence.

In Italy, the Ultras that follow all of the leading clubs are well armed, often with guns, and have quite an extraordinary influence over clubs the size of Juventus and Inter Milan. They have murdered other fans.

In Spain there are still political affiliations in soccer, with Real Madrid having a vocal and organized fascist following because it was Franco's favorite team. Again, fights are common.

In Argentina mass violence is a regular feature, with hundreds if not thousands of shirtless thugs running at each other with weapons. The use of tear gas and baton charges by the police is frequent and, again, governments have launched investigations.

English soccer hooliganism reached a filthy pinnacle in the 1970s. Since then the elimination of standing areas in stadiums, the banning of alcohol, skilful policing and a certain embourgeoisement of the game has all but eliminated the stupidity. It is when the English national team travels abroad that trouble sometimes arises, caused by a hardcore of perhaps 100 or 200 men, many of them with links to neo-Nazism.

There was a time when the liberal media blamed all this on poverty, inner-city decay and Margaret Thatcher. Nonsense. It costs money to visit foreign countries, to buy cell-phones in order to organize attacks and to bail yourself out of jail. The people who commit these acts are short of brains, not cash.

But journalists are also to blame. I've seen press photographers buying English supporters drinks and daring them to smash windows and attack rivals. I have seen the packs of reporters swarming around English fans, waiting to exploit the situation and hoping it happens.

I have also now read too many articles by the ill-informed about how English fans and even the English team should be banned from world football. In other words, include countries that are ruled by military dictators, where political dissidents are murdered and where there is no freedom of speech or assembly, but ban England because of a bunch of morons.

Like a magnet, the English attract any local tough who wants to prove himself, so fights become almost inevitable. Anybody who looks closely at the composition of the English crowd on television would see young women, middle-aged men with small children and smiling fans. The idea these people are intent on causing trouble is absurd.

Could it just be possible the otherwise angelic North African street gangs of Marseilles, notorious for their cowardly attacks with razors, might have had something to do with the violence surrounding the England against Tunisia game? Or is it that the English are all psychopathic – just like all Canadians are so terribly dull and speak French as they ski through Toronto in the middle of August?

The European Championships were held in England in 1996 and were a major success, and English clubs have played in Europe now for many years with very little trouble. To punish England, English soccer and English supporters for the behavior of a small group of politically repugnant and socially grotesque idiots would be to let those idiots win.

At the risk of sounding like the representative of a special interest group applying for a government grant, I have to say there seems to be some good old tribalism in all of this finger-pointing. Simply, there are people out there who are just lining up to take shots at a country they resent or envy. Which is precisely the sort of attitude that leads to, well, soccer violence.

A Man, and a Message, for the Ages

The award-winning drama A Man for All Seasons is running at the Stratford Festival in Ontario. It is a good production, but it is a great play and about an even greater life.

Robert Bolt's account of the 16th-century statesman, author and lawyer Thomas More, and his resistance to what he saw as oppression and injustice, is soaked with lessons for today.

More's struggle was against a brutal king who let lust overwhelm logic, and fervor get the better of fairness. More was eventually executed for his refusal to, well, change with the times.

Come with us, said his friends in the political and cultural establishment, come with us and all will be well. You will be revered by the powerful and the rich, doors of opportunity will be opened wide for you and the world will accept you as a hero and a giant. But he refused.

The essence of More's argument was less that he had to follow his conscience than that he had to go along with what he considered to be the truth. Some of his opponents were ideologically opposed to him and others were simply opportunists who bent with the wind, but both demanded that for the new world order to succeed More had to adapt.

In other words, he had to find a new truth.

We cannot tolerate dissent, they said, because if enough people dissent from what we say is true it will no longer appear to be the truth at all.

These new rulers called themselves open-minded and rational men, but were not prepared to tolerate views with which they disagreed.

More embarrassed them, made them look at their ideas afresh and, as a consequence, shamed them.

He also opposed them with humor and intelligence and that was something they really could not accept.

Some members of the court accused More of being insane; others said he was evil; a few said he was foolish.

But they were all proved wrong. So in the end they bribed a weak, ambitious man to lie under oath to convict More and send him to the block.

That weak and ambitious man, Richard Rich, served under various regimes in this period of profound change, doing extremely well under both Protestant and Catholic monarchs. He was a politician. Unlike More, he did change with the times, held prominent posts and made a great deal of money.

At one point in the play Rich is seduced into the darker side of political subterfuge and scheming. At first he feels dirty and violated. His seducer sees this and tells him in an icy phrase it will be "easier the next time."

The banality of evil. It gets easier to be evil the more you get used to it.

Then we have a theatrical device used by author Bolt in his stage play, but not in the superb movie of the same name. This is The Common Man. He is a survivor, an observer, a commentator. He watches the scene and has opinions, but does not intervene. He prefers a safe, easy life to the hardships of standing up for what is right. After all, why should he risk everything for a belief when it is a full belly, a roof over his head and a good income that matter most?

More's son-in-law is a zealot. And a zealot for changing causes.

Whether he is a harsh conservative or a dangerous reformer, he refuses to listen to anybody else and is always certain he is absolutely correct. He is young, recently a student, and is contemptuous of other people and their views.

Not so his mother-in-law, More's wife, who is a simple woman incapable of reading or writing. But although she is illiterate she is also wise. Behind her bluster and plainness is a visceral knowledge of right and wrong.

A cultural elite arrogant in its foolish power. Scheming politicians. The caress of evil. Extremism without thought. Intolerance disguised as sophistication. A good man victimized for truth and the courage to proclaim it. As relevant now as it was then. A life and an example for all seasons.

Believe it or Not,
Pro-Lifers Have Rights Too

I have held off writing about the closure of Toronto's Wellesley Hospital and about its work being taken over by nearby St. Michael's until now, but I can no longer sit back and say nothing.

It is, of course, a dark day when any hospital is closed, and I do not believe the Wellesley should have been thus treated.

But this, apparently, is no longer the point. The fuss now is St. Michael's Hospital dares to be a Roman Catholic institution and consequently believes in the sanctity of human life from conception until natural death.

In short, abortion and surgical contraception will no longer be offered.

Few people have actually complained about this but those who have seem to have an unusually easy and generous access to the media. Their voices tend to be heard. Which is surprising, in that all the new hospital policy will mean is that those women who want to abort their unborn babies will have to drive another half a mile for this publicly funded procedure. As for vasectomies, they are virtually available at the corner store.

The truth is Toronto drips red with abortion clinics and the Ontario government, in spite of many gestures to the pro-life movement while in opposition, has done nothing to curtail abortion since coming to government.

Much as I wish the St. Michael's policy would drastically reduce the number of abortions, in reality it will save only a few tiny lives.

Yet the venom of some opponents of St. Michael's is extraordinary.

In their passion for pluralism they demand the Roman Catholic Church abandon its most fundamental beliefs.

In the name of tolerance, they seem to be saying, we refuse to tolerate your religion.

Interestingly enough, as unborn life is also sacred to evangelical Christians, orthodox Jews and practising Muslims, this paradoxical interpretation of pluralism might be in for a rough ride in the years to come.

The irony here is the reason hospitals like the Wellesley are being closed in the first place is so cuts can be made to the health care budget. And one of the largest unnecessary costs to that budget is financing the elective surgery of abortion. Surely even those who support abortion must accept there is no moral or logical argument for the government to be firing nurses so it can continue to fund violent birth control.

It is also the case that a hospital that refuses to perform abortions would be a much more inviting place for the millions of Canadians who are vehemently opposed to the phenomenon. Surely they are entitled to a hospital in Greater Toronto that is less repugnant in their eyes. Irritating though it might be to some people, pro-lifers have rights too.

The Roman Catholic Church was providing universal and free health care before the modern secular state even existed, and without such a system socialized medicine could not have triumphed.

As for the marginalized of society, leper hospitals were, and often still are, staffed by nuns and priests and Christian doctors and nurses of all denominations were working in the developing world long before the United Nations. Christian health care in North America has a sparkling record and a belief system that features at the top of its list a commitment to treating people of any and every faith.

Such is the anger toward this church and its hospitals, however, that in New York some politicians are threatening to impose abortion by force on the city's many Catholic institutions. The church has replied it will close its hospitals down before allowing such a thing. If this happened, the entire health system of one of the world's largest and busiest cities would come to a standstill.

Why, then, the extremism from the pro-abortion movement and why the lack of respect for the views of others? Because this isn't about the Wellesley or St. Michael's or any other single hospital but about a new authoritarianism that refuses to accept dissident and different views. Anyone who genuinely believed in choice would be applauding the courage of St. Michael's Hospital, but then this isn't really about choice at all.

That has been obvious for a long time.

A Helping Hand Lopped Off

Although this story takes place in downtown Toronto it could, unfortunately, be set in any city or town in Canada.

It is about business, about the homeless, about compassion and about indifference to those who have the misfortune to slip through the cracks of consumerism. It is also about the burying of heads in the sand and refusal to deal with an issue that won't go away simply because we ignore it.

The Salvation Army has been forced to close a 50-bed hostel and fire 15 staff members because the city of Toronto has withdrawn funding, even though it had originally promised money would be available as long as there was a need. The hostel was given just 10 days notice.

This occurred after various businesses in the area complained that having homeless people nearby caused insurmountable problems. It should be noted, however, that not every business owner agreed with this. The hostel will now open as a drop-in centre from morning until early evening five days a week, when the essential service for the homeless is a safe, warm and healthy place to sleep.

According to the councillor responsible for the area, Kyle Rae, there are "drug deals and fights in the area and people are frightened. It's scaring people away, scaring customers away, scaring tourists away."

When asked where the 50 homeless will now sleep, Rae replied "I don't know." Others do know. On the streets.

This is all interesting stuff, particularly from Rae, who has until recently largely played the role of liberal activist, an outspoken leader of the gay community and an opponent of conservative ideas and leaders. He is correct in saying there is crime in this area, but self-respecting drug-dealers don't usually sleep in hostels. After all, where would they recharge their cellphones?

Indeed, the clumsy stereotype Rae offered was one that would probably have provoked mass criticism if it had come from a Mike Harris or a Ralph Klein.

The fact there are problems in this part of Toronto has little to do with the homeless, but a great deal to do with a social decadence and permissive attitude created by generations of politicians. If we want to point fingers we should actually ask who gives out the permits for the many strip joints and pornographic video stores in the area. Or to the dowdy dollar stores that sell items such as lethal knives and drug paraphernalia. Such places might stimulate tourism, but surely not the sort that would improve a grey, troubled part of town.

The Salvation Army, on the other hand, has a well-won reputation for being street-wise, responsible and moderate in its care for the homeless. Its workers know the troublemakers and deal with them in an appropriate manner. They believe in self-reliance, character reform and strong Christian virtues. They have even distanced themselves from the protests that have taken place since the closing, aware that political activists of all stripes should be treated with a certain degree of suspicion.

They also tried to respond to local business concerns by hiring security guards and closing the hostel's doors at 11 p.m.

More than this, when local businesses requested lighting in an adjacent parking lot, the hostel provided it within 24 hours. It also hired a street person to keep the sidewalks clean and offered to provide the female staff of local stores and restaurants someone to accompany them to their cars or the subway. But it seems none of this was good enough.

It is sadly significant at a time when governments are telling the private sector to pick up the slack on welfare cutbacks, the Salvation Army, which in this case provided $150,000 as well as volunteer work and time, should lose its public funding because of a few ugly caricatures about the homeless and a misconception of what causes crime.

The irony about this sad tale is that the people who were spending their nights in the Salvation Army hostel have said they will now be sleeping in the doorways of the stores and restaurants whose owners made such a fuss. Which should do a great deal for their businesses and increase their profits substantially.

The Army's no Place for Gender Equality

I was not enormously impressed with allegations in Maclean's that incidents of rape and sexual harassment are rife in Canada's Armed Forces.

As soon as the story was published there were female soldiers who painted a different picture and, anyway, the subject of sexual politics is now so muddy the truth can become somewhat obscure.

Rape is, of course, an obscenity and any man who commits such a crime has to be severely punished. But there is also something extremely significant here – and something that will probably get me into all sorts of trouble. I would have hoped a young woman who wants to be a front-line soldier and whose job is to kill or be killed for her country could perhaps cope with the odd bit of teasing or sexual innuendo. If she cannot cope with an annoying come-on, how will she cope with an enemy commando?

If the alleged harassment becomes violent, then action must be taken. But in any army worth its name the non-commissioned officers know when their soldiers breathe, let alone when they try to assault a comrade. Even in Canada's ridiculously top-heavy structure there are still highly experienced sergeants who know their job.

But an army is not meant to be a place of particularly elegant manners and a barracks is not meant to be a daycare centre. There has always been and always will be confrontation and rivalry as well as fraternity and support within any military organization. But it is difficult to believe all the men who we routinely celebrate as internationally respected peace-keepers and courageous humanitarians suddenly become sexual monsters when they see a woman with short hair wearing a baggy uniform.

Predictably, it was one of Canada's many military leaders who immediately told the media that sexist behavior from his men was unacceptable. He did not in any way wait for concrete proof but simply parroted the Ottawa line about gender equality and how if you didn't like it you should not be wearing the uniform.

Shed blood for Canada, risk your life for Canada, be forced by low pay to send your wife to the food bank for Canada, but if you have different politics from the liberal establishment you might as well leave now. You have about as much chance of promotion as a war hero who doesn't speak French.

The underlying point in all this is that the people who push gender equality in the Armed Forces care not a jot for the Armed Forces but care everything for gender equality. They follow an obsession, which at its logical conclusion will obliterate the differences between men and women.

Feminism was at one time a means to an end, a way of improving the lot of women. It has now too often become an end in itself, confused in its ideology and confusing in its intentions. Feminism embraced peace and was opposed to war. Now it wants women to drop bombs on the enemies of their government.

Equality does not mean the elimination of differences. Women can be prime ministers, women can be editors, women can be business leaders, women can be almost anything they want to be. They have a fundamental right to equal pay, equal privileges and equal dignity. But the right to not be women any more is not a right at all but an abuse of nature.

Countries such as Israel, with years of bloody war experience, experimented with using women in combat roles but quickly reversed the policy. In the Gulf war the U.S. used a small number of women. Some performed well, some went to pieces, one was captured and repeatedly raped by her captors. Yet even if all of them had been heroes, we must question a society that increasingly marginalizes motherhood but lionizes women who plunge bayonets and throw grenades.

In fact, women have been in the military for many years, but not in combat roles and not in the same units as men. Such a system helped defeat Hitler but has not, it seems, beaten the social engineers. The day women as front-line soldiers die to defend this country is the day this country is no longer worth defending.

A Little Intolerance Isn't Always a Bad Place

As a teenager in Britain about 20 years ago I, along with millions of others, watched a particular TV commercial for a major financial institution. The advertising slogan from the campaign was successful and became extremely popular. It was simple yet effective: "The bank that doesn't like to say no."

Everybody seemed to be aware of it. I didn't realize as I crept toward early middle age I would be faced with less of a slogan than a national disaster: "The society that doesn't like to say no."

The more things we permit, popular wisdom appears to say, the more enlightened and intelligent we are. The more we tolerate the more sophisticated we become. Tolerance is good, except when it comes to tolerating those people and ideas who are allegedly intolerant in the first place. In other words, tolerate those with whom we agree, which isn't tolerance at all.

It surely goes beyond saying that tolerance of different cultures is a good thing, as is tolerance of different opinions. This has always been the sign of a mature civilization. But tolerance can turn into an obsession and become, ironically, severely intolerant in itself.

Tolerance is now considered to be the quintessence of being Canadian and thus it is somehow unpatriotic to be intolerant of anything. We hear examples of this all the time.

George disagrees with a publicly funded art gallery displaying a picture of the Virgin Mary holding a condom, so he is intolerant. Betty condemns public nudity and acts of sexual intercourse in a park, so she is intolerant. Emilio is deeply disturbed by a pornographic magazine store opening up near to his young son's school, so he is intolerant. They don't understand, the criticism runs, that we now live in a pluralistic society.

Not true. Such people not only understand that we live in a pluralistic society, but are products of the same. They are merely expressing a moral opinion of a certain action. And the logical consequence of expressing a moral opinion is to act upon that opinion. In other words, to get off your backside and do something about it.

This is not intolerance at all, but genuine care about society and country. We can either have a nation of apathetic people nodding in unison every time their beliefs are attacked by governments or extremists or we can have active and concerned citizens who sometimes object to the lunacies of the culture. Oddly enough, we rarely hear labor activists being accused of intolerance toward conservative governments.

The point is, tolerance does not mean and never has meant the automatic acceptance of what is wrong.

I would ask those who argue there is no such thing as right and wrong if they would be upset if someone stole their car or ran off with their partner. The first may be against the laws of the land, but the second is not. Yet the latter would probably cause the most distress and produce cries of, "It's not fair, it's just plain wrong." It is. But we have to ask ourselves why we feel this aggrieved.

Laws, in fact, have little to do with all this. A good country will pass good laws, a bad country will pass bad laws and a confused country will pass some of both.

The South African government acted within the law when it introduced apartheid. It passed its racist legislation and gave its brutal policemen official powers. Yet the world knew it was wrong. Hitler's Nuremberg Laws were declared in public and he was a democratically elected leader of a European nation. Yet we hanged his henchmen at the same Nuremberg after we had defeated his armies.

The realities of right and wrong are not bound by the whims of a lawmaker, the pressures of a special interest group or a country's emotional spasms, but by the certainties of absolute truth. Every person and every nation knew and knows this. Unfortunately, some have chosen to ignore it.

I have to reject the claim of those who state there is no such thing as absolute truth because, according to them, it cannot be absolutely true. Or perhaps I am just being intolerant. I certainly hope so.

A Soul, Not a Statistic

When we discuss the homeless, the people who live on the streets, we tend to objectify them. To some they are "a problem," to others they are "a cause" and to politicians they are "a policy." Because of this, governments of all stripes fail to grasp the fact these people are individuals with individual needs. Until we understand that, we will achieve little.

That is certainly what Jessey believed.

She came from Nova Scotia to Toronto when she young and lived on and off the streets from the age of 14. She wouldn't have done so if she had thought there was any other way, if she hadn't been physically and sexually abused. Easy to know better with the benefit of hindsight, money and a stable family.

She found food and shelter where she could, but refused to sell her body the way some girls did. She huddled in a ball in the park or on the street, on a good day crowded into a tiny room with other kids. At one point she met a man who seemed to care for her. They had a child, lived in a housing project and all seemed to be going well. Until it didn't. She was back on the street, her baby lost to the Children's Aid Society.

Jessey wanted to belong, wanted meaning. Other kids were dabbling in the occult, looking to devil worship to give them a sense of power. Jessey flirted with the idea. But it wasn't really for her. Morality survives poverty; a knowledge of right and wrong is not always smothered by deprivation.

Some of the people who threw themselves into this darkness thought Jessey should not be allowed to just walk away. Motivated by a grotesque mixture of violence, lust and Satanism they decided to brutally rape her and even kill her.

They almost succeeded. She had terrible wounds and the doctors thought she would not make it. Others disagreed. Jessey had spent several nights sleeping on the steps of the Evergreen Centre in downtown Toronto and had become friendly with the staff. They visited her in hospital, held her and prayed for her. She recovered.

Shortly after this Jessey's life was transformed. She became a Christian and described her conversion as like "warm coffee running through my body." Priorities changed, she became more responsible and began to speak to people and organizations about what the streets were really like. It was then discovered she was HIV-positive. This tiny, beautiful young woman with piercing blue eyes and long blonde hair had been given a death sentence.

But instead of terrifying her into submission or depressing her into silence, her illness made her commitment grow. Her dedication to helping kids off the street, keeping others away from it and educating the public appeared to increase in intensity. She changed people, made them think again. Made them love again.

Jessey was frequently in hospital, often in great pain. She spent four months in palliative care and the nurses remarked on the extraordinary sense of calm in her room and all around her. She finally died three years after the initial diagnosis and a friend who was with her at the end remarked, "when she died she looked like a cross between a child and an old woman. It was beautiful to see her get the rest she deserved. It was almost like a sacrifice." She was 26 years old.

Jessey's funeral was remarkable. Community representatives, church leaders, street kids, people whose lives she had touched in so many ways packed the crowd. Her relationship with her mother had been restored and her little son Jonathan now had such a large family, composed of his mum's friends. At the funeral the six-year-old boy took the microphone and said, "I'm just happy my mum isn't in pain any more."

One of Jessey's final requests was for a trust fund to be established for Jonathan's education. She had become quite a skilled artist and painted a series of eight pictures that were made into greeting cards. They are sold for $11 and the money will help make Jonathan the young man Jessey always imagined. She didn't want him to be "a problem," "a cause" or "a policy." He won't be. Neither was she.

To Pretend a Word Doesn't Exist is Madness

When Dr. Johnson compiled his dictionary more than 200 years ago, he remarked to a friend that words are like explosive devices and should be treated with extreme care. If only the great man were alive today.

The publishing house Merriam-Webster has found itself in the centre of a political controversy because of its definition of the word "nigger."

Repulsive and repugnant, the word is nevertheless part of the sinister vocabulary and, as such, surely has to be included in any dictionary worth its name.

Merriam-Webster defines the term as "a black person – usually taken to be offensive." The dictionary also refers to "a member of any dark-skinned race" or "a member of a so-called disadvantaged class of persons."

Obviously aware of the sensitivity of this word and the pain it can cause, the editors of the book went so far as to include an explanatory paragraph, stating this is "perhaps the most offensive and inflammatory racial slur in English" and is "expressive of racial hatred and bigotry."

A moderate, balanced and intelligent piece of work. But no. The publishers have received several thousand complaints, many of them calling for the word to be removed.

The National Association for the Advancement of Colored People has demanded a total revision of the definition and even threatened a boycott of the company if this does not happen. Other threats have been far more unpleasant.

In response to such pressure, the 150-year-old publisher organized a special task force to "investigate" the word and explore a new definition.

Commenting on this conciliatory move the NAACP's president, Kweisi Mfume, said he was pleased with the reaction but that his organization will "determine if a culture within the company has made it difficult for them to recognize why this definition is unacceptable to millions of Americans."

Other critics still insist the word should be omitted from the book and from all subsequent editions.

This is not, of course, the first time a dictionary has faced criticisms over its contents. The listing of the word "Jew" annoyed some people in the past because it included a pejorative definition. Merriam-Webster has been attacked for including such words as "whitey," "queer," "Kraut" and "cracker."

But the purpose of a dictionary is not to define those words and meanings of which we approve, but simply to define those words of which we are aware. This entire argument is, or should be, about knowledge and not about politics.

The moment we apply a politically correct veneer to information, the moment we curtail what people may know because of the demands of various groups within society, no matter how justified they may feel, we are in serious trouble. Vocabulary and language tend to be the first victims when freedom is attacked.

If the opening Webster definition of "nigger" as "a black person – usually taken to be offensive" is so provocative, then there might be an argument to move it further down the entry and to first explain the racist origin of the term. Here there is room for compromise, although until now dictionaries have always listed the oldest definition first. But to call for an adult, respectable and respected dictionary to pretend a word does not exist is madness.

It is all rather self-defeating madness as well. Better to define these words as being the hurtful and vile things they are than to refuse to acknowledge they are known and used.

There is nothing more a Klansman could ask than for his favorite term of abuse to be considered so unpleasant, and so effective, that it has to be hidden from the dictionary.

It is also significant that some abusive words have been taken by their victims and used ironically as a weapon against their oppressors. I would like to know how this came about and I would like the dictionary to tell me. More than this, I demand that the dictionary tells me. It is my right as a thinking person to know, to learn and to understand.

There are other unpleasant words, such as "authoritarian," "obsessive" and "intolerant" – but they should remain in the dictionary as well. It helps us to understand what they mean and, more important, whom they describe.

A Manifesto of Hate

This year marks the 150th anniversary of the first publication of a long obscure but now infamous political program outlining the ideas and beliefs of a tiny revolutionary society. The small and secret group was known as the League of the Just. The two men who wrote the party's policy document were Karl Marx and Frederick Engels. It was The Communist Manifesto.

It's odd that a glorified pamphlet that inspired so much bloodshed should be celebrated in 1998, but celebration is nevertheless taking place. New editions are being produced, some in splendid color and most, irony of ironies, with the money of international capitalism behind their publishers. The booklet that fuelled the ideologies and murderous policies of Stalin, Mao and a legion of dictators and war criminals is once again fashionable.

The predictions and analysis of Marx and Engels were fundamentally flawed. World revolution was certain, they said. Germany would soon be a socialist paradise, they said. Capitalism would wither away, they said. The people would embrace communism, they said. But they said much more, most of it conveniently forgotten.

Of a mutual Jewish acquaintance, Engels wrote to Marx, "As a true Jew he was always only too ready to exploit anyone for his private purposes under some party pretext. Then his eagerness to thrust himself into elegant society, to climb up, if only for appearance, to plaster over the grimy Breslau Jew with all kinds of pomade and make-up – all this was always repugnant."

Marx himself was Jewish but he was perversely self-hating, which may explain some of his overall bitterness and misanthropy. "What is the secular basis of Judaism? Practical need, self-interest," he wrote. "What is the worldly religion of the Jew? Huckstering. What is his worldly God? Money."

He went on to say about a fellow revolutionary and an alleged friend named Lasalle. "The Jewish nigger ... fortunately departs at the end of this week. It is now completely clear to me that he, as is proved by his cranial formation and hair – descends from the Negroes who had joined Moses' exodus from Egypt. The obtrusiveness of the fellow is also Nigger-like."

Referring to Paul Lafargue, a man of mixed race who was a political candidate for an area of Paris that contained the city zoo, Engels wrote, "being in his quality as a nigger, a degree nearer to the rest of the animal kingdom than the rest of us, he is undoubtedly the most appropriate representative of that district."

Of the Chinese, Marx said they were a people of "overbearing prejudice, stupidity, learned ignorance and pedantic barbarism." About Turkey he lamented the country had "the misfortune to be inhabited by a conglomerate of different races and nationalities, of which it is hard to say which is the least fit for progress and civilization."

Engels and Marx seemed to hate the Slavonic peoples as well. The former wrote a future conflict would "wipe out all these petty, hidebound nations down to their very names. The next world war will result in the disappearance from the face of the earth not only of reactionary classes and dynasties, but also of entire reactionary peoples. And that, too, is a step forward."

Of the Irish, Engels said they were "little above the savage" and "his very crudeness makes him incapable of sharing, his filth and poverty, all favor drunkenness."

Both men were violent imperialists who wrote in enthusiastic support of the brutal conquest of Mexico by the U.S., Algeria by France and India by Britain. This was the only way, they claimed, that socialism could be advanced. They believed, "the most determined use of terror" would be absolutely essential.

So it really should come as no surprise the followers of these two authors exterminated millions of people merely because of their ethnicity or class and incarcerated and oppressed an entire continent. What is surprising is there are still governments and movements that believe Marx and Engels were not only great but correct. We conduct international trade with some of them.

Ask two questions. Why did so many ostensible intellectuals and progressives take these callous individuals seriously? And how did they and their followers get away with it for so long? The answers speak volumes.

Another Speech, Another Place, Another Time

Last week Ontario Premier Mike Harris said that by abolishing the monthly $37 food benefit given to pregnant women on welfare less public money would be wasted on beer. In a parallel universe another Ontario premier made the following speech to an assembled press corps.

"Now let me get this completely straight. I do not want to remove the tax allowances for the very rich. But this is the real world and this money, even if it comes to only $40 a month, could make us all more financially sound. It's not as though these people actually need what amounts to a fairly small lump of cash. And it's time they learned to stand on their own two feet.

"I also have to say that, well, to be honest we all know where this money is going to go. Don't quote me here because this is not scripted and it's off the cuff, but you and I know the very rich tend to waste the money on imported brandy. Come on now, boys, this is definitely not on the record so you can put those pens and tape recorders down right away. I don't mind telling you that if Leslie or Alistair or David or anybody else who decides my policy knew what I was saying here today I'd be in a whole pile of trouble.

"Did somebody ask me about how my cabinet colleagues might react? Please! Are you serious? Cabinets are only good for storing cups and saucers.

"Anyway, getting back to the point. We're saving these people from themselves. It's pretty well known that rich people drink brandy whenever they get the chance. I've actually seen them coming out of liquor stores with it. I mean I've seen them buying it and I know plenty of people who'll back me up on this one so don't give me any of your arguments about me needing proof or statistics or the idea that we shouldn't indulge in offensive and ugly caricatures.

"Okay, I'll grant you that it's not always the rich themselves who'll spend these tax breaks on bottles of Cognac but often they let their wives go out and buy the stuff. I'm not blaming anyone here, perish the thought. The idea of me making scapegoats of people is as likely as Hugh Segal winning a general election. But you can't avoid the obvious. Mr. Banker gets home from Bay Street with the tax break in his hands and his wife – if they're even married in the first place – nags him until he gives her the cash. She runs out the door and before you can say 'spin doctor' there's a crate of Armagnac parked in the BMW, paid for by your money.

"Someone in the caucus proposed a system of food stamps, so that instead of squandering the money on a dozen bottles of Remy Martin we can make sure it goes on what these people really need, like Cuban cigars. At least that way there will be some accountability. But in the end the guys in my special research unit decided that it would be humiliating and patronizing for us to act in such a way. So we just took the money away from them completely."

Suddenly the premier's cell phone rings. After a hurried conversation with someone in Toronto he returns to his speech.

"Two schools of thought here, my friends. One says I didn't actually say what I just said and once again you've twisted my words. Another says I said all of what I just said, but the bleeding hearts hate me anyway and the faithful will support me all the way on this one. Apparently I have to be strong, just like Maggie and Ronnie.

"Just one last thing before I go, and I tell you this in the utmost secrecy. If we gave the money to a bunch of pregnant women on welfare who had the guts to raise a kid, at least the cash would go to beer. And beer is made in Canada. But don't get me started on that because someone will call me a bigot. Which, of course, I am not. And to call me one would be a stupid generalization unworthy of an elected official."

Don't Sugar-Coat Easter

Titus Brandsma was a small, gentle, bespectacled man. He spent years working with the Dutch underground movement to smuggle Jewish people out of the Netherlands and away from the threat of the Nazi murderers. As a monk he rejected violence and so would not, could not, pick up a gun to use against the oppressors of goodness and all he held dear. But night after night, week after week, he struggled in his own way to do what had to be done.

Until he was caught. Until he was tortured, beaten, smashed and sentenced to death. As the Nazi nurse gave him a fatal injection he looked up, gave the uniformed killer his rosary beads and said, "I forgive you, I'll pray for you."

Not far away, in Germany itself, a young Lutheran minister called Dietrich Bonhoeffer had returned to his homeland from abroad even though he knew the extreme danger. Precisely because, in fact, he knew of the extreme danger. He joined the German resistance and worked without pause to bring down the regime of the Hitler gang. Like his comrade across the border in Holland, he was arrested and imprisoned. Unlike his Dutch brother, he was on one occasion presented with the chance to escape. He did not take it, aware that if he had done so the Nazis would have arrested and murdered his entire family. Bonhoeffer was executed at the age of 39. He died forgiving his captors and smiling in the certainty of his future.

The reason I write of these two men is that this is Easter Week, Holy Week, the week of Good Friday and of Easter Sunday. It is the most sacred time in the Christian year and commemorates the death and resurrection of Jesus Christ, the precise reason why Brandsma, Bonhoeffer and so many others were able to live and die with such splendor. They did not "change with the times" as so many did then and so many do now, they did not become hateful and they did not surrender. They fought and they forgave. And they did so not because of liberalism or relativism or nationalism or socialism, but because they were utterly convinced that what happened on the first Easter was completely true. Oh, for a few more Canadians who thought the same in 1998.

Easter, however, is getting a hard time of it. The culture and the state have transformed what was the motivation for Brandsma and Bonhoeffer into a few days when we can buy and sell chocolate eggs and chase a little yellow bunny around the backyard. There has been an attempt, conscious and unconscious, to expunge Christianity and meaning out of Easter.

But without Christianity there is no Easter and without Easter there are no Christians who devote their lives to ending slavery like William Wilberforce, no heroes who give their all to do away with child labor like Lord Shaftesbury, no champions of racial equality and non-violence like Martin Luther King. The body politic, Canada and the modern world would be very different without people like this, people who worked tirelessly and courageously not because of nicely packaged candy, but because of their certain knowledge of Easter and all it represents.

Indeed the very political foundations of Canada are based on a European enlightenment that was Christian to the core. Of course there are abuses and of course we have made mistakes, but notions of pluralism, tolerance and human dignity do not come from thin air or from the backroom of some party conference. They did not exist in the Pagan world and they do not exist today in many parts of the non-Christian world. We only need to look at the history of the vehemently anti-religious Soviet empire to realize that.

So Easter is about more than a day off and a sugar rush. It is about a Dutch monk, a German theologian and about tens of millions of people persecuted across the world for their beliefs. It is about love, forgiveness, hope and charity. It is about freedom, the goodness of Canada and about a young Jewish man who died in agony in a faraway corner of an ancient empire. And about his resurrection. Believe it or don't believe it but, please, don't ignore it. You really can't. Happy Easter.

Kid's Needs Come First

A study by two University of Toronto economists has stated Canada should invest a massive $5.3 billion into child care. The paper also suggests children should be "educated" by the state from the age of 2 and argues this would result in large economic and social benefits.

That a report by university economists would call for such financial support and barely mention any negative aspects to socialized child care is as predictable as another losing season at Maple Leaf Gardens.

In this day and age no thinker, politician or teacher who is in any way opposed to shipping off our children to institutions as soon as they can toddle is asked to make judgments on the success and ethics of child care. The establishment has already made up its mind, it is now just arguing about how much it should all cost.

Let me say immediately I fully understand those couples who are forced by economic circumstances into using daycare and I intend no personal criticism of their actions. But many people choose such a system not out of necessity but out of indifference and because of confused priorities.

Late summer. The sun is casting exquisite shadows on the scorching street. Three dozen beautiful children, their smiles subdued, uniformed in matching blue hats and T-shirts, were roped together and being pulled along the road by a trio of young minders. Those in charge, teenagers themselves, were trying their best but it is all so artificial, so forced and so sterile. It was child care, it was daycare.

Yet in the last 10 years a subtle and somewhat sinister campaign has begun in which we are told "child care professionals" are somehow preferable to biological parents. Mothers who make financial sacrifices so as to be home with their children are marginalized and their partners are mocked as being of another, lesser era.

The state has bought into this by not providing appropriate tax breaks and benefits to such men and women. Rather than giving billions of dollars to the destruction of the family, the basis of any civilized society, the government should give huge financial incentives to people who want to raise their children in the appropriate and normal way.

And the point really has to be made. In spite of the propaganda from the entertainment industry and the media that communal daycare is healthy and wise, it is not. It is perverse. There are no valid historical or biological precedents for suddenly jettisoning tiny children into groups to be nurtured by strangers with a flimsy state qualification.

Feminist advocates of daycare argue that it increases choice.

Not really. Money and societal pressure cut a woman's freedom in this matter and daycare is merely a grey Band-Aid. We all know of examples of the "smiles in the boardroom tears in the washroom" syndrome.

As for the child's rights, I have yet to hear a plea of "Mummy, let me be raised by the nice lady I have never seen before and who will forget my name after I leave because I'm just one of thousands of faces." The idea of a 2-year-old still in diapers being pushed out into a child-rearing centre is, I'm sorry, the stuff of dark fantasy.

The phenomenon of the nanny is equally problematic. One journalist whom I know thought it amusing to tell people her children now spoke better Filipino than they did English. An ugly comment.

Inherent in the guilty humor is a selfishness and a flabby racism that implies immigrants should clear up after the offspring of the white middle class. What was particularly upsetting about this story is the woman was wealthy and her husband was not working full-time and did not need to. He simply rejected being a real father.

Such refusals to accept family responsibilities should provoke peer disdain. They don't. Partly because we have largely confused personal licence with individual liberty. A parent's right to do whatever he or she wants is now more important than the child's fundamental need for stability, love and family.

We ignore duty and love, and worship what we call freedom. But the freedom of the swimmer to float out to sea is actually better known as drowning.

Divorced Dads Everywhere
are Cheering

Last week a Mississauga woman was given a 60-day prison term for disobeying a court order requiring her to allow the father of her 4-year-old daughter access to their child. (She was released after nine days and is appealing the order.)

I don't know the details of this case and I'm sorry for all those who lose their freedom. But such a punishment for such a crime is long overdue.

Let us be direct. Any man who is allowed access to his child but still withholds support payments should not lose his driving licence or his passport. He should go to jail. For years, if necessary. For as long as it takes for him to understand, by force if necessary, his paternal responsibilities.

But there are men who have stopped paying child support because they are no longer allowed to see their children. As a first step to countering this the law should immutably connect access to support payments and should make joint custody genuinely "joint."

Day after day in this country and abroad, divorce courts award joint custody to broken families and in far too many cases the mothers involved simply break the law at will, knowing that judges, lawyers and police officers do not have the political courage or the moral strength to do anything about it.

Take the story of Dave and Stephanie. This couple in their mid-40s divorced 10 years ago after a sorry marriage. Both were to blame. There was one child, a gorgeous little girl named Tessa.

Dave had been a loving and devoted father, arguably spending at least as much time with his daughter as had Stephanie. The judge ordered joint custody, Dave dutifully paid his ex-wife each month and that, as they say, was that.

Not so. That, as we will see, was not that at all. After some early visits between Dave and Tessa matters did not run according to plan. Whenever Dave went to fetch his daughter, she and her mother had gone out. More visits would be arranged, more no-shows. Dave asked for an explanation. Stephanie said she didn't want Dave to see Tessa any more. Dave explained the law, Stephanie implied the law was a ass.

Dave withdrew his savings to pay for a lawyer and took the issue back to court. The judge ordered Stephanie to comply with the earlier decision. Stephanie agreed. But when Dave arrived for the next visit the same thing occurred. And occurred again and again and again.

Dave had no money left and the police told him there was absolutely nothing they could do or would do.

He was told, however, that if he made a fuss outside his daughter's house and the police were called by Stephanie or the neighbors he would be arrested, handcuffed and put in jail for at least a night.

Dave spent many evenings looking at photographs and crying. He waited outside Tessa's private school – for which he was largely paying – and watched her as she went in and came out. Like a pathetic criminal spying on a child. But the child was his daughter, his flesh, his blood, his love.

One day Dave received a letter from Tessa explaining she hated her father and never wanted to see him again. The vocabulary was far too sophisticated for a girl of Tessa's age and had obviously been dictated. Just as the thought has been imposed.

Stephanie married again and Tessa has a new daddy. As for Dave, who cares? He is just one of those men so commonly and easily objectified and marginalized in media and in drama.

If Dave was unique I would smile. But he is incredibly common. It could be worse, he could have been one of the men falsely accused of sexual abuse of their children by ex-partners so full of hate they will do anything to cause pain and to win.

His new wife holds him and listens to him and wonders how she, a woman, has benefited from the feminist attack upon the law that did this to her husband. And they both mouth the mantra the Daves of the world know so well. "When she's old enough to be independent she'll know that I loved her and that her mother was wrong."

Perhaps, Dave. Perhaps.

Because of Dave I say it again. Harsh punishment for the denial of access is long overdue. Pray God it makes a difference.

In Arts Funding, Quality Doesn't Count

One day there will be a Canadian movie made about Canadian movies.

About how the public funding of films, film-makers and literature about films really works. And nobody will believe it. They will think it just too ridiculous and too far-fetched.

The story so far:

A highly readable and entertaining movie magazine called Take One is suddenly denied a grant by the Ontario Arts Council, after receiving between $10,000 and $15,000 annually for some years. Whatever one thinks of the public funding of the arts, if such funding does exist it should at least be given to quality work. The case of Take One says much about the whole quagmire of ineptitude and insularity known as Canadian arts funding.

Take One is a highly regarded quarterly publication with a circulation of more than 5,000. It employs writers of the quality of Geoff Pevere, Doug Fetherling and Gary Michael Dault. Many people within the movie industry consider it one of the finest magazines in the country but, as one respected critic had it, "Unless you are printed on recycled toilet paper and contain obscure, ultra-leftist nonsense, the council is not willing to give any help."

In rejecting Take One the Ontario Arts Council's literature officer, Lorraine Filyer, described it as indulging in industry boosterism and lacking "critical edge." A little surprising, in that its editorial board and regular contributors include some of the busiest and harshest critics in Canada.

Two film magazines were funded, however – POV and Cineaction.

The former receives $6,000 a year while the latter is given an extremely generous $20,000. Yet Cineaction contains dreary and pseudo-academic articles of interest to only the tiniest of readerships. POV is a hardline feminist journal with close links to the grant-giving community and seems to be most interested in left-wing documentaries.

"I'm being punished because people are reading the magazine," says Take One editor Wyndham Wise, who used his personal savings and financial support from friends to maintain the magazine.

"We have a popular culture in this country but some people don't want to believe that. There's no accountability here, no logic. They simply won't allow any room for artistic divergence, everything has to be rigidly critical. People really have to know the absurdity of it all."

Allegations that Take One is somehow mainstream and bland certainly don't seem to stand up to scrutiny. The new issue balances a piece on the making of Titanic with a story about lesbian films and includes articles about a Winnipeg documentary maker and one on the dreadful television series Twitch City.

The other justification offered by the Ontario Arts Council is that the provincial government has cut back on grants and that Take One is "a low priority." Anyway, the council adds, "The writing is not good enough."

The latter suggestion is, frankly, ludicrous. The former is more significant. If a serious movie magazine is of low priority, what constitutes high priority for the rather well-paid bureaucrats at the Ontario Arts Council?

One is Brick, a literary periodical that receives $25,800 a year. Another is Descant, also a literary journal, that receives $25,800. A third is This Magazine, a sadly tired Marxist publication that tends, in the words one of its contributors, to be about as exciting as watching paint dry. This Magazine is given $25,000 of your money.

Interestingly enough, Brick is edited by novelist Linda Spalding, who is married to the highly successful and highly wealthy author Michael Ondaatje. This Magazine has included many members of the well-funded liberal establishment on its masthead, and its former managing editor now works for the Ontario Arts Council. Her name is Lorraine Filyer.

What the tale of Take One, its defenders and its attackers really shows is that if we are to retain public funding of the arts in this country we must start all over again and do it correctly, fairly and intelligently. If we don't, the cries of protest when the axe lands once and for all will fall on deaf ears.

If you don't believe me, just ask the people who work at the CBC if they believe they have a future.

There's a Time to Fight, But This is Not

If you'll excuse the pun, it's time to talk turkey about Iraq. Time to ask why so much western foreign policy currently resembles a bad action movie starring Harrison Ford or Chuck Norris. Time to wonder why we're preparing to kill more innocent Iraqi women and children when the last round of slaughter achieved so little.

Saddam Hussein is a repugnant, small-time dictator who should have been, and could have been, removed many years ago. The U.S. and its allies did not do so because they preferred a lunatic they thought they could control to the Islamic fundamentalists who seem to be sweeping the region. The thug with the big moustache had been murdering his own people and killing the Kurds for some time, but only after Kuwait's oilfields were threatened did the West become so morally outraged. Cheap gas was worth, it seems, a few mangled foreigners.

Some history. During the long and bloody war between Iraq and Iran the western powers let their arms dealers make money and let their generals test their weapons. Washington had a soft spot for Saddam because he was giving the Iranians a bloody nose and Iran had, of course, humiliated the U.S.

Most of the Arab world supported Iraq in this conflict, and Kuwait and Saudi Arabia were particularly satisfied the war they backed against the religious fanatics in Tehran was being fought to the last Iraqi. As a consequence, Baghdad expected to be given financial help by its oil-rich neighbors after the war as a token of appreciation. Not so. The bank accounts of the sheiks remained firmly closed.

Bitter and obsessive, Saddam made it clear to the U.S. ambassador he would like to take from Kuwait what he considered to be rightfully his in the first place. Through incompetence or misplaced zeal the diplomat in question made it appear she did not object to such a scenario. Thus the invasion of Kuwait. Thus the granny of skirmishes rather than the mother of all battles.

Saddam could have been brought down quite easily during the last stages of the Gulf war, but the allies chose not to do so. They still thought he could be controlled and they were so terribly wrong. Proving that while smart bombs are sometimes not so smart, allegedly smart politicians are even less so.

If we do bomb Iraq again it is highly possible Saddam will escape and highly probable more impoverished and oppressed Iraqis will die. There is nothing particularly heroic about a pilot dropping a bomb from so high he cannot see his victim, or the shack in which his victim lives. Particularly when the bomb in question costs more money to build than the average Iraqi family will earn in a lifetime.

Nor is the proposed war really about defending righteous nations. Neither Kuwait nor Saudi Arabia has full democracy or freedom of religion and both have been criticized for their human rights abuses. As for Israel, its security is absolute and must be protected. But I cannot help thinking if the Israelis seriously believed they were in profound danger they would already have acted.

Unfortunately, some of the people who oppose any attack on Iraq are less than appealing.

First there are the usual suspects, the hairy peaceniks who seem to be more interested in silly dramatics than in genuine humanitarianism.

Second are more sinister, if equally ridiculous, people. They call themselves anti-Zionists and oppose any policy that appears to help Israel. A large number of these types are too cowardly to admit their real motivations. They just don't like Jews.

But those groups are in a minority. Many people now realize that oil, cash and the twisted motives of the Clinton administration are inadequate reasons for stealth bombers and stealth foreign policy. There is a time to fight, but this is not it.

One footnote, British Prime Minister Tony Blair embarrassed many of his countrymen with his recent fawning over U.S. President Bill Clinton. The same week Blair mobilized his troops to bomb Iraq something called the Christian Socialist Group announced that fox hunting is cruel and unacceptable because of the "dignity" of the fox. Blair is the group's leading member. Save the foxes, unless, of course, they speak Arabic.

The Man Who Invented Maggie Thatcher

The British politician, philosopher and author Enoch Powell died on Sunday at the age of 85. He had been suffering from Parkinson's disease for some time and close friends have described his passing as a release and a liberation.

Which was precisely the feeling experienced by many of Powell's opponents after they had finished debating the man. That's because for 50 years he was one of the most impressive and electric political personalities in the English-speaking world. Sadly, though, he will be remembered by some people for just one belief and for just one speech.

In 1968 Powell made a series of statements in which he criticized Britain's immigration policy and, in one infamous address, warned of "rivers of blood" if the program continued. He argued for a halt to what was then referred to as "colored immigration" and for so doing was removed from the shadow cabinet and not given a government post when Edward Heath's Conservatives came to power two years later.

Powell's views on this subject were not only offensive, they were quite simply wrong. He predicted a racially divided and bloody Britain, but such a nightmare did not emerge. Yet he said, did and thought so much more, most of which was of enormous importance.

Unlike so many modern politicians, he understood war, had a distinguished military record and became a brigadier in the armed forces. He was also academically brilliant, becoming a full professor at a startlingly young age. And this was at a time when being a professor actually meant something. He was also a noted biographer, a gifted poet and a brilliant orator.

He championed the ideas of the free market, personal freedom and ideological conservatism long before they were fashionable and probably did more to create Thatcherism than any other person. In that the ideas and ideals of Margaret Thatcher ruled Britain directly for 15 years and have largely shaped today's Labor government, he was a man of extraordinary influence.

He came into constant conflict with the red Tory leader and one-time prime minister Heath, arguably the most incompetent British leader of the century.

There are partial parallels to be drawn in contemporary Canada. One, for example, being the antagonistic relationship between the Reform and Tory parties.

I had only one conversation with Powell, in which we discussed the idea of me writing his biography. The project did not materialize and I must say I was, and am, rather glad. In some ways he was a frightening man, a hypnotic character who was as unnerving as he was fascinating. He would fix people with a piercing stare and, while always acutely courteous and charming, would shake even the most hardened interviewer and critic. It was not advisable to let one's guard drop.

His literary editor at the Independent, Robert Winder, was a close university friend of mine and Rob once told me he hated telephoning Powell to discuss the man's book reviews for the newspaper. I asked why.

"Because I'm always afraid he will correct my grammar," said the young man who had gained a First Class English degree from Oxford.

Extremists on the left as well as on the right tried then, and will try now, to paint him as some sort of fascist. Not at all. He was a man soaked in compassion and humanity, renowned for acts of kindness and charity. Nevertheless, some of his statements were used and abused by lesser souls to further the cause of racism and to manufacture discontent.

Tara Mukherjee, president of Britain's Confederation of Indian Organizations, said, "Mr. Powell loved India and the Indian people, he was not a racist but an extreme nationalist."

The view was echoed by many. Such nationalism, however, contains seeds of destruction.

Whatever Powell did wrong, he was one of the last of the grand old Tory politicians who had a direct link with the working classes, who felt the pulse and understood the mood of ordinary people. Because of this he took on the mock patricians and the social engineers and did it with a poignant brilliance.

For all Powell's failures and fantasies, the world will be a lesser place without him. He had an effortless contempt for those politicians who wear their banality, their mediocrity and their consensus cowardice on their sleeves with a perverse pride. Powell made these people look like, well, like mere politicians. As such, he could not have survived in a world where they dominate.

Abortion is Killing, There's Nothing to Debate

I wasn't going to write about the 25th anniversary of the Roe vs. Wade decision in the U.S. and the 10th anniversary of there being no abortion law in Canada.

I thought I'd ignore the fact that 37 million abortions have taken place south of the border, one million up here, since these dates. But I have to comment. The eruption of propaganda and nonsense in the media leaves me with no alternative.

Can we begin by scrapping the "I don't approve of abortion myself, but I wouldn't stop someone else from having one" line? If abortion is not about the taking of life and the killing of children then it should be legal and protected. The only argument left is whether the state should fund such elective surgery at a time when it is closing down hospitals and firing nurses.

If, however, it is about the taking of life and the killing of children it should be banned and illegal. For everyone. For all time.

Thinking people cannot argue that they personally disapprove of killing but are prepared to allow other people to kill. So, is it killing?

Let us call her Mary. Because Mary is a nice name. Mary is genetically complete at conception and there can be no other starting point for her life. Her heart is beating by the 25th day. Three days later Mary's arms and legs have started, her eyes and ears are also forming and her brain has uniquely human features.

Mary's milk teeth form in the seventh week and her ankles and fingers have developed. Three weeks later her limbs and organs are established and Mary can turn her head and is sensitive to touch.

By the 12th week Mary can swallow, her fingernails have started and her ribs and vertebrae have turned into bone. Mary's vocal chords are complete and there are even recognizable inherited physical features.

"Hey," Mary's mum could say, "our baby looks like me."

At four months Mary is half her birth length and her heart is pumping 50 pints a day. At this point Mary looks just like a small baby. Her eyebrows and eyelashes begin soon afterward and she is kicking and sucking her thumb. Mary's birth, four months later, is merely an incident in a process that began long ago.

Mary is born. Suddenly she is protected by the same state that would have financed her destruction just weeks earlier.

Such destruction was once championed by the doyen of the abortion movement in the U.S., Dr. Bernard Nathanson. The man pioneered abortion techniques and became a hero to the feminist movement. Until, that is, he witnessed the results of ultrasound and realized what he was doing.

This U.S. version of Henry Morgentaler changed his position and has spent the rest of his life working to stop abortion. In a ground-breaking book on the subject he recounted his time as one of the leaders of the abortion cause and admitted he and his people had lied, had made up figures to promote their case. He apologized and asked for forgiveness.

There can be anger and lack of charity on both sides of this issue and a great big helping of empathy served to all concerned would help matters enormously. But even those who believe that abortion should be preserved surely see the lack of balance in the coverage of the issue in the media. Suppression of truth and a perversion of objectivity can do nobody any good.

As a father of four children I take my stand. Life is sacred, from conception to natural death. I condemn all violence around the abortion issue, whether it is committed against the unborn or against a doctor being paid to carry out abortions.

I also know that when I put my ear to my wife's womb I do not say "Darling, I can hear the fetus" and that my wife does not scream with joy "Love, I felt the fetus kick." We had a baby, have a baby. Baby.

I also know this entire issue is not just about the idea of choice. It is also about money, about power, about control of society and about the dignity and the definition of the human person.

And it is about a little woman called Mary. And Mary's right to choose.

Facts Always Beat Cocktail Party Gossip

I suppose I should be flattered. Once again the Globe and Mail has given me some free publicity by attacking me.

That the contents of the attack don't tell the whole story should come as no surprise. This is, of course, the newspaper that listens to the private dinner conversation of a rival editor, prints the dialogue and then defends such behavior as being ethical.

Be that as it may, it is always a good thing to be mentioned by name, particularly by people whose names mean nothing. The piece describes me as "A frequent critic of public funding to the arts," who hypocritically applied "to the Ontario Arts Council's Writers' Reserve program (and has, indeed, benefited from that public trough at least once that we know of)."

If the Globe had relied on facts rather than cocktail party gossip it might have discovered I have applied to this program several times – no secret in these pages – and, in fact, received quite a few grants. Never for much, but always enough to help me complete my books, which are then published in various countries and languages. The tax on these international sales is paid in Canada and thus the country is slightly richer because of it. Which to my mind constitutes a fairly good argument in favor of a grant system.

The item provides me with an opportunity to discuss arts funding.

Contrary to what the Globe might claim, I have never been a "critic of public funding" but a critic of gratuitous and incestuous public funding.

There are two polarized views with regard to all this. One says the market should dictate all and there should be no cultural funding whatsoever. The other claims almost every artist deserves state support. Or at least every artist whose work falls into a strictly defined left-of-centre framework. There are other ways.

   – A loan system. A writer, for example, who might be at work on an important, but not lucrative, biography of a Canadian historical figure could be supported by the public until enough money is made to pay back the initial loan. If no money is made and the loan is outstanding the writer in question will not be helped again.

- A means test. The cultural establishment cringes at such a suggestion, but it is only appropriate that wealthy people do not receive government financial support. Unfortunately, many people of independent means think it their privilege to be given a little, or a lot, more. Nor should artists become dependent on grants. A Canadian poet and songwriter once remarked, on camera, that it was his "bloody right to have grants every year." Not so.

Juries must be composed of people who are objective and not hindered by personal bias toward those who apply for grants. This is not currently the case. Too often jurors are also applicants for other grants and everybody seems to know each other in a nepotistic little world.

I once had to listen to a distraught juror in Toronto on the edge of tears as she told me how an award jury was unfair, dishonest and a sham. She was surprised. I wasn't.

Grants should be given to individuals and organizations that are more in tune with mainstream Canadian concerns. There is simply too much money given to tiny circulation extreme magazines and perverse art galleries that attract hardly any visitors.

While Stratford, Niagara-on-the-Lake, Canadian ballet and opera companies – and many more – bring in tourists and dollars and boost our own and outsiders' sense of Canadian culture, I cannot see where yet another radical art exhibit or Marxist monthly does anyone much good.

- A voucher-funding scheme. Such a system would allow taxpaying citizens to direct their arts dollars into a specific area. This mirrors the educational voucher proposals being proposed by so many parents and educators. We should also make sure ideas of so-called positive discrimination and quotas are expunged from the grants system. The bureaucrats will deny such notions exist. But they do.

Indeed, we should also improve the quality of those who administer the grants bodies. So that, amongst other things, information about who applies for grants is not leaked to friends on newspapers for the sole purpose of cheap and misfired political pot-shots.

A few ideas to consider over this Christmas, which I hope is a merry one.

The Words
We Dare Not Whisper

Happy Holidays from all the businesses, corporations, politicians, banks, schools, government departments and individuals who are too cowardly to risk annoying someone.

A very Happy Holidays from all those who are prepared to abandon their history, identity and faith in the name of contemporary banality and the aching blandness of the politically correct lexicon.

The obsessive fear on the part of those who refuse to say Merry Christmas seems to be that if they refer to the season of love, forgiveness and salvation they will slightly offend other Canadians. Causing offence. The great sin of our time. And the great lie. In fact, by trying not to offend anyone, people who say Happy Holidays offend almost everyone who has any common sense. Most people have thicker skins, larger brains and a more stable grasp of the righteousness of majority will than secular liberals would have us believe.

This is Christmas because, quite simply, it is Christmas. The only reason the season exists is that our society, founded as it was upon the principles of Christianity, injected the diamond-bright time of charity and hope into our year. The great mythical dragon of offence is apparently easily provoked, however, so we have to be extremely careful.

But if we are going to be truly atheistic about all this we should at least be consistent. Happy Holidays still drips with religiosity. Holiday is the shortened version of Holy Day. It must go. I suggest Jolly Day of Recreation, Merry Time Off or even Happy Hangover. Otherwise, we might offend someone.

Then there is the calendar we observe. Goodbye to all that. The calendar we use was introduced by Pope Gregory XIII in 1582 as a correction of the one adopted by Julius Caesar. It might be ingenious and accurate, but that is hardly the point. Old Gregory was a Roman Catholic, a Pope and a European. Thus, by origin the calendar is, obviously, deeply offensive.

If you live on the St. Lawrence River, in St. Catherines or perhaps in the capital of Newfoundland – well, time to move or to change the name of your city. We really cannot allow such religious intrusions into our way of life in case someone is offended. How about Living Zone 14, Dwelling Area 24 or even State Approved Community 823B? Some of the beauty, romance and originality might be lost but this is, I think, a small price to pay for not offending anyone.

If your name is Christine or Christopher, or for that matter any name inspired by a saint, disciple, apostle or any Biblical character, get thee another. This would mean a great many new names. But such a chore must not stand in the way of progress. After all, words can offend.

The provincial flags simply have to be adapted. So many of them contain a cross, a symbol that, according to our masters, causes millions of Canadians to scream in disgust and outrage.

These could be replaced by large red banners emblazoned with pictures of that terribly fashionable immoderator of the United Church of Canada, or perhaps a rampant Stephen Lewis. By doing this we cannot possibly cause any offence.

There is hardly any point in my referring to "thou shall not kill," "love thy neighbor" or "turn the other cheek" being unacceptable. They are drenched in religion and hugely offensive. The list goes on.

What this is all really about is fixing something that is not and never has been broken.

When I see the millions of signatures affixed to the petitions calling for an end to Christmas I might think again. When I see the tears of thousands of children driven to despair because someone wished them a Merry Christmas I will reconsider.

Until then I will remain convinced the people trying to expunge Christmas from our lives are the same people who wish to dismantle all that is good, all that is healthy and all this is right with this country and this culture.

A very merry and completely unapologetic Christmas to all of you. From a man named after an overly aggressive male who stabbed a poor, innocent fallen angel named Lucifer and has thus provoked and, yes, offended, the devil community ever since.

If only he had been more sensitive. If only we were more willing to change with the times.

Hollywood Decrees: Thou Shall Not Smoke

The timing was pure Hollywood. Four events of dramatic significance occurred in the space of just one week. They were all linked,
and they were all overwhelmingly indicative of the hypocrisy
and moral corruption of the entertainment industry.

First, in response to criticisms from U.S. Vice President Al Gore,
the Screen Actors Guild, the Directors Guild and the Writers' Guild
in the U.S. agreed to work toward expunging cigarette smoking
from the movies or at least to make the habit appear ugly and
repugnant. This was after Gore cited a study that found 77% of all
films released in 1995 depicted smoking, frequently in an attractive manner.

It is enough to make one have a coughing fit. For decades
family groups, Christian organizations and citizens' lobbies have
pleaded with Hollywood to cut down on the levels of grotesque
violence, the manic degree of promiscuous and loveless sex and
the plague of filthy language in the movies. Repeatedly, the cinema establishment, led by the three unions named above, has
treated these critics with derision and marginalized them as being
extreme and prudish.

"We are simply catering to what people want," the directors
and writers have said, "and there is no proof there is any connec-
tion between what we present on the screen and what people do
in real life. Anyway, we're just giving you reality."

Indeed, when another vice president, Dan Quayle, suggested
Hollywood should be more responsible in what it portrayed in a
positive or romantic light he became the whipping-boy of the
small and large screen. Different political parties, different friends,
different causes.

The arguments offered by the princes of the cinema are ludicrous. The average U.S. police officer does not draw his gun in an
entire career and most people never witness a murder. Yet the

rate of violent death in movies and on television is so high that, if authentic, the entire population of North America would have been wiped out more than a decade ago. And when did Robocop last visit your home?

As to giving people what they want, year after year the most watched movies are not films like Natural Born Killers but films like Beauty and the Beast. Nor have I ever heard movie audiences complaining about the lack of bad language and the insufficient number of exploding heads.

The double standard is obvious. Smoking is not desirable. And Gore and his buddies in Hollywood have confirmed there is a direct link between smoking on screen and smoking in real life.

Violence and pornography are even less desirable. And the logic and consistency of Gore and his friends tells us there is a link between violence and pornography on the screen and violence and pornography in the big world.

It comes down to a Hollywood contempt for what is perceived as "the ordinary person" and that person's views.

This was well illustrated last week when ABC announced it would extend the run of a television series called Nothing Sacred. This show is not particularly bad or particularly good but it is particularly offensive to

Hollywood's least favorite people these days – Roman Catholics. There have been numerous complaints about the series and its fatuous and wild depiction of a young priest.

This aside, Nothing Sacred came 94th in the official television ratings, a position so low that even prayer will not help. In the past, such a wretched showing would mean instant scrapping, even after the first few episodes. To extend the run of such a failure is unprecedented and goes against all television and business logic.

It seems positively perverse. Not at all. ABC will stick by Nothing Sacred not in spite of it being so offensive to so many people but precisely because it is so offensive to so many people.

Now to the last two of the four events. The police have said the 14-year-old boy accused of murdering three classmates in Kentucky may have been influenced by the 1995 film The Basketball Diaries. And Walt Disney chairman Michael Eisner, who labelled critics of his movies as crazy people, sold shares worth $514 million and became even richer.

Be at peace, however. Neither Michael Eisner, the boy in Kentucky nor the priest in Nothing Sacred smokes cigarettes.

Compassionate Murder: A Modest Proposal

I consider the following to be merely a modest proposal. It is this.

Let us kill all able-bodied people. Let us murder the healthy and slaughter the fit. Let us sterilize the ones we don't kill so they cannot procreate and, as a pre-emptive strike, abort them in the womb for the sakes of their parents and of greater society.

Now let me make myself completely clear here. I do not for one moment mean we should be sadistic or cruel in our actions, although killing is never completely clean or painless. But whenever possible what some have defined as "compassionate murder" should involve the least amount of agony possible for those we kill.

They are not, after all, animals.

Then again, animals apparently have rights these days and enjoy the protection of celebrities and the support of extremely well-financed pressure groups.

We have to be coldly realistic. Many, if not most, of these able-bodied people lead futile, vacuous lives with little point and less hope. They might not actually ask us to end their sordid little existences, but that is hardly the point. Their suffering is obvious and they are, after all, nothing at all like us. It is for their own good.

Many of them complain about their lot in life and about how hard it is to keep going every day. Goodness me, it's not as though any able-bodied person is ever going to be famous and brilliant, like a Stephen Hawking or someone.

Apart from anything else, the healthy and the fit are extremely expensive to maintain and are prone to be dirty, parasitic and even criminal. We shouldn't forget that Stalin was able-bodied, as were Hitler, Mao, Ivan the Terrible, Attila the Hun and even Paul Bernardo and Karla Homolka. In fact, it is a proven point that almost every murderer, rapist, pimp, fraud, abuser and thief is able-bodied.

Obviously, I have heard the arguments from those lunatics and fanatics who moan about how life is sacred, how the so-called culture of death is so pervasive and how we have no right to play God.

I've heard them say able-bodied people are frightened to go to sleep at night because they are terrified of what might be done to them. I've also heard the story about that tiny able-bodied boy who looked up at his mother after some court decision and said, "I know I'm a lot of trouble mummy but I'll try to be better in the future. Please don't kill me. Please let me live."

All these arguments in favor of the able-bodied are nothing more than sentimentality and extremism. I mean, who knows what is best for the able-bodied, young and old – us or them?

The question is rhetorical, the answer is obvious. We're trying to build a New Jerusalem here. Okay, it might sometimes look more like the old Gaza Strip, but nobody said a perfect society would be easy to create.

We must also make sure our judges and lawyers are willing to change the fundamentals of the legal system and the nature of justice so any of us who do kill able-bodied people serve only a few months in prison for what we do, followed by a few more watching television in the comfort of our own homes. When judges do treat murder as if it were a speeding offence we must praise them for being brave and compassionate. This shouldn't be difficult, as so many people in the media are already onside.

Nor must juries contain any able-bodied members, otherwise they might not understand our intentions, might empathize with the able-bodied and might even call us murderers and make us serve 10 years in prison or something ridiculous like that. Natural law must be ignored and we must be protected against what we like to describe as cruel and unusual punishment.

It might sound harsh but it comes down to this. Kill, kill, kill them, for goodness sake. There are many precedents in our history. Just a proposal. And a modest one at that.

Falsely Accused,
He Still Awaits an Apology

I shall not name the man I write about in this column. Even though he was found by the courts to be completely and absolutely free of any guilt, a mere accusation in such a case is enough to destroy a person's life. It has done so in the past. I shall therefore call him Innocent.

Last year Innocent, a Toronto teacher, was called into his principal's office. There were two police officers in the room, who informed him he was being charged with sexually and physically assaulting a student some 10 years earlier. They took him away, read him his rights and told him that in such a sensitive case his anonymity was guaranteed.

At the police station, Innocent, incredulous and understandably frightened, was placed in an interrogation room, his eyeglasses were taken away because they were considered to be a potentially dangerous weapon and he was told if he signed a confession it would be much easier on him, his wife and his two children.

He replied that the police had the wrong man.

The police did not seem to be interested.

He then asked if he could phone a lawyer.

He was told he had all day to contact a lawyer and it was more important that he signed a confession.

He was then put in a holding cell for seven hours, with no mattress or toilet paper. He paced. He sweated. He shook. Periodically the officers would visit him to again urge a confession.

Innocent's wife came to visit him, but was initially denied any contact. Only after she argued with the police and demanded her rights was she allowed to see her husband.

The police then told Innocent it was too late to find a justice of the peace and he would have to stay the night in a cell. He was moved to another police station in a van in which, handcuffed and vulnerable, he bounced around like a sack of potatoes.

When a JP was found there were certain conditions imposed on Innocent's release, one of them being he should have no contact with children. He asked about his own children. The answer was there was to be no contact with them either. Innocent refused to accept this and eventually, after much pleading and disputing, the conditions were altered.

Innocent returned home. The guaranteed anonymity lasted only days. To his horror, various newspapers and television and radio stations announced his name and some made it appear he was already guilty. Innocent then received a telephone call. Did he know hundreds of posters announcing he had been charged with sexual misconduct had been placed around the area?

No, he didn't.

Did he also know these posters asked for more information about him from people he had taught in the past?

Again, he did not.

The person on the phone said she had seen a policeman pinning up the posters, which were enlargements of a recent newspaper article.

When the case actually went to court it did not take long for the judge to decide Innocent, a highly respected and experienced teacher with a glowing reputation, had done nothing wrong.

There were some very basic problems and inaccuracies in the accusations, many of which the police should either have noticed before pursuing the case or should have put to Innocent in the early stages of their investigation.

Unfortunately, the story does not end there. In the Toronto Star a ournalist wrote that while acquitting Innocent of the charges, the judge in the case did not accept his side. In fact, the judge had said the opposite stating in acquitting Innocent that the defence made the former student's story "difficult to accept." It took the Toronto Star a full month to give a very small correction to its original story.

Innocent developed a heart condition following his ordeal. His teenage daughter suffered nightmares. His wife went through what she describes as "persecution and hell."

Innocent is still waiting for things to be put right and for someone to say "Sorry."

Is this the Best Our Supreme Court Can Do?

Last week the Supreme Court of Canada ruled by a 7-2 decision in favor of the court of appeal of Manitoba, agreeing it was wrong to compel a pregnant woman to be confined in order to prevent her from sniffing glue and endangering the life of her unborn child.

This, in spite of the fact the woman in question had previously delivered two brain-damaged children.

In writing the majority report, Justice Beverley McLachlin made several arguments. She repeatedly stated it was not the place of the courts to interfere in such a case, but the job of the Manitoba Legislature. She said if the woman in question had been confined it could lead to the incarceration of other men and women for "conduct alleged to harm others." She also claimed there would be a risk that expectant mothers with an addiction might fear state detection and avoid medical care.

Another argument was that the issue was not one of biological or spiritual status, but of legal status. The court dismissed biological evidence that there is little difference between the born and the unborn and said again the law was all that mattered.

If this is the best our Supreme Court can do we are in trouble.

First, the right of the courts to intrude into public policy. Courts and judges have changed the fundamental nature of this country for a very long time. Just recently the basic notion of what is appropriate behavior was revolutionized by allowing female toplessness. Courts have also intervened to contradict the legislatures on issues of sexuality, marriage and benefits. Such activism here, but such indifference on the issue of the unborn.

If the courts had not intervened in the past Canadian women would have not been classified as people. In 1929 this ridiculous law was thrown out by a court with the words: "To those who would say that women are not persons, the answer is, why not?"

230

I would ask the same question to those who claim unborn children are not people. I would ask them, if life does not begin at conception, when does it begin?

As to the idea of limiting the freedom of people who might cause harm to others, this is hardly a new idea. We do such a thing every day. Regarding expectant mothers with drug habits somehow avoiding medical care, there is no evidence of this being the case. Abusive parents, for example, are caught every day precisely because they have used the medical system.

Then there is the statement that the biological evidence for there being little difference between the unborn and the born is less important than legal precedent. Dangerous ground indeed. When a black man in the U.S. first tried to change the law so as to be treated as a person, the court said Negroes were not people because they had never been treated as people under the law in the past.

Then there is language. The court consistently used the word "fetus" to describe the child in this case. It used, in fact, a term that dehumanizes what is essentially, and can only be, human.

When a pregnant woman puts her hands to her womb and smiles she does not say, "I just felt the fetus kick."

When we gather together to celebrate a friend's pregnancy we do not describe the event as a fetus shower and I for one have never put an ear to my wife's stomach and cried, "Darling, I heard the fetus!"

While we spend large amounts of money on campaigns to tell pregnant women that "smoking can damage your baby," we have also decided that in the balance between the right of a child to a healthy life and a woman's right to sniff glue, the freedom to sniff is the greater and the more important.

Perhaps the woman whose behavior caused all the fuss should have the last word. She has managed to overcome her addiction and plans to marry the father of her child. She says she has concerns about the court's judgment and is "worried about the fetuses out there."

She has cause to be.

Who's Afraid of the Promise Keepers?

Last weekend about one million men from all races and classes gathered in Washington, D.C. to proclaim or reiterate seven promises.

These included a commitment to "build strong marriages and families," to "practice spiritual, moral, ethical, and sexual purity," to break down racial barriers, to honor wives and children, to live a life of love and compassion and, above all, to be accountable.

The Promise Keepers, with three million adherents in 60 countries, had arrived.

This is a Christian organization, though with strong support from other religions and communities. What makes it so different from other men's groups is that rather than blaming the state, feminism or anybody else, these men take full responsibility for their failings and for the failings of their societies. Instead of banging drums in a forest they bang themselves over the head and opt to change their lifestyles and to try harder.

Opponents of the group are certainly having a hard time of it. They all seem to have used one Internet site for their attacks, that put out by the largest U.S. radical feminist group, the National Organization of Women.

Critics delivered the same old quotations and accusations and, to use one of their own favorite words, seemed rather "threatened." The Promise Keepers, they argued, want to turn back the clock, want women to be submissive and do not believe in women's rights or equality.

In fact, the ideal marriage advocated by the Promise Keepers is one of "mutual submission," a relationship centred on a husband and wife sharing life in a selfless love based around their faith. In that they take an oath to be "men of integrity" these people promise fidelity and truth, to spend more time with their families, to openly accept criticism and to share their feelings.

I do not know many women who would be offended by such a commitment from a man.

One Promise Keeper leader even said that men should be prepared to "wash their wives' feet," and he was being literal as well as metaphorical.

Certain women, of course, act as if no man has ever been willing to wash the dishes, let alone a woman's feet.

Patricia Ireland, leader of the National Organization of Women, announced, "I see the Promise Keepers and I am afraid. I am very afraid."

Come on, Pat. Mass starvation in the developing world is frightening, ethnic cleansing is frightening, inner-city squalor is frightening, but there is nothing frightening about men who promise to give themselves to duty, to their wives and to universal decency.

There are obviously some vital public policy issues involved here. North American and European governments, including our own, are spending billions of dollars trying to help single-parent families, dealing with domestic violence and coping with the results of an irresponsibility that often comes from fathers and husbands. The war against drugs is also becoming astronomically expensive and increasingly futile.

What the men in Washington were saying, and what their Canadian brothers believe, is that personal accountability can often achieve a great deal more than state intrusion. Surely we have learned that lesson by now.

Just a few days ago, for example, it was announced that men who do not pay child support will lose their driving licences. But nobody seriously believes this will have a major influence on most of those men who don't even care about the well-being of their children.

Equally, no amount of money thrown at the domestic violence issue will do much to dig at the fundamentals of the problem.

Far more effective is a wave of moral outrage created by a nucleus of men, supported and affirmed by one another in their views and virtues.

There is something else, something that is less tangible but certainly most noticeable. There is an overwhelming sense of happiness and joy about the Promise Keepers and about their meetings.

Instead of outrage there is satisfaction, instead of angst there is gratitude. From the men present and, very important, from the women as well.

Oddly enough, I think that it is this that makes some people so upset and so angry.

Mother Teresa
Rebel With a Cause

Death often walks the world as part of a gang. It is cowardly, and cowards need company.

Last week, of course, Princess Diana and Mother Teresa died. Back in 1963 the British author C.S. Lewis, author of, amongst others, The Lion, The Witch and the Wardrobe and The Screwtape Letters, died on the same day that John F. Kennedy was assassinated. Because of the massive coverage given to the death of the president it seemed as if Lewis did not die so much as simply disappear.

That was very sad. Because Kennedy, for all his glamour and fine intentions, was a terribly flawed man who had much to answer for. Lewis, on the other hand, was a deeply committed Christian who gave all of his book profits to charity, led an exemplary life and who with his writing had a far greater impact on the world than President Kennedy could ever have had.

Which brings us to Mother Teresa. It was as if God decided to take the lady home just before Princess Diana's funeral, so as to remind us of what a real saint looked like. Though the diminutive nun was hardly physically attractive in the conventional sense, she was, in fact, the most beautiful woman in the world.

Yet it is fascinating to see how that world has tried to define and understand the saint of the gutters. Liberals have, of course, applauded her work for the poor but they have ignored, or chosen to hide, her views about other matters. Mother Teresa believed that abortion was murder and that artificial contraception was not only selfish but immoral. She championed all of the Vatican's teachings on sexuality, sin, marriage, divorce and life issues and she thought western decadence was appalling.

She did not help the poor in spite of all this but precisely because of all this.

234

In fact, the contemporary, modernistic idea of goodness had very little to do with why Mother Teresa did what she did. She devoted her life to the destitute because of her pure, pristine belief in Christianity and in an orthodox Roman Catholicism that is routinely and savagely criticized by the world.

Her religious opinions are difficult for many people to accept, but to relish and cherish only some of what Mother Teresa did and said is to reject her completely.

Conservative newspapers and commentators, on the other hand, have refused to accept the fact that Mother Teresa was obliged to work with the poor and the starving only because there were such people. These wretches exist for no other reason than the fact a developed and western world is unwilling to make tangible sacrifices or introduce meaningful reforms. Ironically, and tragically, since Mother Teresa has died hundreds of thousands of people have succumbed to starvation or starvation-related diseases.

She remained poignantly aloof of politics, but implicit in her life was a stabbing criticism of the existing economic order and its plump complacency.

So she was a true rebel with a cause, a true revolutionary, who did not fit into the banal categories of left and right. Very much, in fact, like the man she worshipped and in whose name she labored. Her faith gave her strength but it also gave her the capacity for relentless love. A love that now often dares not speak its name.

She thought that to ignore what she called sin was not compassionate but callous. She would tell people when they were right but she would also tell people when they were wrong. This in an age when universal truth is severely out of style.

There is one final point that has to be made. Recently the Canadian Radio-television & Telecommunications Commission made an interesting decision, one that I wrote about last month. It ruled that a television broadcaster named Sister Angelica, a nun whose views and theology are identical in every way to those of Mother Teresa, should be barred from the Canadian airwaves.

How quickly a saint can become a devil.

As Elton John might have sung about consistency and truth, sometimes they are merely candles "in the wind."

Send in the Tanks –
It's a Nun

They quake in their boots at the sound of her approach.

They fight her progress at every turn. She must be stopped.

Is she a warlord leading tank divisions, or the linchpin of some huge mafia intent on destroying our country?

No, she is a plump, elderly, bespectacled nun from the U.S. by the name of Sister Angelica.

And for Canadian liberals, nun is too many.

Last month the Canadian Radio-television & Telecommunications Commission (CRTC) decided that Canada was too vulnerable, too fragile and too atheistic to need or want Sister Angelica's Eternal Word Television Network.

Broadcast to 56 million people in more than 30 countries, the show consists of what is essentially a fairly ordinary woman preaching orthodox Roman Catholicism. And love.

Other countries and broadcasters are lining up to receive the 76-year-old nun, but the CRTC, while agreeing to let Playboy TV be broadcast on one of the new cable outlets, rejected the Sister.

The entire incident speaks volumes about the CRTC. As the state body monitoring what we see on our televisions, it currently allows the weekly depiction of graphic sexual murder by serial killers, death-a-minute police shows, all sorts of anti-social and perverse behavior and waves of mind-numbing verbiage that destroy the intellect and drowse the imagination.

Interestingly enough, the CRTC has also allowed an ostensibly religious channel, Vision TV, to broadcast in Canada but then Vision's own shows wear their radical liberalism so brightly and so clumsily on their sleeves that only a fool or a fellow traveller would fail to notice.

Vision TV was one of the groups that lobbied against Sister Angelica being allowed to broadcast in Canada.

In the spirit of its own liberalism, it said the nun's values were somehow not Canadian. In the spirit of its own selfishness, it said that she might hurt it financially.

If the censoring of Sister Angelica reveals the authentic nature of the CRTC, it also cuts to the heart of Canadian liberalism. The core of the creed, or what a liberal perceives as the Canadian identity, is toleration. The more we tolerate the more Canadian we are, and the more Canadian we are the better we are.

But tolerance surely concerns not the acceptance of that with which we agree, but the toleration of people and ideas with which we do not agree.

Difficult of course, but all-important. When we read the names of the other people and groups that opposed Sister Angelica we find the usual left-wing organizations and activists.

"Canada is a tolerant society," they shout, "and we don't think that Sister Angelica is sufficiently tolerant of other people. So we won't tolerate her in our country."

Plato must be rolling in his cave.

So here we have the fundamental hypocrisy of that philosophical "Push-Me-Pull-You", the modern liberal. We used to have twin-headed monsters, now we have two-faced politicians and public figures.

Nor are they being honest even to themselves and their own flabby thinking. Almost half of Sister Angelica's broadcast subscribers are not Roman Catholic and evidently do not find her views to be so terribly threatening to their ways of life. And what she says differs not at all from the teachings of the

Vatican. To be consistent, surely these good liberals will have to stop the Pope and his people from ever visiting Canada again.

There are indeed reasons to control television broadcasting, such as the censorship of pornography, of hatred and of calls to violence. There is, in fact, a broad consensus concerning what is too explicit or too provocative to be on our screens and the CRTC has a duty, let alone a right, to control in such a manner.

But when control mechanisms are used in a political way to ensure that certain ideologies and groups have a monopoly on air-time, then we have lost our way. Terribly. Perhaps Sister Angelica could teach us the lesson we seem to so badly need.

Putting Animals First Perverts Our Priorities

At the end of the 18th century, shortly after Britain lost the American War of Independence, a rousing tavern song became extremely popular.

The lyrics spoke of "the world turned upside down," of all that was natural made unnatural and all that was appropriate made inappropriate. A modernized version would make some musician a millionaire.

For the uninitiated, let me explain. Last week in Alliston, a cardboard box full of discarded kittens was found by the Alliston Humane Society. Many of the small cats were dead, others were dying. Nasty stuff.

But the reaction of the people who discovered the animals bordered on the hysterical. One humane society official wept, another vomited and both spoke of the necessity of catching the evil person who treated the cats in such a way.

"My society wants this person bad. Only a monster would do something like this," said one, in a language more suited to describing a serial killer or a concentration camp guard.

The Alliston Humane Society offers rewards of up to $1,000 to help it catch animal abusers, but in this case it immediately volunteered $2,000 of charity-status cash for any information that might lead to the arrest of "the monster."

The place where the kittens were found was termed "the deathbox" and numerous newspapers, television and radio stations covered the story in enormous detail for the best part of a week.

At almost the same time as the kittens were discovered, a 6-year-old-child was savaged by two Rottweilers in a public park in Welland. The two men to whom the dogs belonged sped off in their black sports car without even checking to see if the tiny, bleeding youngster was alive or dead.

The story barely made the news at all and at the time of writing no reward has been offered to catch the culprits.

On the weekend before the Great Alliston Kitten Incident it was revealed, amongst other tragedies, that 36% of Toronto's children live in poverty and that torture gangs are still raping and murdering people in the Balkans. A far from untypical offering from a sorry world.

Neither story, however, produced anything like the same response from the media and the public as the tale of the kittens without their mittens.

Now there is nothing wrong, and much right, about having compassion for animals. But there is much wrong, and little right, about perverting our priorities. We have created a league table of what provokes our outrage and philanthropy and currently animals are enjoying the No. 1 spot. If there is a No. 1, there has to be a No. 2. The runners-up happen to walk on two legs.

The argument we often hear is that people who love animals also love people, but last week's antics seemed to contradict this. Nothing else explains the popular indifference to the child in Welland and the general apathy shown to so much human suffering. We seem to be falling, without even knowing it, for the now infamous statement from one of the founders of the animal rights movement that "a rat is a dog is a boy. They're all mammals."

Our reactions are terribly wrong. We have grown layers of fat around the muscles and nerves of sensitivity that maintained our moral bodies for millennia. We find it easier to sympathize with a cute, cuddly kitten than empathize with an African child with a distended belly or, for that matter, a hungry baby in Canada's most prosperous city. More than this, while we weep at the plight of the former we find reasons to ignore or even justify the suffering of the latter.

The logic used by everybody involved in this case is deeply flawed. If cats matter so much and their tormentors are so repugnant, why is it that the state encourages doctors to dissect animals and cause them discomfort and pain for scientific research? Why are we allowed to skin animals to keep us warm and kill them so as to eat their bodies? Because, quite simply, animals are not as important as humans, and neither is their suffering.

I make no apology for such a statement, but I do ask you to spell my name correctly in the hate-mail.

Terrorism: Who's Really to Blame?

The photographs are horrific. Blood, terror and tears. Suicide bombers, motivated by a manic fervor and a perversion of religion, murder a group of Israelis in a market.

The actions of the killers are applauded by various Islamic fundamentalists. They are, naturally, condemned by the world's leaders. Nation by nation, various prime ministers and presidents exhibit their revulsion at such an act.

They are abundantly right to do so. But are they being completely honest when they do so? While the good and the great must take a stand against the barbarism of others they must also look more closely at their own.

The reason being that terrorism is not confined to revolutionary organizations and murderous gangs. Terrorism is best defined as the use of intimidating methods to coerce communities or individuals. As such, a government may be terroristic when it tries to subdue internal opposition.

We conveniently ostracize some countries that sponsor and train terrorist groups, but we embrace other nations that use terrorist tactics on a regular basis.

Jean Chretien, for example, wasted no time after the Israeli massacre in expressing his detestation of terrorism. Yet the prime minister has worked hard at increasing Canada's support for, and trade with, China.

The old men in Beijing have used terror as a vehicle of governance for generations. They executed young men and women who dared to ask for basic democratic rights. Many of the protesters did not, and now never will, know the embrace of a lover or the smile of their children. They were shot to death by state terrorists. Their families had to pay for the bullets.

The Canadian government's argument is that by trading with China the country might be liberalized and become more tolerant of contrary opinion. If we apply this logic, why not trade with Hamas and other Middle Eastern terrorist groups and thus make them more humane and acceptable people?

An absurd suggestion.

Chretien was also a key player in the Liberal governments that became so close to many of the world's more brutal state terrorist regimes, particularly in Africa.

He has also spoken up for Cuba, where only last week a group of dissidents was arrested for its politics. There are more political prisoners and torture victims under Castro then there ever were under the last rancid administration.

Cuba is a terrorist state and also a supporter of international terrorist organizations.

Canada is its ally.

Only a few years ago our government insisted on increasing sporting and trading links with the former Soviet Union, while Moscow trained or armed half of the world's terrorist organizations and made itself a model terrorist state by its use of horrible internal security measures.

But Canada is not alone.

In the U.S., President Bill Clinton expressed horror at the atrocity that occurred in Israel. But Clinton invited the leader of Sinn Fein, the thinly disguised political wing of the Irish Republican Army, to the White House. He welcomed Gerry Adams as a friend.

Adams was a member of the army council of the IRA, an organization notorious for planting bombs in civilian areas and killing children. Very much, in fact, like the Islamic fundamentalists in Israel. When the families of IRA victims, many of them Irish Catholics, begged Clinton not to be so friendly to Adams, the president simply ignored them.

Britain's Tony Blair added his voice to the list of those standing firm against Arab terrorism. Blair seems to be a good man, but he recently allowed arms and aircraft to be sold to Indonesia, knowing that they will almost certainly be used to subdue Indonesian dissidents as an extension of that country's domestic terrorist activities.

One of the British prime minister's predecessors, Margaret Thatcher, gave valuable support to South Africa, a nation that used internal and external terror as a central means of dealing with opposition. The evidence linking the former apartheid regime with national and international terror grows by the week.

Michael Coren

It is essential that we throw stones of criticism at Hamas and other mass murderers. But while doing so we must move out of our metaphorical glass houses. Because hypocrisy contains within it its own very special kind of terror.

"Thank you President Clinton ... you can't imagine how dreadful a weight I'm carrying!"

No Room for Racial Meddling in the Judiciary

Last week an official complaint was received by the Canadian Judicial Council from the Samson Cree Band and the Canadian Jewish Congress. It concerned an alleged remark made by Justice James Jerome, the Federal Court of Canada's associate chief justice, in a telephone conference call with several lawyers representing the Samson Cree and the federal government. The call concerned Jerome's removal of Justice Douglas Campbell from a case involving the natives because Campbell knew four Samson Cree people from a community of more than 5,000 members.

During the conference call Jerome allegedly said he would not put a Jewish judge in charge of a case involving war crimes and wouldn't appoint an aboriginal judge to cases involving aboriginals. In that Justice Jerome administers our federal court these alleged comments are extremely serious and controversial.

But Jerome is no stranger to controversy. He was previously reprimanded by the Canadian Judicial Council for scheduling only one day of pre-trial motions concerning Nazi war criminals in an 18-month period.

Such an argument concerning Jewish judges is not unique, and neither is its defence. Indeed James Jerome is already being championed even before his remarks have been proved. The justification being offered by some of the defenders of the alleged remark is that Jewish judges would somehow be biased and subjective in dealing with a war crimes trial because of Jewish suffering during the Holocaust. As Jews they would be unable to expunge personal or family pain and it would be impossible for them to judge only according to the facts and to legal precedent.

What is ironic about all this is that the people who are making such arguments tend to be on the right of the political spectrum.

But what they are actually promoting is an extremely socialistic view of the world. They presume that individuals are less important than groups and communities and that personal integrity is less significant than ethnic experience.

If this is true we must immediately accept the demands of those black radicals who want to change a system where predominantly white policemen, lawyers and judges arrest, prosecute and sentence people of color. Juries must be subject to a racial quota system and all past trials of black people must be re-examined.

Further, as our law is based on European and Judeo-Christian principles and is essentially a "white man's law" no aboriginal must be judged by it. The judiciary is also, by foundation, patriarchal. According to some feminists it fails to understand that most women who commit crimes do so because of abuse or the subconscious fear of abuse. Often so subconscious that neither they nor anyone else know about it.

There is more. The logic of the argument surely insists that no woman can judge a man, no Catholic a Protestant, and no anglophone a francophone. And all judges must be tested for anti-Semitism before they are allowed to sit in a case involving a Jewish person.

Ludicrous perhaps, but merely consistent with the arguments put forward by those who support the alleged comments of Justice Jerome. We could also extend them into the workplace. If we believe in the group rather than the individual and in the impossibility of people from one race being fair to another, then we must support employment equity.

Then there is the problem of how we decide who is a Jewish judge. Is half-Jewish sufficient, or should we take the pernicious National Socialist interpretation of one Jewish grandparent? Many Jewish people do not have obviously Jewish names and keep their religious lives quiet. Imagine the fuss if one such person were allowed to judge a war crimes trial and was then discovered.

We already require that judges declare conflicts of interest before accepting any case and also take an oath of honesty before becoming a judge.

There is case law, media attention and governing authorities to monitor their actions.

There might be arguments for greater accountability and even for an electoral process in the judiciary, but not for racial interference.

The Smell of Money Overpowers the Sulphur/Calgary Ran Marilyn

The scene is grimly familiar. A rock singer who has apparently dedicated his professional life to evil treads the stage in an ugly fog of dry ice, sweat and hurtful lyrics. The audience, mostly composed of impressionable teenagers, cheers and screams. The performer parades in a perverse imitation of a fascist rally, encouraging his followers to chant in adoration. This is just the sort of thing the liberal pundits and left-wing social scientists have warned us about and told us to prevent. It is the social and emotional indoctrination of young people.

But just hold on one moment. This time the majority of the liberal pundits and left-wing social scientists, especially those based in Toronto, are defending the right of this particular musician to hold concerts. It is all a matter of free speech, they say, and those who oppose the man are simply "ignorant" or "hysterical."

Let me explain. What is good enough for neo-Nazis is not, apparently, good enough for someone called Marilyn Manson. This singer, whose latest album is entitled Anti-christ Superstar and whose songs include a little gem by the name of Deformography, was scheduled to play in Calgary in the last week of July. But a collection of church groups and family organizations managed to persuade the concert hall to cancel the arrangement. The promoter of the event has responded with threats of litigation.

Manson goes much further than shock-rock predecessors such as Alice Cooper. He has stated many times that he is a full priest in the Church of Satan. According to the Concise Oxford Dictionary, Satanism is, "the worship of Satan, with a travesty of Christian forms. The pursuit of evil for its own sake. Deliberate wickedness." Now a priest in such an organization is, one presumes, rather accomplished and experienced in being, well, devilish. Goodness, even a reformed Satanic minister must be wicked and evil on most days, perhaps just being lazy and smelly on, say, Wednesdays and Thursdays, with the weekend left for being cruel to animals.

It could be argued that Manson's actions influence young people, just as do the hateful moans of Holocaust-deniers and racists. It could even be that the Satanists have a much more tangible effect on the young and naive.

Witness the grotesque violence surrounding satanic cults, the attempted and accomplished suicides, the horrors of flirtation with authentic evil. If you doubt this, ask a priest, a minister or a social worker. These are the people who pick up the pieces, who do their best after Marilyn Manson and his defenders have done their worst.

If Manson changed his name to Hilary Himmler and sang songs glorifying the Third Reich we would, rightly, condemn him as a monster and try to close the doors of our concert halls to such repugnant nonsense. But Manson not only gets away with it, he is encouraged by people who should know better.

Nor is this the only example of the current hypocrisy. Manson's entire persona, entire point, is provocation. In fact, his career is about nothing else, and certainly not about his musical talents. His taken surname is that of a serial killer and child mutilator, his stage clothes often reveal a naked backside, his statements promote the pursuit of evil. The transformation of little Brian Warner into Marilyn Manson was contrived and deliberate. The assumption was, surely, that by provoking people he would be successful and, important this, become rich.

Yet when people are actually provoked, when they respond to Manson's pathetic pleas with concern, they are condemned and marginalized.

The good people of Calgary reacted to Manson's provocation in a time-honored, democratic and Canadian manner. They used moral muscle and intelligent argument to make their views heard. But they then committed the terrible sin of being successful. Christians and conservatives are simply not meant to win.

As for Manson, there may well be more of the whiff of dollar bills than sulphur about the man, but either way it will be of great benefit for him to discover that sometimes the good guys fight back.

An Odd Way of
Seeking Public Acceptance

Last week Toronto Police Sgt. Peter Harmsen commented on his time spent supervising the recent Gay Pride Day parade. He was disturbed by the men who marched along in the middle of Canada's largest city with their genitals exposed, with pierced testicles on display or who took part in acts of sado-masochistic sex.

In what seemed like an eminently reasonable statement the officer concluded that, "It just seems to be escalating past the point of fair play and common decency. We're certainly concerned. If this type of thing happens next year, we'll stop the parade."

But the good sergeant was wrong. In fact the police were not concerned by all at these acts of flagrant law-breaking.

Within 24 hours, in a series of statements from police headquarters, it was announced that Deputy Chief Robert Molyneax had "no problems with the parade," that the parade would definitely continue, that a debriefing meeting would be held "but the issue of nude revellers" would not be discussed and, in what must be the quote of the summer, that it was doubtful whether "concerns over some male parade-goers exposing their genitals will even be raised."

That the law was broken is beyond doubt. There is a great deal of footage of naked men strolling around in the parade, of acts of indecent exposure and of bondage and whipping. What is extraordinary is how quickly and how vehemently the bureaucrats and high-ranking officers in the police department contradicted Harmsen and how eager they were to excuse the lawbreakers.

It is worth comparing all this to the same police department's handling of the annual Caribana parade. This valid and vibrant manifestation of Canada's multicultural fabric was under severe threat last month when the police temporarily refused to supervise the event. There was talk of Caribana not being "our parade," and it took several days for the police to come to their senses and to agree to work with and at the West Indian festival.

Caribana encourages tourism, fills the hotels, boosts trade and sends a buzz through the core of Toronto. There was a tragic shooting last year, but this had nothing to do with the carnival itself and was, thank goodness, entirely atypical. Yet the police questioned the very future of the event because of a relatively trivial disagreement over the parade's route.

Double standard or just a case of political pressure?

I'm not sure.

Let me state that the people who behaved so neurotically and so pathetically at the Gay Pride Day parade represented a minority of those present. They were obviously broken and hurting people who deserve our charity and sympathy rather than our condemnation. We must temper our righteous outrage with compassion. We must also ask why their actions were not criticized by the managers of the event.

Parade organizer David Dent, for example, said the bondage floats and nudity were "quite tame" and that he did not find them to be "unacceptable." Thus we move from the appalling behavior of a minority to the sanctioning of such behavior by parade officials.

Homosexual activists frequently try to change the laws of this country to accommodate or protect their way of life. That is their right. It is odd, though, that while they want the majority of the population to accept such new laws many homosexual zealots seem intent on mocking and breaking the laws that already accommodate and protect that same majority.

Nor must we tolerate any nonsense about homophobia, a contrived and artificial word invariably used to silence free debate. If a section of Canadian society wants to change the country so radically that public sex and genital exhibitionism are standard, so be it. Let them, however, be honest about it. And let the politicians who control our police departments be honest as well.

A single person walking along the street without any clothes would be stopped and, if necessary, arrested. Two heterosexuals whipping each other's semi-naked bodies in the middle of a city would, again, be stopped and, if necessary, arrested.

The law must apply equally to every Canadian. Otherwise, it is no law at all.

Only You and I
Can Destroy Racism

A Toronto policeman faces charges after allegedly making a series of grotesquely racist comments to another officer who, unbeknown to the accused, was himself black. Racism. As old as it is repugnant.

Thirty years earlier, and 3,000 miles away, an 8-year-old-boy, Ginger, runs to the local park to play soccer, as he does every day of the summer vacation. He meets another little boy, Jim, and they become friends, brothers-in-arms, fellow musketeers. They run and laugh all day and then as the sun begins to set Jim asks Ginger if he would like to come to his house for tea.

"Yeah," says Ginger, "that would be great."

They set off together to Jim's house where they drink a fizzy English pop called Tizer and eat cookies. They play board games, like each other very much and are certain they will now be inseparable.

Jim's dad comes in. He is a large man and doesn't smile. He looks at Ginger and asks Jim about him. He speaks not in a kindly, but in an aggressive, way.

He demands answers. Jim answers his dad and looks a little nervous.

"He is, isn't he?" shouts the dad. "He is, he bloody well is!" Jim is scared. He says he doesn't know much about Ginger, just knows he is a nice boy. He asks why his dad is shouting, why his dad is so red in the face.

"He is, now get him out of the house, get him out right now," shouts Jim's dad. Jim is embarrassed, almost in tears, but asks Ginger in shy tones to leave. Ginger is confused but has no choice. He leaves the house, walks home and goes to his room. He tells nobody about what happened, not even his mum or dad or other friends.

Later Ginger thinks more about what had occurred. His innocence begins to evaporate, like the lifting of a fog. As the mist clears the real shape of events comes into sight. The gaps are filled in, the empty spaces disappear. Ginger realizes what was said.

Jim's dad had actually shouted, "This kid is a Jew isn't he?" Jim did not even know what a Jew was. Jim's dad had continued with, "He is a Jew, now get him out of this house. I don't want a Jew in this house!" Ginger was a child, a half-Jewish child, a half-Jewish child who did not know there were such things as racial or religious differences.

Ginger's delicious innocence received a knife-wound that, without a loving family and a loving God, might have led to the slow, bleeding death of his faith in humanity. But one nasty slash from the tired body of British fascism was not capable of such an achievement. Ginger recovered.

I am largely bald now. But as a child I had a full head of curly red hair.

My friends called me Ginger. Just as my father had been called Ginger by his friends and my grandmother, a refugee from massacre, had been called Ginger by her little friends in her Polish village. My dad and my grandma had suffered far worse than being ordered out of someone's house. And they knew such hatred was not typical and was merely the screams of ancient and pathetic hatred.

Back to Toronto. If the police officer in question did make those comments he should be fired. Any such comments, made by white, black, Jew, gentile, about white, black, Jew, gentile, are unacceptable. We are all, irrespective of our race and religion, capable of hatred and we are all, irrespective of our race and religion, capable of love. It is not our ethnicity, but our morality that dictates our behavior. Until we understand that, we understand nothing.

The state will not destroy racism, the law will not destroy racism and politically correct intrusion will not destroy racism. We will destroy racism.

Ginger will try his best. And so will Jim. He grew up to be a fine man, a police officer, and married a fine Jewish woman. They have children. Jewish all. And none of them is ever ordered out of the house.

Some Questions Vital at
Blood Donor Clinics

Well, it had to happen somewhere. Carleton University has banned the Red Cross from its publicly funded campus.

The internationally respected organization usually holds a donor clinic at this Ottawa university in February. Not this year. Because the Red Cross dares to ask male donors if they have had sex with other men since 1977. If the answer is yes, they cannot give blood.

The reason for the policy is, of course, that many people have died from receiving tainted blood. One would have thought, then, that such a screening procedure was moderate and extremely necessary.

Carleton's several homosexual student groups disagreed, accused the Red Cross of discrimination and exerted pressure on university authorities. Now there is no Red Cross on campus and a diminished blood supply.

The fact that probably more than 95% of those giving blood were not homosexual, or that some homosexuals might understand the policy and not object, was ignored. The more vociferous, the more the influence.

The university is willing to let the Red Cross back on campus only when its staff attends a series of – wait for it – sensitivity workshops. The ubiquitous "workshop" is much in demand these days by our special interest groups, and it is always paid for by the public. When I was a child, a workshop meant learning to saw wood and hammer nails. Now it involves propaganda and rigid control of our opinions by extremist factions made powerful by our apathy and our governments' cowardice.

Those fortunate to live in a democracy are obliged to pay for their privilege by dealing with numerous clashes of freedom. Some thinkers argue there are two types of freedom – freedom from and freedom to. Others explain the freedom of one citizen's fist

251

stops at another citizen's nose. When liberties of equal importance collide we have to consider, discuss and decide.

But here we have two freedoms that are not of anything like equal importance. On the one hand we have the freedom for a gravely ill person to accept a blood transfusion safe in the knowledge the blood is not infected with a deadly disease. On the other is the freedom for a person who is not, anyway, required to give blood to maintain the privacy of his sexual life.

Agonizing death vs. social manners.

Nor is the Red Cross some bigoted organization likely to advertise someone's homosexuality or exploit the information for amusement or gain. Indeed, the man who exposed all this, Glen Hansman, has admitted he went to a donor clinic with the sole purpose of proving his point. He says he knew he would not be accepted and, thus, was more interested in the special privileges of his group than with giving blood to save lives.

He is obviously not ashamed of his sexuality or he would not have engineered this issue in the first place. He stated the Red Cross implied that "some people might be bad" because they were homosexual. Nonsense. They were trying to protect the people of Canada.

I would also expect the Red Cross to ask potential donors if they were intravenous drug users or hemophiliacs, two other groups with a tragically high infection rate. The vast majority of people who are HIV positive in Canada, however, are male homosexuals and while we must all weep at such a horror, the Red Cross has a right to information that might protect the greater citizenry.

Any number of organizations have any amount of information about any number of us. We sacrifice these small liberties for the greater good. Most of us appreciate that such minor compromises are necessary.

The usual wet snowball of "homophobia" has been thrown at the Red Cross. If the Red Cross was motivated by prejudice it would also ask women if they were lesbians. It doesn't, because lesbians are not a high-risk group, and the risk of infection is the only criterion here.

The logic of these tax-funded extremist students and their flaccid teachers is most reassuring. If you collapse with an agonizing disease, die with a smile knowing that no homosexual has been asked about his love life.

Peaceful Protester, or Common Criminal?

Last week I saw someone arrested. Her name is Linda Gibbons, a 46-year-old grandmother. She is little more than five feet tall and weighs only 100 lbs. But for some reason it took four police vehicles and six large policemen to carry her away.

It was difficult to understand what crime this tiny lady was committing.

She was merely walking along, slowly and silently, in front of a group of houses. From one of those houses a video camera recorded her, and the person operating that camera called the police. As the police arrested Gibbons she said nothing, but just sat down on the dark, damp street. She was shivering just a little and I think she was praying.

When the policemen picked Gibbons up her body became limp and it took several minutes to force her prostrate body into the cruiser. All the time people were cheering her and car horns were honking in support.

Actually, Linda Gibbons has been arrested several times and has served more than three years in prison. The reason is that she does what she does outside an abortion clinic. Let me emphasize that this is not a column about abortion. This is a column about freedom of speech, freedom of movement and freedom of protest.

In 1991 the former socialist government of Ontario launched an enormously expensive and crassly tendentious political and legal campaign that resulted in an injunction preventing any pro-life activity from taking place within 60 feet of an abortion clinic. The reasons given were flimsy and arbitrary at best, but were based on the alleged probability of violence.

The pro-life movement in Canada has no history of violence, however, and no pro-lifer has ever been convicted of a violent act. All Gibbons seeks is to say a few words to people entering a clinic. This "counselling" is sometimes successful. On the day I saw the arrest, a woman with a beautiful 3-year-old child was present. Four years ago Gibbons had spoken to this young woman, then pregnant, who was on her way into the clinic. Gibbons changed the woman's mind. The result was the little girl in front of me. As the police cruiser drove away the young mother sobbed "We love you Linda, we won't forget you!"

Such a "rescue" would have cost the clinic several hundred dollars, the price charged for an abortion. This is invariably covered by the taxpayer, the cost rising depending on the lateness of the pregnancy.

In the past when Linda Gibbons has gone to court, the Crown has asked for a six months sentence, which is longer than that usually requested for violent assaults and thefts. A comrade of Linda's, who also served half a year for his actions, shared a cell with a man serving only four months. He had just committed his second assault with a deadly weapon.

Throughout Gibbons' ordeal the people inside the abortion clinic videotaped not only Linda herself, but the small, law-abiding protest across the street and outside of the bubble zone. At one point the wife of the chief abortionist insisted to police that a poster across the busy two-lane road was 18 inches within the zone and demanded it be removed. It was.

How different from an industrial dispute. Here a picket has the legal right to stop someone entering his or her place of work and to harangue that person for several minutes. This right will be protected by the police, even when the language used is heated and perhaps threatening. Intimidation, kicks and screams are frequent. Yet there is no bubble zone.

So why the double standard and why the mythology about pro-life violence?

The answer is the law has become politicized. Those who support abortion and manage clinics have become a privileged group and have engineered rights above and beyond those of the rest of society.

As long as protest is peaceful and lawful it must be allowed, in every context. It defines us as a free country.

And while people like Linda Gibbons are in prison that definition is pathetically and tragically blurred.

Prize-Winning Porn Disguised as Art

Welcome back to the wonderful world of public funding for the arts.

This time we travel not to the usual location of Toronto, but to Winnipeg.

Yet fear not. Extremism and cultural parasitism seem to be just as nauseating in Winnipeg as they are in the nation's largest city, the favorite grazing patch of the tax-supported Canadian artist.

Late last year Meeka Walsh, editor of the arts magazine Border Crossings, and Wayne Baerwaldt, director of Winnipeg's Plug In Gallery, judged a contest in Los Angeles organized by The Tom of Finland Foundation. Tom of Finland is renowned for drawing pictures of homosexual acts, often involving bondage and leather fetishes. This particular competition was called the Emerging Erotic Artist Contest.

The winning illustrator was Garilyn Brune, and both Canadians voted for this entry. Rather than describe the prize-winning entry in detail and cause offence to many people, let me merely say the work consists of a graphic depiction of a priest having oral sex with Jesus Christ. I believe the picture is obscene, immature and hurtful, that it is as hateful as the rantings of a Holocaust denier or the screams of a Klansman.

Now it goes without saying that the artist involved, and those who awarded him his prize, are not courageous. Can we imagine them, for example, being so committed to the truth of their art and the fight against so-called censorship that they would have replaced Christ with Mohammed and would have entered a contest in North Africa rather than North America? The act would have been just as vile, but the result might have been a little more interesting.

Michelangelo was a hero when he dared defy the Pope, the Prince of Rome and a mighty warlord, and painted the ceiling of the Sistine chapel the way he and not the pontiff saw fit. He risked exile and death. Even Picasso was a hero of sorts when he defied the cultural and political elites with his work. But rather than defy the artistic establishment Brune, Walsh and Baerwaldt merely ape its more vulgar manifestations.

Nor is the figure in the picture merely of Christ, but of Christ crucified.

Even for those who are not Christian or religious in any manner, this is particularly significant. Here we have a person at his most vulnerable, his hands and feet nailed to a cross, his body recently whipped and tortured. The sado-masochistic connotations are obvious. The picture implies that it is permissible to take perverse sexual advantage of a bound figure. The awarding of a prize to such a picture legitimizes the very picture and the very action.

What must immediately concern us here, though, is the involvement of the two grant-aided Canadians. Walsh's and Baerwaldt's defence is that they were two private citizens judging an award and as such they are answerable to nobody. But they were only asked to judge the contest because they have a certain standing in the artistic community. They have that standing in part because of their positions as magazine editor and gallery director.

One reason they have these positions is that taxpayers contribute tens of thousands of dollars to the institutions in question and, indirectly, to the salaries of the two individuals.

The first task is to remove all public funding from the pair and let them survive, or not, in the arts world on their own abilities and with whatever money they manage to earn from the free cultural market.

The second step is to ask ourselves whether Border Crossings and the Plug In Gallery should be funded in any way with public money. After all, I am sure our artistic friends in Winnipeg would be the first to remind us that money is needed to feed the hungry and to clothe the poor.

The ultimate step is to consider censorship of all forms of pornography disguised as art, and I intend to make the arguments for this case in a forthcoming column.

In the meantime, pay your taxes with a smile, knowing that Walsh and Baerwaldt are most appreciative.

Justice For All... *Even Your Enemies*

I despise the Heritage Front, I despise its racism and I despise all for which it stands. I also love justice, I love truth and I love all for which they stand. Thus, this story.

In March, 1996 the Federal Court of Canada, Trial Division, heard a case in which the Canadian Human Rights Commission charged June Louise French, Wolfgang Droege and the Heritage Front with being in contempt of previous court orders prohibiting them from making certain political statements over their so-called telephone hotline. The commission alleged that a subsequent message broadcast by the Heritage Front had broken the law.

The judge dismissed the case, but our interest should be not in the decision but in the contents, bearing in mind that the financing of the case itself and of the human rights commission came and comes from our tax dollars. During the trial the human rights commission officer leading the case, Mervin Witter, claimed the Heritage Front's telephone message had referred to the "Jewish mafia" and had said the Jewish community was seeking "vengeance" against people they thought were war criminals. Nasty and malicious language indeed.

And untrue language as well. In fact, the tape referred not to a Jewish mafia but to "Jewish lobbyists" and not to the Jewish community seeking vengeance but to it seeking "justice." Slightly different. Witter testified that the error was an honest mistake and that he had no intention to mislead the court.

Now just hold on one moment. Presumably Witter and his colleagues had heard the tape in question dozens of times, because they were spending a great deal of public money on a case that rested on the very words used on that same tape. Odd, then, that such fundamental mistakes should be made. How could someone confuse lobbyists with Mafia and justice with vengeance? They are totally different in length and sound and the original tape was extremely clear.

Witter was, naturally, grilled by the counsel for the defence about his confusion and his misleading transcript concerning the language used by the Heritage Front. He was asked if he agreed that any use of the term "mafia" conjured up thoughts of organized crime, brutal murder and illegal conspiracy.

In his judgment, Justice Bud Cullen stated Witter's responses were particularly evasive, very vague and that his supposed "lack of knowledge about mafia did not ring true; after all, he had been a police officer for a number of years." He wrote that Witter's "mistake was serious" and had a "bearing on the evidence of other witnesses." He also stated that Witter only "reluctantly admitted that the word (mafia) was emotive."

In fact, the word mafia drips with sinister connotations, while the word lobbyist is quite innocuous. Similarly with vengeance and justice. The first implies something spiteful and dark, the second defines a notion that is decent and admirable.

If we believe that Mervin Witter or his superiors made only a series of mistakes, then they demonstrated such incompetence that we have to wonder why such people are employed in positions of authority and responsibility. If it was not a simple mistake ... well, the consequences are terrifying. The law applies to all. It even applies to those with whom we fundamentally disagree and to those whose views are severely distasteful.

At this point Justice Minister Allan Rock becomes a player in this costly farce. The minister was contacted by one of the defence lawyers in the case, John D. Gibson. He wrote to this member of the Privy Council and former treasurer of the Law Society of Upper Canada last September because he was concerned about Witter being further employed after such a waste of public money and such a gross – let us be generous – lack of professionalism. There has been a further letter, but still no reply.

Last week, in the Brian Mulroney case, Rock learned how to apologize. Let us hope he has now learned how to take firm action, and also that the Canadian Human Rights Commission acts in a Canadian, a human and a right manner. We will wait and see. And while we wait we will hope Mervin Witter does not make a transcript of anything we might say.

Public versus Private Radio

Last year I wrote of the struggle between CBC Toronto's AM station and a group of competitors to fill the vacant and coveted 99.1 FM spot. I said the CBC already has an FM spot and that there are any number of religious, ethnic or mainstream proposals for 99.1 that should be given priority. I said the CBC was being greedy and dismissive. I now believe they are being unfair.

In the last quarter of 1996 the CBC distributed a leaflet entitled You Deserve to Hear CBC Radio! The flyer outlines various reasons why the CBC should receive another FM spot and asks the public to write in to demonstrate support.

Several hundred thousand flyers were sent out. The CBC is reluctant to reveal how much they spent on the exercise but when we factor in the cost of printing, design and distribution, the total must be significant. And it was paid by the public, including those who do not listen to the CBC and do not want the CBC to have a second FM station.

The leaflets were distributed around the time of a crucial radio ratings period organized by the Bureau of Broadcast Measurement or BBM. This organization mails out ballots and the results dictate success or failure for a private station and employment or unemployment for its broadcasters. They are the main indication for advertisers as to how well a station is doing and how much should be paid for commercials.

The BBM ratings book is a detailed diary. An official-looking leaflet from the CBC arriving at the same time might influence the way some people kept that diary, or suggest that somehow the two mailings were connected.

An Angus Reid poll taken at the time of the flyer showed a significant jump in CBC 740 listeners, even though the station's format and personalities remained the same. Official complaints about CBC Radio's behavior have already been made to the BBM by private broadcasters.

The flyer states, "Earlier moves by CBC Radio from AM to FM in Halifax and Ottawa have resulted in top ratings." Quite true. Given such an unfair advantage in Toronto, CBC's ratings would also improve. This is exactly why competitors for the FM spot should compete on a level playing field.

It continues, "With its non-commercial format, CBC Radio's move to FM presents a revenue-neutral approach." Untrue. The government is bringing enormous pressure on CBC Radio to take ads and become more self-sufficient. If the press and public know this, so do the people who wrote the leaflet.

Then we have, "CBC Radio 740 has demonstrably the worst signal quality of all Toronto radio stations." Nonsense. All AM stations in Toronto have poor receptions but CBC has one of the best. The myth of 740's poor signal is perpetrated by CBC managers who want the FM spot.

We are then told that CBC Radio is "Original programming by Canadians to Canadians." There is a sinister implication here.

Every Toronto AM station's programming is made by Canadians for Canadians and much of it is far more original than that produced by the CBC.

In a similar vein is the statement that "CBC Radio contributes to the development of citizenship and understanding among Canadians." What rot! Contrary to what some at the CBC believe they do not have a monopoly on truth and patriotism. And all surveys demonstrate that most new Canadians listen to stations other than CBC, developing their sense of citizenship elsewhere.

I am not alone in believing that CBC Radio evinces a political and social bias, that it enjoys a commercial unaccountability, and that it no longer represents this country in all of its contemporary diversities. Times change, and so does radio. Men used to run away to sea.

Now they run away to the CBC.

Happy Holidays? Humbug!

Let us talk turkey, if you will excuse the pun. Tomorrow is the anniversary of the birth of Jesus Christ. As a Christian, the day represents for me the beginning of everything. As a participant in the public discourse it raises for me a series of political and social questions. So as a Christian journalist I have one or two things to say this eve.

I will not wish anyone "happy holidays." This is Christmas. To pretend it is some incidental vacation is insulting to a world religion and to the intelligence of the Canadian people. A similar argument can be made for other religions that have a festival in December. I have enormous respect for Judaism and for the Jewish people. As such I will not dilute Hanukkah, an ancient celebration of liberation and the evidence of God, to a generic and banal phrase that stinks of political correctness.

In our obsession with inclusiveness we have, ironically, excluded almost everyone who possesses anything more than the most trivial of belief systems. Differences of faith always have and always will exist, and to pretend they do not is to deny the very importance of those beliefs in the first place, which is in itself discriminatory. When we try to meet in the middle we meet nowhere at all. Better to acknowledge our differences and to disagree with mutual respect and, vital this, with love.

The British rabbi who said recently that assimilation was a greater threat to Judaism than the Holocaust was roundly condemned. But he had a point. Religion is killed not by cruelty but by kindness. Christians best retained their Christianity when the state hated them. Compare Poland or Uganda with Holland or Canada.

Yet nor must we forget that modern Canada was founded by Christian people on Christian principles. The country is now post-Christian, but its laws and virtues are solidly rooted in Christian morality.

The reason so many of the world's immigrants want to go to Canada, the U.S., Britain, Australia and Europe is precisely because those countries, founded on Christian ideals, are so accepting and pluralistic. This is not and never has been the case with, for example, the vast bulk of the Islamic world.

Unfortunately it seems that every Christmas a few parents decide to object to something like the singing of carols in their children's school. They impose their minority will because an oversensitive teaching staff no longer knows when to tell some people to shut up.

In Buffalo just last week a crib was removed because of a handful of objections and in some public schools every indication that Christmas might be Christian is aggressively expunged. Oddly enough, there is also a trend to invite wizards and sorcerers into schools at Halloween to explain the feminist and humanist significance of witchcraft.

This year we will also all be able to work and shop on Boxing Day. And if we are allowed, it means that most of us will. It would take a brave person indeed to lose customers because he refuses to open up store on Dec. 26. Society is tearing at the seams because families are hurting; families are hurting because they spend insufficient time together; Boxing Day was a time when families relaxed as a unit.

I applaud the capitalist work ethic but I also know that a healthy capitalist system requires a bedrock of tradition and community structure. Capitalism developed as a direct result of the Protestant Reformation and out of the admission by the great reformers that Christianity must accommodate business and commerce, and that business and commerce must accommodate Christianity.

What actually lies at the root of all this confusion is an ambivalence, even an embarrassment, about who we are. Practising, nominal and even merely cultural Christians have for 20 years been apologizing for creating in the western world what is the most tolerant, civilized and productive society in the history of humanity. Until we stop it, until we refuse to surrender to the whims of liberal revisionism, we cannot advance.

I wish you all a very happy Christmas, I wish you prosperity, and I wish you the peace of Jesus Christ.

Breast Ruling Strips Power from the People

So once again a group of judges has altered the fundamental direction and beliefs of Canadian society.

Last week the Guelph exhibitionist, Gwen Jacob, won a hollow victory when an Ontario Court of Appeal overturned her conviction for committing an indecent act. In 1991 the young woman had walked the street with her breasts exposed, receiving a great deal of publicity — which I assume is what she wanted. The new ruling means that not only can women now wave their mammary glands around in public, but also that the long-cherished notion of the separation of powers is at death's door.

The latter point first. Our democratic system is built upon a clear division between judiciary and legislature, between judges and government. That division, so important in the history of western society, has now become dangerously obscured in Canada.

Earlier this year a group of judges made a court decision allowing same-sex benefits for homosexuals after our elected leaders, being an extension of the people, had rejected the idea. Our courts are manufacturing decisions that run against the will of the electorate.

If a handful of detached, ivory-tower legalists can change in a few hours what has been debated and held dear for decades within the democratic process, then we as citizens have been made virtually powerless. The right of a woman to show her boobs to any boob who would look represents a profound change in what we believe to be decent and moral. If the people want such a change, fine. But they have not even been consulted.

The practical consequences of the decision itself are equally worrying.

Take the example of two bare-breasted women standing on a street corner, one a prostitute and the other a radical feminist. The former will be arrested, because she is not allowed to expose herself for commercial reasons. The latter is not even spoken to by the police, because she has no financial gain in mind. Before long the most subtle dressers downtown will be the hookers.

The argument put forward by the equality fanatics is that because men are permitted to bare their chests women should be allowed the same right. Women's breasts, however, are directly sexual, the second most erogenous part of a woman's body, and are also more biologically intimate in that they are used for nursing children.

Also, only certain types of men will walk along the street topless. Be they the owners of beer-bellies or of perfect pectorals, those men who want to show their upper bodies to the greater world are usually making a deeper, more neurotic point. We should be dissuading them, not persuading others.

The only generally acceptable form of exposure is during nursing, when we should encourage women to feed their children whenever and wherever they want. Breastfeeding represents much of what is best about humanity, such as love, procreation and family. But the so-called Breast-Walkers' reasoning represents the precise opposite of the nursing scenario and their behavior is the contrary of natural. It is full not of care and bonding, but of egotism and perversity.

Then we have the great modern myth of tolerance. The more we accept the better we are. Thus, some people will welcome the breast decision as a progressive action. I would ask them two questions: how many of them would feel comfortable conducting a conversation with a 70-year-old lady who had her breasts exposed; and how many of them would allow their children to be taught by a bare-breasted woman?

Finally comes the argument that few women will take advantage of the ruling anyway.

It is true that no emotionally, sexually and politically mature women would act in such a manner — but some politically extreme women are not particularly mature.

The social engineers and the lawyers want to change human nature because at the heart of their philosophy lies an invincible arrogance. The common people are against it, so it must be sophisticated to be for it. We impose, therefore we are. It all makes me weep, when I suppose it should just make me titter.

It's Madness to Deport a Woman Like This

By the time this column is published Jacqueline Ross-Jenkins may have been deported from Toronto to her native Guyana. The reason for the deportation is, according to immigration officials, that Ross-Jenkins is in the country illegally and on welfare.

The 34-year-old woman has been in Canada for 20 years. Her marriage to a Canadian lasted long enough to produce three children, but not long enough to complete her spousal sponsorship for citizenship. A decade ago, Ross-Jenkins worked briefly as a prostitute and received a minor conviction for loitering. Since that time she has turned her life around, embraced Christianity and, according to members of her church congregation, "become an upstanding, good woman, a fine mother and a responsible citizen."

There are many non-citizens in Canada who should be deported immediately, and recent history has shown how tragically weak we have been in enforcing the law in this regard. But this is a different case. All of Ross-Jenkins' children are Canadian citizens and know only this country. Immigration Canada has said the children do not have to go with their mother and can be left behind with the Children's Aid Society. An offer so generous it might almost be described as Jacqueline's Choice.

Ross-Jenkins' lawyer, Davies Bagambiire, says the reason his client is on welfare is because she has been refused a work permit. He says there are jobs waiting for Jacqueline, if only she is allowed to work. Members of her church confirmed this and even raised $4,000 so Ross-Jenkins' case could be fought until this point.

"I want to work, I want to stay, I have shown for more than 10 years that am a decent person," said Ross-Jenkins from her place of custody near Toronto airport, with a security guard looking on. "My children cannot go to Guyana, the authorities know that. I can't leave them, they know that. I don't know why they are doing this."

The reason "they" might be doing this is that in the past the immigration service has failed in its job – or not been allowed to succeed – and has suddenly been told to enforce the law, quickly and without exception. In attempting to compensate for past disasters they are pursuing strict law but ignoring strict justice.

The Ross-Jenkins case comes only weeks after a man dying of AIDS was to be deported back to Portugal after spending all of his adult life in Canada. He had a criminal record and should probably have been expelled many years ago. But it was curious, and callous, that the authorities would act when the wretched man had only months to live, placing his family in a grotesque position.

Similarly, if Immigration Canada wanted to deport Ross-Jenkins why did it not do so 10 years ago rather than now, when she has three Canadian children?

Apart from the ethics of the situation there are the finances. The cost of arresting, guarding and deporting four people is enormous: tickets for the family, return tickets for two immigration officials to accompany them, the wages for staff and security, the rent for the room, the purchase of food, the time of the four police officers who took the family into custody and the legal battles that have gone on for months.

Cheap at twice the price to deport a gun-toting pimp or drug-dealer. A little excessive, however, to eject a young mother who simply wants to build a Canadian life.

The solution is simple, and is one that would test the credibility of Ross-Jenkins, her supporters and the morality of the immigration authorities.

We remove the woman's welfare privileges and provide her with a work permit. We then give her six months. If she is without employment at the end of that period Ross-Jenkins is deported. If she is working, she and her friends have been proved correct, the state is receiving her tax dollars and the nation has another model citizen.

And, by the way, true conservatives are people who place as much importance in the exceptions as they do in the rules.

Irish Potato Famine has Lessons for Today

A century and a half ago Ireland was even greener than usual. This was not the glorious green of the fields and the hills, but the grotesque green of the mouths of the children, salivating that color because they were starving to death and in their agony had eaten nettles and grass.

The Irish potato famine occurred between 1845 and 1849, killed a million people and forced another million to emigrate, thus decreasing the population by more than a quarter. Apart from its moral significance, the famine is of vital memory because it represented an example of a government deciding to let the free market dictate economic policy. As to any lessons the famine may have for us in Canada today, I leave this entirely up to the reader.

All of Ireland was part of the United Kingdom in the 19th century, but generations of neglect and indifference by some London governments, hostility and contempt by others, had laid the foundations for crisis. Anti-Catholic discrimination and exploitative absentee landlords had devastated the country and, with the exception of Ulster, there had been little industrial development.

Phytophthora Infestans, a fungus that destroyed potato crops, had already been seen on the English mainland and on the Isle of Wight, but in a country not dependent on potatoes it had caused limited damage and little concern. When it crossed the sea to Ireland it wrote a different story. For three years the staple diet of the Irish people simply did not materialize. First the weak and ill died, then the children and the old, then the able-bodied adults.

The Tory government of Sir Robert Peel tried to do something about the situation. The founder of the modern police force – Peelers or Bobbies – introduced a public works program to provide employment and inject money into the economy.

It did some good. He then rigidly controlled food prices throughout Ireland and brought in Indian meal to be distributed to the hungry. Although the famine still ripped its way through the people, Peel's policies began to have an effect.

But Robert Peel lost the following election and was replaced by a Whig administration committed to non-intervention and laissez-faire economics. The new prime minister, Lord John Russell, was a follower of the Scottish philosopher and economist Adam Smith, who is a hero to many neo-conservatives.

Smith was a profound, if obsessive, thinker who believed the invisible hand of the market had to be left to its own devices. He was also extremely impractical and absent-minded, famous for walking around Edinburgh only half-dressed. Smith never married, lived with his mother and had very little understanding of the real world.

The British government removed the policies of the interventionist Peel, dismantled his programs and decided to let the market sort out the famine. London gave out soup rations to the Irish, but this charity was not very helpful. It also sent Queen Victoria on a state visit to Dublin, and as far as we know the good lady did not sign any copies of her books. Even if the Irish had eaten the queen, she would not have fed enough people.

The country quaked, its death-rattle heard from Europe to North America. Ireland has never recovered and neither has England, if we judge by the deaths of British soldiers and civilians.

The Irish potato famine should never be forgotten, particularly in Canada where there are entire towns founded by and for the victims of this slaughter.

In fundamental ethical and human terms London let hundreds of thousands die or be forced into exile. In selfish, political terms the British government created mass hatred from the Irish and initiated, by the forced North American diaspora, waves of Irish-American men and women who distrust or despise England and all of its works.

A little economic practicality and a little political moderation would have gone a very long way in the 1840s.

Oddly enough, they still do in the 1990s.

One Mom's War with the
School Board Bully

Home-schooling is a growing phenomenon where parents withdraw their children from school and teach them at home. Some of these parents are concerned about declining morals, others about declining standards.

Under the Ontario Education Act, children are not obliged to go to school as long as they are "receiving satisfactory instruction at home or elsewhere" and, in fact, school boards are encouraged to help home-schooling parents. This often happens. Sometimes not. The following is one woman's story. And a story, according to home-schooling lawyer Chris Corcery, "that is far too common."

Judy, a single mother, decided to home-school her three children, one of them physically handicapped, after receiving a letter from her 13-year-old daughter.

"I could not read it, I thought it was in code" said Judy. "If she'd written 'Help! I'm being kidnapped,' I'd never have known." Judy asked her daughter, about to enter Grade 8, to spell circle. "Srkl" was the reply. Judy asked her to use vowels. "Sicuil" came back.

She informed her board, Roman Catholic, that she would be home-schooling.

She was told, vaguely but threateningly, that she would be charged if she withdrew her children and shortly afterwards her family benefits were suspended, even though the Family Benefits Act recognizes that a child may be taught at home. At this point Judy went to the local newspaper and, surprise, her benefits were restored.

Judy then had a meeting with the public board. It asked for written plans, timetables and continuous evaluation. All were provided, but after three meetings it was clear the local school principal and board officials were more interested in getting Judy's children back in school than in their educational progress.

While at no time naming any problems with Judy's home-schooling courses, the board wrote several letters complaining about her decision.

One letter stated "Joey's education is very important and we have the learning and psychological/social support programs that he needs." They had never even met Judy's son.

The school board then demanded an inquiry under the Education Act. Judy agreed. An education ministry official arrived at Judy's home and expressed concern that she had a lawyer present. He then referred to possible "charges," implying child welfare legislation. The lawyer objected to what he saw as threats, and in response the official said he would only deal directly with Judy. The lawyer reminded him that in Canada all people are entitled to legal representation. The official became a little more conciliatory. He was shown several boxes of teaching notes and records but said it wasn't necessary to see all of these.

Only weeks later a social worker appeared on Judy's doorstep, unannounced, and demanded the children attend school because the inquiry had found their work to be unsatisfactory.

Several more letters were then written ordering school attendance and Judy's family benefits were again withdrawn.

Another letter demanded a meeting to ascertain "the real causes" for the children's non-attendance. Only last week Judy received a letter again threatening charges unless her children "return to one of the secondary schools."

Judy and thousands like her, in Ontario and the rest of the country, still pay their tax dollars into the education system, thus giving us money and lowering classroom sizes in the bargain. The children tend to be exemplary, the parents model educators. It seems, however, that the last person allowed to teach a child is that child's mother or father.

Why would certain school boards treat parents like criminals? The answer, is two-fold. First, we have in Canada a state that has become arrogant and out of control, concerned not with the good of the individual but with its own power. Second, some within the educational establishment will not admit other people can do their job at least as well as they can.

Both Judy and her lawyer now almost want charges to be laid. They believe it is the only way to get rid not of the schoolyard bully, but the school board bully.

Was a Country Like This Worth Fighting For?

In giving its support to the American-led coalition that fought in the Gulf war, the Canadian government gave its backing to a struggle to expel a brutal dictator.

Iraq had invaded Kuwait, depriving that country of numerous basic freedoms and liberties. The small Gulf state was rescued by the might of North America and Europe. As such, Kuwait now has a fundamental responsibility to maintain those very same rights its invaders so detested and its protectors so valued. One of the most basic and vital of these rights was and is a citizen's freedom of religious observance. And Robert Hussein knows that this freedom does not exist in Kuwait.

Hussein is a 44-year-old Kuwaiti, a successful and wealthy businessman who converted to Christianity from Shiite Islam in December, 1995. Immediately he declared his new faith, three Muslim lawyers brought an action against him in religious and family court.

In ruling for the lawyers and finding Hussein an "apostate" from Islam, the judge said that "People like the defendant must be killed." In addition, he made it clear that being branded an apostate meant Hussein would be automatically divorced from his wife, lose all his custody rights to his children and relinquish his family inheritance. The judge also referred to the Muslim law which says "The Imam should kill him without a chance to repent," that "His blood should be shed by Muslims," and that "It is obligatory for Muslims to kill an apostate like the defendant."

This was the first public case of religious apostasy in Kuwait, but the court procedure lasted for less than one minute. At no time was Hussein allowed even to speak to the judge or the prosecution lawyers. Nor had he any legal defender because no Kuwaiti lawyer has been willing to act in such a sensitive and poten-

271

tially dangerous case. Hussein was, however, obliged to pay for the entire cost of the case.

The court's decision also made it possible for the Kuwaiti interior ministry, if requested by one of Hussein's opponents, to deprive him of his citizenship. More than this, it would certainly have encouraged some orthodox Muslims to try to murder Hussein, particularly as one Kuwaiti member of Parliament has already called on him to be killed.

The Kuwaiti government claims it protects the religious freedom of its citizens and the country still operates under a civil code as opposed to Islamic law. The government has also said the killing of any Kuwaiti citizen would be regarded and treated as a crime. But after Hussein admitted to being a Christian his house was attacked and his wife assaulted, with the police refusing to give him protection. He subsequently went into hiding with various European and North American Christian families living in Kuwait.

In fact the Kuwaiti government is caught in a difficult position, one not uncommon in the Middle East. It is relatively moderate and secular in itself but it is also intensely worried about the Islamic militants in the country and about alienating strict Muslim support just before the extremely important parliamentary elections this month. Its ambivalence became too much for Robert Hussein and in August he fled Kuwait for the safety of the U.S., leaving his wife and children behind.

It is a necessary and even a noble thing for strong nations to sometimes go to war for the freedom of weaker states, but those for whom they might fight must in turn safeguard the freedom of all their people. Kuwait is in moral and physical debt to the West and should honor its values and traditions.

Soldiers of the Christian religion died freeing Kuwait and its people and many of the families of those young men pray in Christian churches to the Christian God for the sake of their dead sons. Kuwait owes them. It also owes Robert Hussein protection, dignity and complete liberty of faith.

As for Canada's foreign policy, surely it must show some sort of consistency. The government routinely protests against international discrimination on the grounds of race and gender. Let Ottawa now exhibit its anger at religious bigotry as well.

Revenge is Sweet, But Mercy is Sweeter

The following is one of the most significant stories I have ever heard. If its moral and morals were followed to a lesser or greater extent by the world's governments, leaders, businesses and citizens the entire universe would change immediately, and change for the better.

It was 1974 in Miami, only a few days before Christmas. A 10-year-old boy named Chris Carrier stepped off the school bus, his head filled with thoughts of the presents he was going to receive from his parents. Or maybe, just maybe, from Santa Claus. As the small, trusting boy walked toward his home a man approached him.

"We're arranging a surprise for your dad" he said. "Could you come with me and help?"

Chris loved his dad. He got into the truck with the nice man.

After a few minutes of driving the man told Chris he had to look at the map and check directions. Chris nodded his head. And then, suddenly, Chris was on his back and the man was on top of him, slashing at him with an ice-pick. The thrusts did not hurt as much as shock the boy. The same questions, drenched in terror, smashed into his mind. Why was this happening, what did the man want, where is my dad?

As suddenly as the attack started it stopped. Silence. The man seemed almost apologetic, and then drove on until he and the fear-frozen child reached the Everglades.

"Get out of the truck and I'll call your father and tell him where you are" said the man. The boy got out, walked a few yards and then sat down on a rock.

The man followed, then turned away. As he did there was the loudest crack the boy had ever heard. And then blackness.

Chris Carrier had been shot through the head. The bullet entered his right temple and exited through his left, leaving him

273

blind in one eye. Dazed and semi-conscious, this starving, bleeding little boy wandered around in the wilderness for almost a week. It was on Boxing Day that he was found, 120 km from his home, and returned to his father.

It was, of course, a miracle that Carrier survived. The medics found that not only was the boy shot and stabbed but his body was also covered with cigarette burns. The police had a suspect but did not have proof. They believed that the abduction, torture and attempted murder was committed by someone who had worked as a nurse for Chris Carrier's aged uncle but had been fired for drinking. The case was forgotten and Carrier learned to live with the injuries and restore his life.

The scene moves to 1996 and Chris Carrier is a 32-year-old bookstore owner, married with two children and very happy. Suddenly he receives a telephone call from a police officer who worked on the case two decades ago and has never quite let go. He explains that the man has been found and has confessed to his crimes on tape. He is in a North Miami Beach nursing home, blind and wasted. A pathetic wreck of a man.

His name is David McAllister and he is 77. He will not be charged because of the statute of limitations.

Chris Carrier drives to the nursing home, gets out of his car and walks to the room of his persecutor. He stops. Then enters.

"I am the boy you tried to kill," he says. The man says nothing. Then a pause. Then this from Chris Carrier: "I forgive you."

And he has and he does. He visits David McAllister every day, cares for him and reads him the Bible.

"I have everything, he has nothing," says Carrier. "I no longer see the man who hurt me, just a figure near death who has nobody."

So what are we to make of this? Simple. Justice is paramount, but in a world where so many of our policies and actions are infected by violence we need to hold up Chris Carrier as a torch of inspiration. "As we forgive those who trespass against us." Not new, but still revolutionary.

The Write Stuff,
But the Wrong Colour

Canada is a country that places great value on fairness, justice and equality, and on the importance of the elimination of discrimination and prejudice. This is one of the reasons it is highly regarded in the rest of the world, and the main reason I have written this column.

Virginia Kelley is a mother and author who lives in Hamilton. She spent many years in Jamaica and the Bahamas, where she won the Longman Caribbean's Publishing Award of 1979 and was awarded a distinction in the Bahamas National Arts Festival of 1980. This really should not matter, but Kelley is a white woman married to a black man. They have five sons and one daughter. One could say, then, that Kelley knows a thing or two about literature, about race and about children.

Back in 1991, Kelley submitted a manuscript of a children's story to a small publishing house in Toronto called Sister Vision. They were impressed, and wrote back that "We are in receipt of your manuscript, the contents seem quite interesting. Nowhere in your short bio is it clear whether you are a woman of colour. Because we are a woman of colour publishing house and our mandate is to publish works by women of colour we need to know. We hope to hear from you soon, in the meantime we'll continue to read these most refreshing and enjoyable stories."

Evidently the stories became less refreshing and enjoyable when the women at Sister Vision discovered Virginia Kelley was white. They proceeded to send another letter to her, stating they were "not able to consider your manuscript for publication at this time." It is worth noting that Sister Vision has for some years been partly funded by the Ontario Arts Council, which means by tax dollars.

This story was brought to my attention only recently and I duly spoke to Sister Vision's Nadia Halim. She said Sister Vision had slightly altered its policy recently and had published some work by men and white women. But, she admitted, "this means that they would have to understand the experience of women of colour and, to be honest, I will believe that this is possible when I see it."

At hearing this I asked if Kelley could re-submit her work.

"Well, not really," said a hesitant Halim. "Our grant has been cut this year and we're really blocked with material, right up until 1998. So there wouldn't be any point."

I do not believe Sister Vision's policy has changed; at the end of the day a de facto colour bar still exists.

The plot then thickened. Halim told me she had been contacted by someone from the Ontario Arts Council who told her "Michael Coren had received grants in the past and has also been published by people who receive grants."

I replied that this was true but irrelevant. I am not an opponent of government funding of the arts, only of government funding of unrepresentative fringe groups, and of artists who could not and would not ever pay the country back through income tax.

At this point I asked why the Ontario Arts Council contacted Halim and volunteered such information.

"They knew you were researching the subject of Sister Vision," was Halim's reply.

So they wanted to arm you, I suggested.

"Well, not so much that, but they were networking."

When I pushed her to tell me who she had spoken to at the arts council she first said she did not know , then that she had forgotten it. It was, in fact, the overseer of the entire literature branch of the council, Lorraine Filyer.

Kelley has discussed this issue with her friends in the West Indies, black writers and teachers, and they are amazed such attitudes, and publicly funded attitudes at that, can exist in such a country as Canada. As for Kelley herself, she only wants to write good stories and try to bring the races together. She has bravely said she will try her luck with Sister Vision again, in two years.

I think I know what the publisher's answer will be. But with any luck the taxpayer will not be funding such lunacy by that time, unless of course the "network" is more ensconced than we think.

Forget About People, Free the Whales!

There was a protest last week at the Marineland theme park in Niagara Falls, Ont. More than 100 protesters gathered to express their opposition to whales, dolphins and other such creatures being held in captivity and displayed to the public.

The demonstrators came from around the world and six people were arrested after chaining themselves to gates and doors around the facility. Being arrested had, according to protest organizers, been part of the civil disobedience plan. One man was arrested for assaulting the police.

Many people, including myself, might agree with the protesters that it is unfair, unwise and even unethical to keep large creatures like whales in such confined conditions and that we are better off experiencing the beauty of dolphins in the ocean, where they are what they should be and do what they should do. But the aspirations of most of the protesters go much deeper than a few reforms and a dose of common sense.

I interviewed a group of those involved and, after realizing they were devoted to an entire package of fundamentalist animal liberation, gave them a straightforward scenario:

You are driving along a narrow road. Suddenly you see a small child to your left, a dog to your right. You cannot stop the car in time and there is no room to maneuver around both of them. Which do you choose to hit, which do you miss?

First was Rob Laidlaw of Zoocheck Canada. He refused to answer the question but said everyone involved in the struggle for animals was also concerned with human issues such as housing.

But the question had made him rather angry. After our telephone interview he called back, used foul and obscene language for five minutes, threatened and called me some nasty names. I cannot help thinking that while Laidlaw opposes medical experiments on the likes of rats and mice, he might rather like them being done on the likes of me.

Next came Catherine Ens of Niagara Brock Action for Animals. She took longer about the question but also refused to answer. She did, however, ask me a question: what if the choice was between your child and another child?

I replied that I would miss my own child, however selfish and ignoble this might sound. This seemed to leave her rather dumbstruck. I then expressed concern that she should equate the choice between animal and child with that between two children and also said that, as I had been honest with her, why would she not be honest with me and answer my question?

She still would not.

Next came a young woman who believed passionately in freeing the whales and their friends. She did answer the question, stating she would choose to miss the species that had done less damage to the planet. As Ginger, Snowy, Rover and Spot have not been able to develop any technology beyond the tail-wag, this presumably means the woman in question would smash into the little human.

The last animal rights supporter asked said he would hit the animal, but with great reservations and enormous regret and sorrow.

What I saw, and what we all increasingly see, is an ever-widening gulf when it comes to basic issues of animal welfare.

On the one hand, there are those people who love animals, believe that hunting is wrong, that many animal experiments are gratuitous and cruel, that some modern farming methods deprive animals of dignity and that we must do more to protect endangered species. On the other, are obsessives with a perverse and revolutionary agenda who are convinced there is little or no difference between a child and a cat, a baby and a rabbit, a young mother and a dog, an aged grandfather and a duck-billed platypus.

The money spent to assemble the protest at Marineland ran, according to organizers, to tens of thousands of dollars. This could have been better spent helping to ensure no Canadian 4-year-old went to bed with an empty stomach. But it wasn't, because some individuals are more interested in porpoises than people.

The Big Screen is
Home of the Big Lie

When speaking of the newspaper barons who controlled the pre-war media, author Rudyard Kipling used the phrase, "Power without responsibility, the prerogative of the harlot throughout the ages."

Newspapers have been obliged to change their ways and become more chaste. But while they have adapted, the place of the harlot has been taken by the movie industry and those who control it.

While there are still good and great films made, the tendency to exploit, abuse and lie now dominates Hollywood. The last evil is particularly significant, and examples are legion.

Oliver Stone makes a habit of it, indulging in immature, but dangerous conspiracy theories and fantasies about the death of president John Kennedy or the Vietnam war. Then there is Spike Lee smashing his way through reality with his bio-pic about Malcolm X. The work of both film-makers is taken as gospel truth by hundreds of thousands, if not millions, of people.

On a more banal, but still pernicious, level there are the Disney people retelling both history and great literature so it conforms to the liberal sensibilities of the studio bosses and the saccharine-sweet tastes of the now dumbed down American public.

The latest slice of this deliberate falsification is one of the most harmful cases of the phenomenon, in that it involves a conflict that is still killing people. The movie is Michael Collins, the conflict is that in Northern Ireland and the director is Neil Jordan.

Let me say immediately that this film is well acted and skilfully produced, which only serves to make it more detrimental. It claims to be a true account of the Irish Republican leader Michael Collins, a pivotal figure in modern Irish history and a saint in the eyes of the standard IRA terrorist. In fact, it is two hours of sheer lies.

Lie one presents Collins as being faithful and loving toward his girlfriend and fiancée Kitty Kiernan, played by Julia Roberts. Actually, Collins was notoriously promiscuous and treated the woman he was supposed to marry with disdain and disrespect.

Lie two shows a group of armored cars full of British soldiers knocking down the gates of a stadium and massacring the crowd with heavy machineguns. Not true.

But this is minor to the next pair of lies, involving specific deaths that never happened. The movie shows Vinny Byrne, a violent thug who was appointed by Collins to murder British police officers, being shot dead and being mourned by the brave IRA men around him. This will be strange news to Byrne's friends and family, as he lived till a ripe old age and was a famous figure in Ireland.

Similarly with the character of Ned Broy, who was used by Collins as a spy. He is seen being killed by the British. In fact, he became a police chief in the Irish Republic.

Interestingly enough, Broy is played by actor Stephen Rae, who married a convicted Irish terrorist who thought real-life dead babies might help the Republican cause.

We do not know what Collins' rival, Eamon de Valera, who later became Ireland's state leader, thought about dead babies, but we do know he flew the Irish flag at half-mast when Adolf Hitler died and let Dublin become a haven for Nazi spies.

In the movie he is indicated as being behind Collins' murder. Lie five, because Collins was shot by drunken IRA hoodlums who did not even recognize him.

The obvious targets of the film are naive members of the Irish-American community, who in the past have given money to murder gangs in Ireland.

Which raises the question, and one I intend to return to in future columns, of just how accountable we must hold artists of all sorts, including film-makers.

Some might call Michael Collins a guerrilla fighter, I believe he was a heartless terrorist. We can agree to disagree on that.

We must all agree, however, that the truth is sacred, even to Hollywood, and that to bend or break it is a sin crying out for justice.

They're Twisting Your Child's Mind Again

"The schoolteacher is certainly underpaid as a childminder," said the British playwright John Osborne, "but ludicrously overpaid as an educator."

What, then, would the author of Look Back In Anger have thought about the educational bureaucrats and radical teachers who are now throwing their weight around in Canada?

Two political thrusts are currently being felt.

The first is to counter what is now termed "bias" among our 6- and 7-year-olds. So before young Canadians can even read properly they will be taught the evils of racism and the guilty legacy of the white man.

In Ontario an anti-racism kit is being circulated, outlining the dangers and evils of discrimination and helping children to apply their reading, writing and math skills to fighting evil. The latter might sound a challenge, but no. Apparently kids can use mathematics to "calculate the number of white men in positions of power compared to women and people of color." They can combine this with techniques in literary criticism so "they are made aware of appropriation of voice and racial stereotypes in children's literature."

Until the day when it is compulsory for our Grade Ones to read Jack and Jill Kill a Fascist and Willie Wonka Destroys the White Capitalist Chocolate Factory, the anti-bias kits will have to suffice.

According to one of the authors of the kit, "self-esteem is very important and minority children are liberated" by such antics.

We have yet to see what happens to those children who fail to grasp or agree with this part of their education and how they will be treated or punished. Let us hope it is with an obligatory course in Kafka and Orwell.

The second prong of the attack is in the shape of an expensively produced and highly colorful and elaborate children's folder-book entitled What's My Job in Court, produced by, among others, the Metro Toronto Committee on Child Abuse, the Institute for the Prevention of Child Abuse and the Victim/Witness Assistance Program.

"We expect that children will vary in their use of this booklet, depending on their age and interest" write the authors. "Some children may simply want to color in it while they wait to meet the Crown attorney, or to testify. Others might be interested in the activities and more complex concepts."

From this explanation one would think the booklet is given to those children unfortunate enough to have to go to court. But no. The book is being handed out to entire classes, where no pupil comes from a home with a history of abuse, violence, drug or alcohol use or any dysfunctional activity.

The assumption appears to be that a number of the children given the book will have to appear in some court at some time. After all, when the teacher hands a child a special book and explains how important it is and how that child should read it thoroughly and understand it, the child in question believes the teacher and believes the contents of the book are usual. If no child in the entire school would ever have to testify, as is common, then surely the teacher would not be distributing the book in the first place.

We have to ask ourselves if we want our children exposed to intrusive and tendentious interpretations of such delicate issues as literary racism and child-witness procedures at the school level, by teachers who are often just out of university and with all the baggage that entails.

If the children of this country were being taught properly, with a sound grasp of language, history, science and responsibility, then perhaps there would be the flimsiest of arguments for such policies. But the schools are failing, both in education and in discipline. We are turning out not educated citizens, but politically correct freaks who know Mark Twain was a racist and that one day they will have to hide behind a screen and tell the judge about their abusive parents.

John Osborne thought he could look back in anger. I only pray we will not be obliged to look back in despair.

Coach House Killed by Its Own Dependency

If we are to believe some of our newspapers and radio and television stations, a vital foundation of Canadian culture was killed last week due to cutbacks in federal and provincial grants.

A long pause while we wonder what it could have been.

Stop guessing, I'll help you out. Something called Coach House Press went out of business. As I write this piece we are into the fifth day of tearful obituaries.

Canadian novelist Susan Swann wrote to another national newspaper to explain that she was "frightened" by the event, publisher Louise Dennys announced she was "devastated," and Alberto Manguel said "we Canadians are stupid and cowardly. We will not recognize our own riches. We don't deserve a culture. All we deserve is our Mounties being leased to Disney."

In a week when an airliner was blown from the skies and international chaos threatened, our literary politicians write to the newspapers in large numbers to express their terror about the death of Coach House Press.

The fact is that it is a shame Coach House went under. For all of its failures, it also published some promising authors, helped writers who later became successful and became a centre for certain types of Canadian and foreign literature.

But the death of Coach House will not actually change very much, and Canadian culture is not reliant on one relatively insular publishing house.

Its distribution was poor, promotion weak and it was anonymous to the majority of Canadians, those same people who pay some of the highest taxes in the world each year so that, among other things, the arts can be so heavily subsidized.

In fact the Coach House story is not about Canadian culture, it is about public funding.

It took little time, for example, for Ontario Premier Mike Harris to be named as the monster of the whole scenario. Delicious. A publisher does not sell enough books, fails to make a profit and goes out of business and its employees and champions blame the premier.

Yet this is typical, and indicative of a damaging state of mind that tends to dominate the Canadian arts scene. Grants are not perceived a privilege to be earned, but an entitlement to be given to the vast majority, particularly when their politics are to the left of centre.

Someone who knows a great deal about the relationship between the arts and the grant system is the publisher of Coach House, Margaret McClintock. She was previously the head of the literature department of the Ontario Arts Council. There are other people involved with the publishing house who also understand. A member of the Coach House "collective" is Michael Ondaatje, whose last book is about to appear as a high-budget movie and whose novels have sold many hundreds of thousands. Another close friend and supporter of Coach House is the enormously successful Margaret Atwood, yet another is Timothy Findley. It would be inappropriate to discuss the possible wealth of these gifted writers, but it would also be inappropriate for wealthy friends of a struggling enterprise not to support a sacred cause.

Humiliation
Treated with Indifference

An extraordinary thing happened last week. In a civil case to gain damages, three judges of the Ontario Court of Appeal found the Durham Children's Aid Society to have acted with "bias," "lack of good faith," and with "conduct akin to malicious prosecution," and that some of its actions were "utterly unconscionable and indefensible" when it backed false accusations of child abuse made against an Anglican priest by his ex-wife.

I have known this priest, whom I shall call Victim, for some years now and have seen him dragged to hell and back as a series of social workers deprived him of a genuine relationship with his children, lawyers prosecuted him, vigilantes tried to attack him and courts made him bankrupt. He was always innocent, perhaps a little too innocent, but it has taken more than 11 years for his name to be cleared.

In that time he has wept and screamed. Doubled up in terror, he has cried out to heaven and asked why this was happening, why men and women paid to aid children and their parents were doing precisely the opposite.

The story began when Victim was accused of molesting his two daughters. There was never any evidence, only the word of an ex-wife. Even the flimsiest of competent investigations would have ended the story shortly after it began. But no. Enter a social worker named Marion Van Den Boomen. The court notes dozens of examples of this woman failing to do her job and of being "unable to keep an open mind and conduct a fair and balanced investigation." She filed "a false and misleading affidavit," ignored "evidence which should have raised serious concerns," viewed Victim's "conduct towards the children with hostility, cynicism and suspicion," and turned a deaf ear to Victim's "protestations of innocence and ignored information from him which should have led to further investigation." She was even willing to allow Victim's ex-wife, the accuser, to be a co-investigator in the case.

The court concluded that "Van Den Boomen was negligent in the performance of her statutory duties and her conduct fell below the standard of care expected."

There is more. Long after Victim's daughters were taken from him, his ex-wife was charged with molesting the girls. Where was the Children's Aid Society when this was going on? There is something else, something so evil that it shakes the soul. The court concluded that the highly-paid social workers and administrators at the Durham Children's Aid Society knew a long time ago that Victim was innocent but refused to drop the case unless Victim dropped his claims for compensation.

Now one would think that this incompetence and vindictiveness, causing the shattering of three lives, would have resulted in massive damages for Victim and punishment for the guilty parties. After all, a lesser man would have given up and lost his children for ever, perhaps even taken his life.

But it seems that responsibility and accountability do not extend to social workers and their bosses. Van Den Boomen is still working as a social worker in London, Ont., paid by the public, and nobody at the Durham's Children Aid Society has even been reprimanded.

Victim is more than $300,000 in debt. He has lost 11 years of his life. He will receive $70,000 from Durham, not even enough to pay off the close friends who loaned him the money to make it through the legal war.

Victim is one of the most remarkable men I have ever met. In their own way some of the people at Durham Children's Aid Society are also remarkable. Remarkable in their indifference towards one good man's humiliation and horror.

Realistic financial compensation for Victim and his daughters, dismissals in Durham, and the firing of Van Den Boomen, should be immediate. Otherwise it might happen again, to someone less strong than Victim. We should all be very, very angry.

Welcome, Art Lovers, to the Gallery of Horrors

Last week I decided I needed some artistic inspiration and so I took a tour of some of Toronto's publicly funded art galleries. I selected four, at random, and gave each some of my time. I had already given each some of my money.

First on the list was YYZ, which receives $220,000 a year, 93.5% of its income, from the federal, provincial and local governments. The exhibition here consisted of several dozen small, clumsy, child-like pictures of faces, hands, airplanes and a penis. One of the pictures featured a large dollar sign. I am not sure whether this symbolized a request for more cash or a metaphor for the gullibility of the grant system.

In another room of the gallery sat a woman watching a movie, which she turned off when I approached. I said I would like to see it too.

"I'm uncomfortable with that," she replied.

I insisted, reminding her this was a publicly funded public gallery and that I was a member of the public. After protest, she agreed to let me see the art I had paid for, which featured a woman being stripped and threatened with a knife by what appeared to be a dwarf with a whitened face.

As I left the gallery, I noticed several posters on the wall. One advertised an exhibition called Gay Gangsters visit Niagara Falls, another Energy Orgasm Workshop. A prominent sign proudly announced that "YYZ follows a policy of non-compliance with any government or other censoring or prior-approval bodies." In other words, we'll take your money, but we won't take your opinions.

There was also an advertisement for the position of co-director of the gallery. This required four days a week, for 11 months. The pay was $28,000.

My esthetic needs not quite satisfied, I wandered off to the Mercer Union. This gallery receives more than $200,000 a year,

90.3% of its income, from the government. The star feature of the exhibition was an enormous rack made for sado-masochists. There was also a picture of a man crucified on a Volkswagen – not even a Mercedes – and photographs of people burning their nipples. Most interesting of all was a large black and white photo of a woman pulling a scroll through her vagina. The actual scroll, covered in dried menstrual blood, was displayed in a glass case. There were also several out-of-focus pictures resembling rejects from some family vacation and another of a woman with her jeans around her ankles, showing her somewhat unappetizing bottom.

A sign on the front desk reminded us it was illegal to smoke in the gallery, the fine being up to $5,000. Singe your nipples, cover the place with menstrual blood and nail your hands to a motor vehicle and you receive a government grant. But don't dare light up a cigarette.

I completed the day's activities with trips to two more galleries, A Space and Inter Access, which receive more than $300,000 in annual grants between them. One featured a set of wigs and eggs with hypodermic syringes hanging above them, another a collection of wire dogs. Outside was a written statement from Toronto Mayor Barbara Hall: "I have learned a lot about contemporary art over the past 25 years from visiting places like this."

Two points. First, art is about more than mindless provocation; and even if it weren't, this sort of stuff is provocative only to those with a banal, suburban imagination. To most of us it is simply dull.

Second, all forms of government are cutting services in a vital effort to reduce the deficit. There may be room for funding the arts, but we have to be extremely selective. Millions of dollars go not to people who want to see art and not even to people who want to create art, but to people who are committed to a stale and extreme political, sexual and quasi-artistic agenda. Let them pursue this without the help of the taxpayer.

As for the man nailed to the Volkswagen, if he gives me a call I might be able to find him a job in a travelling circus.

The Zundel Affair: Much Ado About Nobody

Let me begin with a question. What constitutes a national security threat to this country?

Well, international espionage would be one, foreign invasion another.

Certainly the internal peace and order of the nation is challenged by union thugs who try to bring down elected governments and by drug dealers and murderers who now seem to be invading our inner cities. But the country will, I am sure, win the day. Unless, apparently, one man is allowed to remain in Canada.

The man of whom I speak became a permanent resident in 1958. He applied for citizenship in 1968 and 1993 but was rejected because he was thought by the Canadian Security Intelligence Service to be a threat to our national security. Believe it or not, this ostensibly terrifying individual is he of the soft brain under a hard hat, the porky Holocaust-denier Ernst Zundel.

It sounds ridiculous, but it's true. The intelligence service believes Zundel to be so dangerous there may be moves afoot to deport him back to Germany. He is now arguing his defence in front of the Federal Court.

Zundel has never been convicted of a crime, although he has, of course, smashed his way through the moral law for years. His ideas are rotten and repugnant; his friends are nasty and dumb. He denies the Holocaust and is an important player in the revisionist movement. So what!

There are Marxists with links to international communism and dangerous perverts with links to international pedophilia in this country, a few of them with a certain degree of power. Some are citizens, some are not. Yet nobody is trying to deport them and nobody has described them as threats to our stability as a country.

Ernst Zundel is only a threat to Canada's national security in the minds of two extreme groups – his most zealous enemies, and his most zealous friends.

The intelligence service claims Zundel may have links to fascist groups in the U.S. and Europe and that those groups may have employed violence in the past. But there are Canadians who have links with armed fighters in Sri Lanka, Croatia, Serbia, Afghanistan and the rest. These groups are far more effective and far better armed. No, what this seems to come down to is a hatred and a fear of Zundel's ideas. The former is justified, the latter is not. We must not, dare not, fear a lie.

Not only is the whole attack on Zundel an embarrassment to our dignity, it is also a colossal waste of time and money. If we want to deport national enemies, let us invest cash and hours into catching and deporting drug dealers and murderers, such as the one who killed a young Toronto policeman, and tried to kill another, and was supposed to have been deported to Jamaica long before. He managed to evade the authorities with some ease – or perhaps they managed to evade him.

Hysteria will, of course, be heard, will be used and will be exploited.

We will hear phrases such as "They laughed at Hitler" and "They didn't take the Nazis seriously" all chanted as reasons for deporting Zundel from Canada.

But the point is, this is Canada and not 1930s Germany. And Ernst Zundel is not Adolf Hitler.

If our state is so fragile and if the minds and hearts of our citizens so addled and dark the buffoon Zundel is a national threat, then it will take more than one deportation to save us.

If we are stronger and more sane than some would have us believe, Zundel is no more of a danger than the man who says he is a poached egg. We should treat Mr. Zundel and Mr. Yolk in the same way, with a contemptuous detachment.

Let me conclude by making what really should be an unnecessary statement. I am the son of a father whose Polish-Jewish family was devastated in and by the Holocaust. I have more reason than most to disagree with Ernst Zundel but I also have reason to speak up for a better grasp of political reality.

In the words of my 6-year-old daughter, "Get real."

Exposing the Untruths of Afrocentrism

Did you know that Cleopatra and Socrates were African? That European civilization was founded on the achievements of black people some 5,000 years ago? That Napoleon's soldiers defaced the Sphinx so it would look less negroid? That ancient Greek arts and philosophy were merely a stolen echo of Egyptian culture and that those very same Egyptians were black? If not, you have not attended one of the more fashionable and politically correct universities lately.

The issue is something called Afrocentrism, its radical advocates and a timely book entitled Not Out of Africa by American academic Mary Lefkowitz.

Afrocentrism has caused dismay at U.S. schools for years now, which means it will in time cause dismay at the universities and schools of Canada. It questions the very foundation of racial equality and common citizenship and has led to attempts to influence the debate over the educational syllabus, quota systems and the ethnic composition of juries.

This ideology was written about and discussed more than a century ago but its main thrust began in the late 1960s. Arguments were made that the ancient Egyptians, ruled by sub-Saharan people of black skin, had invaded Greece and left behind not only their dominant civilization but also a "secret doctrine," which the Greeks used to give them special powers. This, in turn, led to European dominance over Africa. If the notion sounds absurd, be patient. There is more.

Socrates was black, the Afrocentrists claim, because busts of him made decades after his death appear to be vaguely Negroid. Lefkowitz points out that to be an Athenian citizen, as Socrates was, required several generations of Greek lineage and that not one of the many vicious critics of the philosopher referred to his being black. Because he wasn't.

Neither was Cleopatra. One of the Afrocentrist claims for her being a Negro is based on Shakespeare's imaginary description of the queen, written in the late 16th century!

Lefkowitz also proves, as many of us already knew, that the Egyptians never invaded Greece and left behind any secret code or mystical cult, largely because there was never any such thing. She also bursts the vainglorious bubble about the ancient Egyptian rulers being black. Cleopatra, for example, had three Greek grandparents and one whose race is unknown. This ancestor, the Afrocentrists argue, was African and, thus, the granddaughter was black. The truth cries out to be heard.

At the root of all this is the pursuit of power, the politicization of history and the ambivalence of contemporary black consciousness. When a group has suffered as much as black people have, through slavery and persecution, some of them are liable to reach out for any support that is at hand. That is more than understandable.

What is not understandable, and not justifiable, is fatuous and fraudulent history and the attempted silencing of those with whom these zealots disagree. This, unfortunately, is occurring on American campuses with an alarming regularity.

One incident is particularly enlightening.

In 1993 Afrocentrist historian Yosef ben-Jochannan gave a lecture in which he said Aristotle had visited the great library of Alexandria with Alexander the Great. Lefkowitz shocked the class by stating there was no evidence whatsoever that Aristotle ever went to Egypt and, even more damaging, that the great library was not built until after Aristotle's death. Ben-Jochannan replied that he "resented the tone of the inquiry" and Lefkowitz was accused of racism by the class.

Others have been made to feel that silence is the better part of scholarship.

Saddam Hussein has spent a fortune in an effort to prove that Iraq was responsible for world culture and Heinrich Himmler was obsessed with finding historical landmarks associated with the myth of Aryan man. The confused racists of Afrocentrism are not the monsters of Baghdad and Berlin but they are engaged in a similar process of telling political lies. Nobody benefits from this lunacy, particularly the black people of North America.

Of Censorship and the CBC

Let me tell you a tale of the CBC, a story about censorship, control and sheer political thuggery.

Three weeks ago I wrote a column in this newspaper about the possible CBC strike. I said corporation employees were divided about withdrawing their labor, with on-air people generally reluctant to strike but technical staff more ready to take on the management.

I quoted one prominent CBC host as saying that some technical workers act like oppressed coal miners, when in fact they are well-paid suburbanites who do not work particularly hard. I argued that on-air personalities were overpaid and that the corporation often demonstrated a political bias.

Some CBC people congratulated me on the column, others criticized me. Fine. This is the stuff of opinion journalism and free expression.

Last Thursday I was asked by Newsworld in Calgary to appear on a show called Coast to Coast the following day, to discuss the issue of leadership. I agreed.

I was told a pre-interview would be conducted at 10 a.m. on Friday. This did indeed happen, and for 30 minutes I discussed the forthcoming interview and the issues involved. I was told to be at Studio 37 of the CBC building in Toronto at 2 p.m., and that the show would air at 2:15. Again, I agreed.

I left my home, went to the library to conduct some background research about recent leadership issues and arrived at the CBC at 1:55 p.m.

I was greeted by an obliging security guard wearing a red jacket and a smile. "The show has been cancelled and you have to call this Calgary number collect."

I assumed a bigger story had broken. I called the number. It was the show's producer.

"I'm sorry, the show is cancelled. They don't want you on," she said.

I was, and this could be a first, momentarily speechless. Who doesn't want me on?

"The people in Toronto who are putting the show on, the technical people."

What!

"They didn't like the column you wrote about the strike, they're not going to give you a warm reception, we have to cancel."

But this is censorship.

"I'm sorry ... but they just won't have you on."

You realize there will be repercussions from this?

A long pause and a background conversation.

"Okay, you can go up if you like but I can't guarantee a warm reception. It isn't a good idea. I'm sorry. But we can pay you an honorarium."

That isn't really the point.

"I know. I'm sorry. I don't really know what to say. I'm so sorry. It's out of my control."

Let me add this entire conversation was overheard by a third party, who was as incredulous as I was.

Now I do not hold the Newsworld producer responsible for this CBC moment. She was in Calgary and probably did not realize just how anti-democratic union activists can be. I asked her for names but she said she didn't have any, or wouldn't give any. She sounded worried, under pressure, and emphasized she was sure it was only a minority of people who were involved and that she didn't want the incident to reflect on everybody.

She's probably right. I have worked with people in Studio 37 in the past and they have always been professional. Perhaps it was from somewhere further up the union ladder that this objection had arrived? There had to be some clout behind it. Not only was I being censored but several CBC producers were being inconvenienced and an entire show had to be changed.

The issue is not, of course, one journalist being gagged by an anonymous group of public employees. It is about the power of political manipulation within the CBC and the extremism of some of its staff. It is not only that they did such a thing but that they assumed they could do such a thing and thought it acceptable behavior.

Let me reiterate my final paragraph from the column that made some people angry enough to act immorally and, arguably, illegally: "Personally, I would like to see the corporation have some sort of future, but a very different one to that which it now seems to assume to be its natural right. It is time for a reality check."

I rest my case.

A Sordid Collection of Double Standards

Toronto Councillor and homosexual activist Kyle Rae thought it quite amusing. Fun, interesting, even exciting.

To what do I refer? The dancers at a homosexual strip club in Toronto, Remington's, who have the fascinating habit of masturbating while on stage and, according to Councillor Rae, also into the audience.

Twelve dancers, three club employees and four of the wretched souls who were in the crowd were taken aback in February when the police brought indecency charges against them.

Societal standards are relatively well formed and we, and our police, political and legal representatives, tend to know where the line should be drawn. Many would argue this was undesirable behavior, in addition to posing a possible health problem with the enormously high incidence of AIDS amongst homosexuals.

One would have thought the pathetic incident would have been concluded extremely quickly. But no, this case was just beginning.

As soon as the charges were brought, a defence committee was formed within the homosexual community to support and champion the dancers and their buddies in bad times. Demonstrations were planned and overtures were made to the police and the media. Clearly this prosecution was not going to be as straightforward as some had thought.

One of the activists concerned with all this, Bob Gallacher, explained that "There have been some very encouraging sounds coming from the police. It's clear a lot of senior people in the department are leery about backing this kind of operation."

Really? I can only imagine that the sounds referred to are sheeplike, as frightened policemen follow politically correct dictates from their bureaucratic masters and refuse to apply the law.

Rae seemed to confirm this when he told the press that senior police officers had no knowledge of the raid and that it had been planned within the "morality squad of Metro's Special Investigative Services." Forgive my ignorance, but surely a morality squad is supposed to do what its title suggests and prevent fundamental and extreme breaches of morality in our society. I have not been informed that this police unit is now called the "Morality In Some But Not All Cases Squad," or the "Morality Unless Special Interest Groups Are Involved Squad."

Homosexual activists have said they now fear a backlash from the greater community because of this police action. They also claim the homosexual tourist trade might be hit because of it. So we have financial gain as well as sexual politics involved here. They are chagrined that a single citizen's complaint could have provoked a 10-week investigation of Remington's and brought about charges against those involved.

But we now have an entire police branch, the Hate Crimes Unit, established on the flimsiest of pretexts, often investigating complaints made by people claiming to be victims of ostensible racial or sexual hatred that are far from beyond question. While other vital police squads see their budgets cut, the hate crimes cops are paid to lecture and gather information.

They have yet to lay any charges against so-called racists or homophobes that justify the amount of money given them.

So what we seem to have is a sordid collection of double standards. While lap-dancing is made illegal, while heterosexual strip clubs are charged with indecency – and I do not necessarily disagree with this – an establishment featuring homosexual strippers masturbating in public is defended by politicians and radical activists, who appear to believe high-ranking police officers are on their side.

And perhaps their confidence is justified. Certainly the somewhat insipid but socialistic mayor of Toronto, Barbara Hall, made a name for herself 15 years ago as a lawyer when she defended various people involved with homosexual bathhouses after police raids.

It is similar people who are now, it seems, defending an individual's right to publicly masturbate, at least if that individual is a homosexual. Not a very noble cause to proclaim, one would have thought. But it does, as the saying goes, take all sorts to make a world.

Yet it should also be the case that all sorts should be treated equally under the law, with no special advantages and exceptions for those with political and media connections.

Bombing Reveals the IRA's Moral Cowardice

My parents' small, East-London home trembled last Friday evening. My father shouted that it felt like "the bloody blitz again." Actually it was a different type of fascist at work this time. The IRA had come to call.

The bomb was planted more than two miles away at Canary Wharf, jewel in the crown of the Thatcher revolution, built to a large extent by the Reichmann family, home to Conrad Black's Telegraph newspapers. The device was timed to explode at 7 p.m., as thousands of people were leaving their offices and legions of children were making their way to the local arena to watch a basketball game.

The IRA had announced the ceasefire was over an hour earlier, but as these bombings demand several dry runs and enormous preparation the terrorists had obviously decided to break the peace months ago. Destruction without concern for life is moral cowardice and political sadism. As I say, fascism.

Irish Republican extremists immediately tried to blame the British and the Unionists for provoking the bombing, in that they insisted the IRA give up some of its arms before genuine negotiations could take place. But there was no alternative. According to its Czech suppliers, the IRA has enough explosives to last it for a century. If just some of this materiel - only a few rocket-launchers, a mere handful of hand-grenades - had been given over as a symbol of the olive-branch the British government would have changed its position. But no. The armed struggle is such a crutch, such an aspect of psychotic dependency for the IRA that it refused to give even a catapult.

As leader of Sinn Fein, the political manifestation of the IRA, Gerry Adams is central to all of this. Adams has been feted by Bill Clinton and the chattering classes in Washington and New York but this so-called man of peace – who held military rank as a

298

terrorist only a few years ago – steadfastly refused to condemn the bombers.

I wonder how he would explain this reluctance to the families of the dead, the parents of the 5-year-old girl who was slashed by broken glass, or the wife of the man whose nose was ripped from his face, one of his eyes gouged from his head?

It is certainly true the IRA is seriously divided and it is possible that Adams was unaware the bombing was being planned until it was too late. Some of his people believe he has "gone soft."

There is another scenario. It is based on the assumption that Adams is playing a good cop/bad cop game, obliging the British to suddenly perceive him as the lesser of two evils and thus abandon their conditions and opt to sit down and talk.

There are, however, some people and organizations that have come out of all this with their heads held high. The Irish government in Dublin, the real voice of the Irish people, condemned the bombing unreservedly and demanded the IRA swear never to do such a thing again. On the other side of the border and of the religious divide, the political representatives of the Loyalist paramilitaries have said violence is no longer the way and that they will not retaliate. This is particularly admirable in that before the ceasefire these men were winning the terrorist war, provoking many to rename the IRA "I Ran Away."

A direct consequence of the bombing is that the men and women of the Royal Ulster Constabulary are once more wearing flak-jackets and carrying submachine-guns, London is again soaked in security barriers and heavy policing and people now worry whether their loved ones will return home in the evening.

In the long run, everything will depend upon the resolve of London and Dublin and the goodwill of the people of Northern Ireland.

And one other thing: the ability of Clinton and his people to avoid exploiting Ireland and Ulster as opportunities to win votes.

If some Canadians believe Clinton should be involved in Northern Ireland, let them ask themselves how they would feel if Washington sent a team of politicians to Quebec, decided they knew everything about the situation and demanded that Prime Minister Jean Chretien should negotiate, on equal terms, with the FLQ and with the French government. Yankee go home, and leave Ireland to the Irish and Ulster to the Ulster people.

Exposing the Myths of the French Resistance

While the Paris-based correspondents have been busy explaining to the world that the death of Francois Mitterrand marks a turning point in French history, another event has occurred that is likely to become far more significant. As is often the case, it takes the form of the publication of a book.

The French Secret Service: From the Dreyfus Affair to the Gulf War, by Douglas Porch, is causing shock waves in this country. The reason? It strikes at the very centre of the pride, self-perception and meaning of postwar France. What we have to remember is that part of France, Vichy, allied itself to National Socialist Germany and collaborated in the Nazi nightmare to a degree that shocked even the Gestapo. The rest of the country was occupied by the Germans but stood, and still stands, accused of being too comfortable and obliging a home for the hell-black invaders.

The saving aspect of France, and what made its post-1945 rejuvenation possible, was its pride in the French Resistance. Although France was occupied by a brutal army, legions of men and women worked against the Nazis, ambushing their patrols, assassinating their officers, supplying information to the British and eventually rising up after D-Day to distract tens of thousands of German soldiers from the front line. Thus could this beautiful nation claim equality with the Allies and take hold of national pride. It has been the cornerstone of modern France.

Now Porch tells a very different story. He recounts Albert Speer, the Nazi minister for war production, being asked what effect the French Resistance had on Germany. His reply was agonizingly simple: "What French Resistance?"

Porch pays due respect to the courage of those who took on the Nazis but also shows that many of those French people who were in the Resistance were incompetent and dangerous to themselves and their friends. Ninety per cent of those captured by the Nazis

300

gave themselves away by their lack of professionalism and almost half of the Resistance's radio broadcasts were sent out on frequencies that could only be picked up by German radio. The information sent to London was, we are told in this intensely researched book, so unreliable as to be ignored by British Intelligence. The Resistance's estimation of the size of the German Army on the Atlantic Wall was wrong by more than 11 divisions!

Worse than this, the motives of many of the people involved in the Resistance are questioned. Information had to be purchased by Allied agents from French people, often for large sums of money. The average rate charged by truck drivers to carry documents into Spain was almost $3,000. Porch also shows that the Resistance gave false industrial information to their contacts in London so that Allied bombing raids would be scaled down and a post-war France would have a stronger economic base. That the Nazis were at the time using this economic base to maintain their armed forces was, apparently, not a factor in the thinking of the Resistance.

Those Resistance leaders who were committed to the struggle complained that the population was often hostile and usually apathetic. When the Allies invaded Normandy there was not, as we have been led to believe, any mass uprising but the somewhat embarrassing sight of a French people waiting for Canadian, British and American soldiers to liberate them before they became involved.

In only five towns in the entire country was there any serious fighting between guerrillas and Nazis. There were also cases of French civilians objecting to the invasion, such as the Roman Catholic priest who greeted young Allied soldiers on the beach with, "Go home, we are happy with the way things are."

Much of the responsibility – credit or blame, depending on your point of view – for the creation of the Resistance story was due to the work of Charles de Gaulle. His anachronistic view of the French identity depended on a confident and morally passionate France. So the revision of history began. And it lasted. It was only last year, for example, that France officially apologized for its appalling treatment of the Jews during the war. Ironically enough it was de Gaulle himself who once said, "The Resistance was just a bluff that came off." It could be that the bluff has now been blown.

Soldier Court-Martialled for Being a Patriot

Ring in the new, and give it three loud cheers. I refer to Michael New, a medic in the U.S. armed forces who has just been court-martialled by his superiors.

Michael New's crime was one of refusal: to serve in Macedonia wearing a United Nations uniform and beret; to take orders from foreign UN commanders; to carry a UN identification card. This volunteer soldier was prepared to give his services and, if necessary, his life for his country but not for an international organization to which he owes no allegiance and for which he has little sympathy.

The issue is singularly relevant to Canada. Because there was a time when our army, navy and air force were separate, autonomous and quintessentially Canadian, and possessed an identity that was not built upon some pretext supplied by a group of politicians who owed their loyalty not to Canada but to the UN. I cannot imagine that many of the men who ran up Juno Beach could recognize their armed forces today.

New's defence was two-fold. First came the constitutional and legal grounds. He said he would never question the orders of any American commander, even if he objected to those orders or thought them to be ridiculous. The only exception would be if an officer told him to commit a criminal act.

But American federal law prohibits a soldier, sailor or marine from wearing any "badge or insignia" from a foreign country or international association unless Congress has first sanctioned such a move. More than this, U.S. Army regulations state it is an offence to wear any foreign symbol on a battle dress uniform. Perhaps most important of all, the UN Participation Act of 1945 prevents American soldiers from serving under UN command unless Congress has first considered and then approved a pertinent set of presidential recommendations.

Congress has not agreed to let American soldiers wear foreign insignia, the Army Regulations have not been changed and President Bill Clinton has not submitted any written document to Congress.

Second came the simple issue of why New and thousands like him joined the U.S. armed forces in the first place. They signed on to defend their country and to do battle for its direct interests abroad. They were motivated, at their best, by an understanding for and a love of the U.S. If they allow themselves to be farmed out as international fighting men they surely become little more than mercenaries.

One of the greatest ironies of all of this is that New's commander-in-chief is a man who has seldom allowed issues of physical courage, moral strength and public integrity to cloud his political or personal behavior. Michael New declined to wear a blue beret, Bill Clinton declined to inhale marijuana while his fellow Americans fought in Vietnam.

There is also the broader problem of the UN. When the Cold War was at its most icy, the Soviets and their moribund satellites possessed a superiority in the UN that was as unfair as it was damaging.

An unholy alliance of the Soviet republics, the conquered Warsaw Pact nations, a pack of brutal Third World dictatorships beholden to Moscow and a rag-bag of ostensibly neutral countries dominated votes, policies and the allocations of budgets.

The KGB used the UN as a virtual annex. We had decision after decision condemning the West. We had repugnant African countries that had expelled their Asian citizens because of their ethnicity condemning Zionism as racism. We had tens of millions of dollars poured into radical and fruitless causes.

Now the United Nations has settled down to something approaching reality and embraced the so-called New World Order. But does this make its control over the soldiers of its member states any more ethical or valid? Michael New certainly doesn't think so. And because of that he will spend the rest of his life branded as a man who was ejected from the armed forces of his country. Every time he applies for a job and every time his records are checked the fact will become most obvious.

Michael New will be perceived as a man who betrayed his country. How deliciously absurd. He appears to be one of the few men in all of this mess who still understands what patriotism and faithfulness are all about.

A Low Blow Against the Canadian Family

A charming tale to warm the hearts between Christmas and New Year's.

The ninth session of the United Nations Convention on the Rights of the Child was held this summer. It praised Canada for playing a "leading role in the drafting process" of its report and noted "with satisfaction the general strengthening of the protection of human rights, particularly children's rights" in the country.

Well, it's nice to be appreciated. But if you're not you can always act like a child, throw a temper tantrum and stamp your feet. After all, nobody will punish you for it. Article 25 of the report announces:

"The committee suggests that the state party examine the possibility of reviewing the penal legislation allowing corporal punishment of children by parents, in schools and in institutions where children may be placed. In this regard and in the light of the provisions set out in articles 3 and 19 of the Convention, the committee recommends that the physical punishment of children in families be prohibited ... and that educational campaigns be launched with a view to changing attitudes in society on the use of physical punishment in the family and fostering the acceptance of its legal prohibition."

For "educational," read spending of public money; for "fostering the acceptance," read political propaganda; for "legal prohibition," read colossal increase in state power and control of families and individuals. For the whole bag of nonsense, read authoritarian socialism and a blistering attack upon the autonomy and sanctity of the family.

If the United Nations and its Canadian lapdogs have their way it will become illegal to spank your children. I do not speak of punching, kicking or the causing of genuine pain. That is abuse and has long been, thank goodness, against the law. No, I speak of a parent administering, with care and concern, a smack on the backside.

The ideology behind this latest campaign is a mixture of personal angst and something called "child liberation." The former emanates from people who come from troubled or abusive backgrounds and refuse to believe that most families are actually safe havens of love, protection and respect. The latter is a warped nonsense that began with the French philosopher Rousseau. He preached that children should govern their own lives and futures but, on a personal level, deserted his wife and kids and didn't give a damn about them.

There is, of course, a major difference between people who do not particularly advocate the spanking of children – I include myself in that category – and those who would dictate by law the attitudes of others. This group advocates, ironically, its own form of corporal punishment, the difference being that it is far worse than a tap on the bum. They wish to abuse, humiliate and even destroy any parent who dares lift a hand to chastise a child.

Consider the repercussions and consequences. If parents refuse to comply with this proposed legislation they could go to prison. So much for the stable family. With a good lawyer they might just get off with heavy fines, thus taking food from the table and toys from the children. The logic is superb.

American journalist Ingrid Guzman has chronicled the rise of state intrusion into the family in a book entitled The United Nations Wants Your Children. She recounts horror tales of children being removed from households on the flimsiest of pretexts.

One case concerned a Christian minister who smacked his 4-year-old child on the behind while the girl was wearing a diaper. The smack was gentle and the diaper was thick. This was a token display of disapproval by a parent toward a child who had repeatedly run in the direction of a busy road. A neighbor did not like what she had seen, however, and telephoned the police. The complainant exaggerated the story, social workers were called in and the girl was removed from her home.

Two months later the Children's Aid Society returned the child. Two months.

Eight weeks of agony and psychological terror.

If I were less rational or if I believed that governments were interested only in power and control I might write something like: they come for your taxes, they come for your cigarettes, they

305

come for your privacy, they come for your guns, they come for your attitudes and now they come for your children. It's a good thing I know better. Whack!

Why the Social Engineers Hate Christmas

Our television anchors appear on our screens in their bad suits and indifferent dresses. They wear white or red ribbons on their lapels, depending on which minority interest group has won the day.

They smile, as they always smile, and wish us a Happy Holiday. What do they mean? They don't know and neither do we. But the great liberal god of inclusiveness, worshipped so devoutly by our politicians and opinion-formers, has told them that any mention of Christmas will alienate, hurt, marginalize and displease those Canadians who are not Christians. It is nonsense of course, but it is establishment-approved nonsense.

Inclusiveness is a modern invention of those who despise our traditions and foundation. It travels in unison with the other modernistic myth of "tolerance." The more one tolerates, goes the lie, the better one is.

This is why we get into so much trouble and woolly thinking over teachers who write about pedophilia, over criminals who claim racial discrimination and over people who break the moral and civil laws of the country. Tolerance in the extreme becomes anarchy and amorality, inclusiveness in the extreme destroys all sense of national cohesiveness and identity.

We have to be aware that immigrants from both non-Christian and Christian countries come to Canada not in spite of, but because of its traditions.

These twin liberal obsessions achieve nothing but a sense of confusion.

Inclusiveness is not about political dictate but individual feeling. It is, simply, not the concern of government.

And if we extend the logic of the argument we should not wish anybody a happy new year. Jan. 1 is, after all, not the new year in the Eastern Christian calendar, the Jewish calendar or the calendar of many other faiths and cultures.

And then we have Halloween. Insulting to witches and war-locks in that we mock and vulgarize their beliefs. Thanksgiving? Well, a Protestant holiday in its American origin. Victoria and Simcoe Day have also to go. Both were British imperialists with the blood of millions on their white, white hands.

In fact there is a smothering double standard at play. We still accept the Christian sabbath, Sunday, as our nominal day of rest and we still include the cross, the symbol of Christianity, on many of our provincial flags. If we are to be consistent we would do better to expunge the holiday altogether or merely re-title it "The December State-Approved Opportunity to Get Drunk."

I grew up with a Jewish father. We had a Christmas tree, Santa always came and I am sure I once saw reindeer on the roof. Some-how my father's Jewishness, after thousands of years of survival, was not dented by a Christian festival, some tinsel and a few carols. He wished friends a "Merry Christmas" and, would you believe it, did not feel persecuted, did not feel excluded and did not need a therapist.

Has anyone asked those Canadians who are assumed to feel al-ienated by the use of the word Christmas if they actually feel thus?

We now have a situation where public school teachers invite wicca priestesses into their classes, members of the wizard com-munity, to discuss the real meaning of Halloween but refuse ac-cess to Christian clergy to speak about the story of Christmas. Yet this country, whether we like it or not, was built through the influence of the latter and not the former.

Non-Christians can enjoy carols; appreciate the beauty of the festival, understand the significance of its cultural influence and respect the need for phenomena that bind and represent this coun-try. Christmas is as much a Canadian as a Christian holiday. It is that fact, I believe, that so provokes the social engineers who wish it would go away.

Briefly changing the subject, I can't resist commenting on some letters that arrived from one or two publicly funded law students at the University of Toronto. You might recall from an earlier column that some extremists tried to have me banned from speak-ing at the university and then called me a Nazi. The language in the letters was delicious. They dripped with socialist cliché and with a vocabulary I thought had been abandoned with the '60s. But no. Best of all was the one that condemned my "loathsome dialectic." Lovely. So, comrades, if you'll excuse the loathsome dialectic, Merry Christmas.

Skip This, and Look At the Pictures

You will probably not be able to read this. The reason is that you are illiterate. I know because a new report from the Paris-based Organization for Economic Co-operation and Development tells me so. And statistics never lie.

According to the OECD survey 42.7% of Canadian adults cannot read or are limited to a few words. Another 30.4% of Canadians can use only simple reading materials. In fact, a mere 23.3% of Canadian men and women have good reading skills.

So in other words – and small ones at that – about every second person you meet is illiterate and under a quarter of the people you run into could read a story in this or any other newspaper.

Hard to believe? It should be. I find it genuinely difficult to understand how anybody could blithely accept these figures without a deep sense of skepticism.

A little test. Take into account the people you know, of all classes and backgrounds, who can read and write. This should not include only your friends but the people who serve you in stores, deliver the mail, drive the buses. Consider the sales of daily newspapers as well. Throw in the number of people who complete school. Soon you have a sizable number of Canadians. Of course many of them might be uncomfortable with Dostoyevsky or Kant but not with a TV guide or a telephone directory. Yet, according to the statisticians, you are wrong. Someone, it seems, is not telling the truth.

Other countries are in an even worse state. Only 18.6% of Germans can read properly, a slightly smaller proportion of the Dutch, around 15% of the Swiss and, get this, 5.2% of Poles. It could be significant that the socialist paradise of Sweden comes off best, with a 34.6% literate population.

The sting from all this was not long in coming. Ivan Fellegi, chief statistician for Statistics Canada, was quick to announce that the results "hold enormous potential for shedding light on a number of pressing social and economic policy issues."

Oh, really. And the OECD itself explained that literary skills were directly linked to type of employment and income.

The consequences are obvious. More money into campaigns and programs, all based on what I believe to be fundamentally unreliable information, collected by politically committed people with a tangible agenda.

The same day as these statistics were issued another survey from Gallup in New York revealed there are 16 times as many cases of sexual and physical abuse of children than are actually reported. How do they know? They don't. If statisticians and sociologists confirmed what we already believed, and what is usually true, they would quickly be unemployed – and be asked questions by pollsters rather than be asking them. It is in their interest to shock us.

None of this should come as any surprise. We used to accept without question the use of the "one in 10" figure for homosexuality, basing policy and spending budgets accordingly. Then, suddenly and with little warning, we were informed that this figure was in fact wrong. It was based on research carried out in the U.S. Navy and the U.S. prison system. A more realistic figure for homosexuality was 2% or 3%. We ought to ask ourselves how and why the lie held for so long, why it went unchallenged.

Government by statistic. We have become so used to such information that we have lost that vital sixth sense, the ability to speculate about the veracity of what we are told.

When the Ontario Conservatives introduced their welfare reforms, for example, several anti-government organizations stepped forward to announce that cases of welfare fraud were almost non-existent. The mass of anecdotal evidence about such corruption that was then supplied was so vast that these activists were made to appear ridiculous. The conclusion was that those arguing the statistical defence had a point to prove. The further conclusion was that one can prove almost anything by statistic.

The context may change from poverty to domestic violence, from rape to religious belief, but the misinformation remains the same. Ask one of your few literate friends to explain it to you.

Survey Reveals the Invisible Man-Woman

Three-quarters of a century ago the great British author G.K. Chesterton wrote a detective story entitled The Invisible Man. It concerned a crime committed by someone who could apparently not be seen.

But no, said the author who delighted in pointing out the extraordinary within the ordinary, the man could be seen by everybody but was unnoticed because he was so much a part of everyday life. He was, it transpired, the mailman. Oh, Mr. Chesterton, if only you were alive in Canada today.

Canada Post has just issued a four-page, expensively-produced questionnaire for its staff called Count Yourself In. It concerns employment equity and says, "This questionnaire allows us to more accurately identify the number of women, aboriginal peoples, members of visible minorities and persons with disabilities within the Corporation and" – here we go – "determine areas where representation of these groups should be improved."

It then gives its employees an elaborate quartet of questions, all subdivided into as many as 11 sections. In English as well as French. Of course.

The first question asks if Mr. Postman is "an aboriginal person." If the answer is Yes, there are several categories of native type and each one with its own box and number, all in extremely large print. Bureaucrats and social engineers always assume stupidity on the part of the people with whom they like to play. "If No," continues the form, "go directly to question 2." Okay children, let's do that.

Question 2: "Regardless of citizenship or nationality, do you consider yourself to be, by virtue of your race or color, in a visible minority of Canada?" This is where it becomes complicated. Box 1 is labelled as Black, Box 2 is East Asian, Box 3 is South-Asian,

Box 4 is South-East Asian, Box 5 is West Asian or Arab, Box 6 is Latin American and Box 7 is Other.

Under the subdivision of East Asian, for example, come the further subdivisions of "Canada, China, Fiji, Japan, Korea." Under the sub-division of South-Asian come the subdivisions of "Bangladesh, Canada, India, Pakistan, Sri Lanka" and under the sub-division of South-East Asian comes "Burma, Cambodia, Canada, Philippines, Laos, Malaysia, Thailand, Vietnam" and so on. How annoying that Canada keeps raising its head in a survey of Canada Post.

The West Asian or Arab section is particularly interesting. "Armenia, Canada, Egypt, Iran, Israel, Lebanon, North Africa, Arabia, Palestine, Syria, Turkey." Palestine? Canada Post appears to have achieved what the intifada and the Arab world has not. And then there is Arabia, as in Lawrence of. Not a country with which I am familiar, but then I haven't scrutinized its postal code.

But dull white people do not despair, not if you are "Persons with disabilities." Yes, Question 3 is here. You can qualify under: l) "Co-ordination or dexterity impairment;" 2) "Mobility impairment;" 3) "Speech impairment;" 5) "Blindness;" 9) "Mental impairment;" and six other exciting and rewarding Canada Post approved handicaps. For those afflicted with blindness this could all be somewhat difficult and a complaint under employment equity legislation might be possible – the sheet is not available in Braille.

One has to ask why such information is required, why it is so clumsily requested and how a corporation ostensibly devoted to the transportation of envelopes dare involve itself in ethnic politics and racial escapades. We might also speculate as to how Canadians of East Asian, Latin American, Arab or any other category might react to this intrusive slice of socialism and waste of money.

Having said that, although the entire enterprise might be financed by you and me we must not forget that all of the leaflets are printed on recycled paper.

And I am sure that in the long run the people who initiated and wrote Count Yourself In will guarantee that our letters and parcels are delivered more rapidly and efficiently. See Question 3, Box 2.* Count Yourself Lucky.

*"Mobility impairment." Or, "Pick up your own damn package."

A Fun-Filled Afternoon of Hate and Intolerance

I have long been a fan of comic opera. So amusing, so entertaining and one always knows when to leave because the fat lady sings at the end.

But I did not expect an opera when I was asked by a group of conservative students at the University of Toronto to speak to them about the media. News of my appearance got around, however, and some left-wing extremists tried to have me banned.

This attempt having failed, other zealots decided to pack the meeting. They arrived very early, just to be sure of getting a seat. Flattery indeed.

Leading the group were two very large women who sat together exchanging notes. These ladies were massive. I felt sorry for them; they seemed so old and so tired, not at all the youthful, inquiring and vibrant people who should be students.

Next to them was a skinny girl with a ring through her nose. This trio was joined by a most upset young man with a T-shirt emblazoned with the words, Boys Will Do Boys. Across from him was a woman who blurted out "This seat is taken" when another student tried to sit down beside her. It is standard procedure during these events for the publicly financed radicals to occupy the middle of the room or the table.

The same woman asked if I minded if she tape-recorded the meeting for "a friend who cannot be here." Again, it is standard to use a tape recorder in a feeble effort to intimidate the speaker.

The first woman of size began the meeting by asking me to justify my presence on campus because I was, according to her, a racist and a homophobe. The pattern was obvious. More comments about my politics from the leftists present and then a little man with a bad beard, his hand shaking with nervousness, approached me with a written list of my crimes, one that had been circulated to other students.

313

The piece of paper consisted of criticisms I had made in this newspaper, and on television and radio, of such things as arts funding, the National Action Committee on the Status of Women and of anti-hate laws.

I ignored the charge-sheet but asked why the poor boy was shaking.

"I always shake when I'm with a Nazi," he replied. This provoked a great deal of cheering.

Later on I considered how my aunts, uncles and cousins – most of my father's family in fact – must have felt as they watched all this from heaven. They had been herded into death camps by the Nazis and gassed. Why? Because they were Jews. They had first been labelled, then disposed of. They had no rights, no privileges. Now I, a Jew from a Holocaust family, am obliged to hear this group label me a Nazi because I do not share its outrageous politics. Irony and tragedy in one malodorous pile.

I explained to the group that these antics were all too familiar to anyone who knows the fascist-left and that if the other students, those who had issued the invitation, wanted to hear me in the future they would be best to organize a private meeting.

The woman of size shouted "Not on this campus you won't," or words to that effect.

So I, a taxpayer who helps financially support the university, will be prevented from speaking to students who have expressed a direct interest in hearing me.

This comment was about the last thing said. The fat lady had sung. I left.

As I write this column I ask myself how I should react. Should I be angry? No, no more than I could be angry at a child. Should I be sad? Yes, a little. Universities are supposed to be arenas of open and civilized debate. Should I be amused? I suppose so. It was, after all, very funny and enlivened a cold November afternoon.

To the ladies of size, the skinny girl, the chap with the Boys Will Do Boys T-shirt and the other troubled youths, thanks for the laughs.

Animal Rights Fascists Won't Spoil My Dinner

I was 10 years old. My best friend had cancer. The medical experts told me and my parents that the situation was hopeless. The kindest thing to do, they said, was to end his misery and put him to sleep.

I cried and said they couldn't, it would be horrible. My parents cuddled me, explained the reality of the situation and handed my pal to the man in the white coat. Five minutes later and Sandy was dead. He was the most affectionate golden retriever the world had ever seen. And we had every right to do what we did. He was only an animal. I repeat, only an animal.

I mention this anecdote of a quarter century ago because of three items that are in the news. First, an animal liberation group has called for the people of Canada not to eat turkeys this Thanksgiving. They are distributing alternative vegetarian recipes and leaflets explaining that "Thanksgiving is Murder on Turkeys." Second, a herd of anti-hunt saboteurs is giving classes to would-be comrades on how to ruin the fun of some of their fellow human beings, mostly by illegal and immoral means.

Third, it is the centenary of the birth of British author Henry Williamson. For those unfamiliar with the man, he was the author of a series of anthropomorphic novels, the most famous being Tarka the Otter. Williamson celebrated the purity, the honesty, the intelligence and the vibrancy of animals and believed that we as humans treated them badly. Williamson was and still is a hero of the animal rights movement. He was also interned during World War II because of his vociferous support of Adolf Hitler and international Nazism.

This is not to say, of course, that every animal rights activist is a fascist. And we must distinguish between a civilized concern for animal welfare and an obsessive commitment to animal liberation. But the animal rights movement has become increasingly politicized in recent years and is now willing to turn a blind eye, or give explicit backing, to violent and extreme action. And those who have an excessive regard for animals tend to have, as a direct consequence, an excessive disregard for people.

An example of this is the anti-vivisection movement. We know that innumerable diseases have been and will be cured by the medical use of animals. Yet activists still insist vivisection is never, ever acceptable.

In fact, the link between the radical animal rights movement and fascism is one that reaches back to the beginning of the black-shirted ideology. One of the founders of Anglo-Saxon fascism was a vet repulsed by the kosher method of slaughtering animals. Hitler, we know, wept like a baby when his pet Alsatian died but smiled benignly at the news of the destruction of European Jewry.

Is this really so far from the animal rights activist who said recently that he cared more for the well-being of a rat than for the life of a laboratory technician, and from the men and women who have murdered and maimed, planted bombs and injected meat with deadly poison?

An animal has no rights but humans do have certain duties and responsibilities. We should treat animals with respect and affection and not degrade them. But if we have to cause them pain in an effort to minimize human suffering then we must do so. As to eating them, we are carnivores as are many of them. We have evolved as meat-eaters and ought not be anything else. Ironically, in overwhelmingly carnivorous countries such as Canada animals are invariably treated with more dignity than in Asian nations where religious affiliation encourages vegetarianism.

Like the eating of meat, hunting is also a time-honored and natural extension of our visceral feelings and emotional needs. That it often controls the animal population and preserves the countryside is merely a bonus.

I will stop eating meat when the lion lies down with the lamb. I will start believing in animal liberation when the manic advocates of the cause stop relying on intimidation and silly, trendy logic. Have a happy and meaty Thanksgiving.

There's No
Mercy in Killing

Dr. Sheila Harding has a little story to tell. The Saskatchewan-based woman has a severely handicapped son, a boy who is obliged to undergo frequent surgery. One such operation occurred shortly after the Latimer case came to light, in which a man gassed his disabled daughter to death so as to "end her suffering."

Dr. Harding's little boy heard about the incident. He was terrified.

"Don't worry mommy," he said in desperate tones before one painful operation. "Please don't worry, I know I can stand it. Please, mummy, you don't have to kill me."

I have held off from writing this column for quite a while. I wanted the bulk of the particularities of the Latimer case and the raw emotions provoked by it to have subsided. But now it is time to speak out on one of the most profound issues facing contemporary Canada.

Time for this columnist to explain why he believes that euthanasia is wrong, wrong and wrong again. And to state quite clearly that the vortex surrounding the culture of death is capable of swallowing up not only evil people but good ones who wrap their misplaced compassion in a cloak of naïveté.

The issue is enormous but it speaks volumes if we explore the fundamental logical and moral basis of the argument of those who support the legislation of euthanasia. It would, they say, be voluntary and be based on free will.

Simply, I do not believe such a state of affairs is possible, even if it were desirable.

First, many people in the final stages of an illness are in no position to request death and the decision would have to be made by their doctor or family.

Fine, say supporters of euthanasia, because families know best.

Yet the same people who fight for euthanasia rights seem to be the first to tell us that families are often abusive. If so, surely we should not trust them to decide on whether a relative lives or dies.

Second, even if patients are clear of mind they would still be liable to enormous pressure from a society that is increasingly impatient with the ill and the handicapped and aggressive about the costs of caring for the terminally ill.

Many seriously ill people become deeply depressed and temporarily suicidal. There might also be influences from families that, although still caring, are exhausted and indicate that life would be a great deal easier without poor old grandpa.

Third, and most important, so-called voluntary euthanasia has already been accepted and attempted in the Netherlands for some time. In a universally respected study known as the Remmelink Report it was discovered that the "voluntary" part of the equation disappears extremely quickly.

The report focused on 1990 and found that out of a population of 15 million there were 2,300 cases of voluntary euthanasia, 400 cases of assisted suicide, where the means of death is provided to the patient for self-administration, and 1,040 examples of involuntary euthanasia.

The latter involved a doctor acting without the request of the patient.

Fourteen per cent of these victims were completely competent when they were "mercy killed" and the majority of the rest had never given any indication that they wished to be "put out of their misery." Another 8,100 people died after doctors gave them sufficient morphine to shorten their lives. Many of these patients were not even consulted about the decision.

Thus, we have a large number of doctors killing an even larger number of patients without their consent. Many doctors also admitted to lying on their medical reports and stating their patients had died from natural causes.

If cases of dishonesty are added to the figures, says the report, the real number of people killed by doctors in Holland in 1990 was 25,306, almost 20% of the total deaths in the country. It is probable that the majority of these were not voluntary.

The Dutch example indicates that any societal acceptance of voluntary euthanasia leads to an acceptance, even an encouragement, of non-voluntary "mercy killing" and a subsequent neglect of palliative care and training. Death has become a viable option.

But of course, we are morally superior to the people of Holland and such a thing could never happen here.

I have seen the future and it stinks of the odor of the morgue.

False Charges, Ruined Lives

I am writing a book about a man who was falsely accused by his ex-wife of molesting his children, fought a decade-long battle to clear his name and successfully sued a Children's Aid Society. His life was smashed in the process.

He is not, unfortunately, an isolated case.

According to people such as Dr. Hazel McBride, an authority on sexual and emotional abuse, false accusations of abuse are now one of Canada's few major growth industries. McBride has dealt with enough people who have been abused to know how harmful a false allegation can be.

"Not only are the men violated but false accusations are becoming so common that they hurt the real victims," she told me. "People who have really been abused are no longer listened to. Before I spoke to you I asked some clients, abused youngsters, what they thought and they said that people must be told how wrong false charges are. They're frightened of a backlash."

Yet the statistic given to the police is that 97% of abuse accusations are genuine.

"Yes, in a way that's true," said McBride. "But that figure only applied to cases where there was nothing to be gained. It did not include money, malice, revenge or, most important of all, custody disputes. When the figures for false charges are gathered in that area you will see a totally different picture."

McBride saw few fictitious allegations of abuse until two years ago, and other doctors and therapists agree. It is almost as if a fashion has developed, as though women are being influenced by what they have heard or what they have been told.

There are certainly many cases of "doctor-shopping," of women going to dozens of doctors before one of them will agree that abuse of a child has taken place. Sadly, there are clinics and doctors who are known to oblige.

"It's usually custody but there are also cases of women suffering from a psychiatric disorder or eaten up by sheer rage – the courts never look at this," said McBride. "If a man is charged, he is in trouble. It's almost impossible to prove a negative. Even when an investigation takes place but the police refuse to charge, the file is left open. So at any time that man's file can be used against him."

The pretexts for police investigations can be absurdly flimsy yet the police are obliged to act. If a woman can convince a social worker – who may be callow and politically tendentious – the ball begins to roll. Its momentum can be overwhelming.

"The stress is incredible. Mental breakdowns, depressive episodes and we're currently looking at figures for suicides," explained McBride.

"These cases can take years to resolve and the man will have to change the way he relates to his child. He'll be less physical, give fewer hugs. The child will also be affected. If an arrest takes place it can happen at your job; well, imagine the stigma. Loss of job and reputation, economic hardship, bankruptcy. Strokes, heart attacks."

And lack of justice for the man when his accuser is shown to be lying.

If over a certain age it is the child who has to be charged and not the mother, the fathers are understandably reluctant to do this. If a woman is prosecuted, and that is extraordinarily rare, it will only be for mischief.

Yet once abuse has been thrown into the maelstrom of an acrimonious custody battle the entire balance is distorted. Judges are frightened of appearing to be unsympathetic to women.

Only last month in a case where false accusation was proved, the judge said he did not think this was relevant to the custody battle. Gross dishonesty is now acceptable, apparently, in certain Canadian courts.

"Tragically, part of the problem is that some of the fanatics on the sexual abuse issue are themselves victims," said McBride. "So they are very angry and sometimes come to mistakenly believe that all men are abusers."

Pray for the restoration to influence of dull, ordinary, normal people.

Thank God I'm not an Arab

Thank God I'm not an Arab. Let me say it again in case any of you didn't quite understand. Thank God I'm not an Arab. Offended, hurt, shocked? Are your politically correct sensibilities dented and bruised? Tough. Because you shouldn't be surprised at all.

The fact is that in North America and most of the western world the Arab peoples are not treated at all fairly and seem to be the final example of where racism is permissible, even respectable.

Hard not to notice this when we read the coverage of the latest violence in the Middle East. Whatever the details of why the situation occurred, the fact is that for every tragic death of an Israeli Jew there are at least fifty Arab corpses. The dead include children, teenagers and medics on their way to help the victims.

The Palestinians do have guns but generally throw rocks. The Israelis respond with sharp-nosed, live ammunition. Over and over again. I have seen many violent and terrifying demonstrations in my time but outside of dictatorships I have never seen them treated in such a manner. And such dictatorships invariably receive the world's scorn and a whole bunch of sanctions.

I do not say Israel initiated the violence in the area, but I am deeply shocked at how it has all been handled. Goodness me, truth cries out to be heard. If the demonstrators were as well armed as their opponents say, they would not be dropping like flies and would have inflicted more damage on the enemy.

Beyond this, however, is the way the situation is being treated in, for example, good old Canada. A journalist in one of our national newspapers actually seemed to allege that Arabs are mentally ill. He was a doctor, he said, and it seemed to him that psychologically speaking appeasing such people only encouraged them. The implication was clear. This is a simple, foolish race.

322

There you have it. The doc has spoken. Take three thousand rounds of Uzi 9mm machine gun bullets three times a day, a dozen helicopter gunship missiles before bed and you'll be as right as rain by the morning.

Not as bad as the man who wrote to me that, "Arabs are animals and only want to die for their ridiculous cause. Good, the more the better." He went on to explain why I was, "an example of why Jews should never inter-marry." You see, whilst three of my grandparents were Jewish my maternal grandmother was a convert. Jewish enough for the Nazis but not Jewish enough for some Jews.

I don't blame this man as much as the culture that shaped him. Arabs are bad guys, Arabs are terrorists, Arabs are cowardly and stupid, Arabs are greedy and primitive, Arabs are lustful and cruel, Arabs are not like us. Not like us.

Movies, TV shows, books, newspapers. Seldom has a people been so objectified and reviled. Most men and women die as individuals, with families and faces and feelings. Arabs only die in mobs, with the terrible grieving of their loved ones mocked by comfortable people who watch the weeping on their televisions just before they turn to the latest episode of Friends or The West Wing.

We read the daily coverage of Israel and Palestine by allegedly clever and objective columnists in the allegedly serious newspapers in Canada and the United States. People who frequently demand justice, understanding and human rights. It's suddenly as if they are speaking of a war against three-headed aliens from a distant planet. Every action by an Arab is the result of hatred and ignorance, every gesture by an Israeli is a considered reaction to thoughtless venom.

Goodness me I support Israel's right to exist. I'm a Zionist who believes in the Law of Return and the eternal safety and security of the Jewish state. But not at any cost. I sometimes wonder what I would be doing now if I had been raised on the West Bank or the Gaza Strip, and how much influence I would have in the media. I think I know the answer.

I also wonder if frustration would turn to anger and anger would turn to disaster. I pray not. Again, thank God I'm not an Arab.

He is my Father.

Mum telephoned from England last week. I knew, I just knew. "I've got some bad news", she said, crying. "Dad has had a stroke." I was at the hospital within twenty-four hours.

There he was. Confused, unable to speak. My dad, swathed in those pungent, antiseptic hospital odors. Odd how smells provoke memory. I remembered the same smells from when he would wash his hands after work, trying to remove the ground-in dirt and oil from his calloused hands.

His skin was so tough. I can still recall the scraping sound of the razor on his evening stubble, still see the darkness of the water in the basin after he had cleaned his face.

He always spoke to me as he washed, told me tales of his own childhood and let little drops of moral tuition fall into my lap. Simple, and marvelous. "A promise is a promise." It was. He never broke one. He was my father.

He drove a London black taxi for more than forty years. It was a job that attracted waves of poor young men after the Second World War, a job that paid a decent wage if you were willing to work a seventy-hour week.

When I was small and we were driving back from soccer matches he would sometimes pick people up who were hailing cabs along the way. He wasn't supposed to, not with me there. But I was six or seven and sat in the hollow space next to the driver's seat where the luggage was stored. I was barely noticed.

I could never understand why the passengers treated him with such contempt, such patronising disregard. He was "cabby" and "driver" and "you!" No he wasn't, he was my dad. But he smiled and said nothing and did his job.

And then he told me more stories from his past, such as about the times he boxed for the RAF. Oh, the pride. And about how his German cousin had gone back to Berlin in the 1930s to rescue his family. The family did not escape and the cousin never came back. A long time ago, said my father, and not for you to worry about. He winked, a wink full of confidence. Never again, he said. I believed him. He was my father.

He always looked so strong, so able to protect me, so powerful. Powerful enough to cry when he felt the need. I heard him weep when my grandmother died. Confusing. How should I react, what should I do? Just be there, as he was for me. He came into my room, saw the fear on my face and recited a short prayer with me for my grandma. He kissed me, held my hand and then drove me to school before putting in his ten hours. He was my father.

I remember his joy when I went to university, the first in the family to do so. Of course he took too many photographs when I graduated and of course he didn't understand the Latin that was spoken before the meal. Who cares? His wisdom was born long before the Romans imposed their language on the world.

He felt a little out of place, but all that concerned this working man in a smart suit was that his son would not follow in his footsteps. "Do you know why I work such long hours?" he would ask me. "So that you won't have to push a cab around and tip your hat to everybody." Then he'd pause. "So that you won't have to."

He didn't come on vacation with us very often, just didn't have the money. He stayed behind and worked. We'd telephone him and said we loved him. He already knew. When my first child was born he said little. Just sat and stared and smiled. He spoke through his eyes. And what eloquence he had.

What eloquence he still has. As I sit by his bed and hold his hand I see the frustration in his eyes. Suddenly he lifts his head, and with all the effort in the world, says just one word. "Michael." Then says it again and again. "Michael, Michael, Michael."

He'll be okay. I know it. Oh God I know it. He is my father.

Hannon

If you went down to the church last week you were sure of a big surprise. Because a rather odd man performed his music and sung in the choir. The church was St. Basil's Roman Catholic, an extremely important parish attached to the University of Toronto. The man was Gerald Hannon, who is notorious for his view on pedophilia.

Hannon published an article entitled "Men Loving Boys Loving Men", in which he favourably discussed homosexual acts with lads as young as seven. He has said that a child-adult sex ring is little different from a hockey school, that both involve a certain degree of fun and risk, and describes pedophilia as "intergenerational sex." He was exposed some years ago as a homosexual prostitute.

On October 27 Hannon was at St.Basil's performing in a choir called Kammermusik Toronto, under the direction of Keith Muller, who is also the music director of St.Basil's Church itself. The concert featured a "Kyrie" composed by Hannon. A Kyrie, or Lord Have Mercy, is a sacred part of the Catholic Mass.

It is far from easy to get permission to use churches and even some faithful Christian organisations are turned down. But not this group, who calls St. Basil's their home venue.

I made several calls to the pastor of the church, Father George LaPierre, to find out what happened. Although he did not return my calls I did finally manage to reach him. I have seldom been treated with such rudeness. I asked about the Gerald Hannon incident.

"I'm not aware of any incident." I explained that I knew that people had called to complain. "I'm not aware of any incident." But you have spoken to people who have complained haven't you, so you do know about this issue. "Call the archdiocese."

But it's your church, I continued, and you're a shepherd of a flock. Surely, sir, with all due respect, people who are Roman Catholics, people who give a great deal of their money each Sunday to help maintain this church, are owed just a little of your time. "Call the archdiocese."

I tried three times to ask, extremely politely, if I could have a conversation, adding that "courtesy is the order of the day." He kept repeating the name of a woman who worked at the archdiocese and then hung up on me. I tried calling back, but as soon as I got through the answering machine was turned on.

An odd way to treat a journalist who is somewhat known for his strong defence of the Roman Catholic Church. Consistent though. One of the people who had earlier called Father LaPierre to question the incident was told, "What makes you think that you can tell me how to do my job?"

Acting on my new priest friend's advice I called the Roman Catholic Archdiocese of Toronto, where I was told, "Oh, we've been expecting your call. Father LaPierre has telephoned us." I asked Communications Director Suzanne Scorsone why LePierre could not have been a little more courteous, at which I was told that LaPierre told her "a different story." I read out the interview word for word.

No response, apart from to say that the archdiocese didn't know "if this is the same Gerald Hannon." I assured her that it was. "We only have your word for that." I said I had spoken to Hannon, as had other people. "We only have your word for that."

Gerald Hannon's views may be grotesque, but he is certainly more polite than Father LaPierre or Ms. Scorsone.

"I won't condemn child pornography because I don't see it as being different from any other representation of children", he explained. "I won't condemn pedophilia any more than I'll condemn heterosexuality. A man's sexual relationship with a seven-year-old child can certainly be acceptable. I mean, what is consent? Children don't consent to being taken to the doctor or going to school."

St.Basil's has a special place in my heart. Two of my children were baptised there and it was in the church's car park that I first kissed the woman to whom I would be married. I suppose I feel that in a funny old way my family has a right to be affirmed and not spat upon.

The Abolition of Britain

From Winston Churchill to Princess Diana
By Peter Hitchens

It can't be that easy being the brother of Christopher Hitchens. The sibling of the sage, as it were. For the uninitiated, Chris Hitchens is the journalist based in the United States who gets away with saying nasty things about Boy Clinton because he is clever, witty and has that raffish style that confuses liberals. Oh yes. And he's British. You say tomato; we say tomato. You say Clinton is a fraud and a liar; we say, "what a swell accent you've got."

Hitchens, the Peter of that name, is similarly the iconoclast but of a more conservative point of view. Same standard of cleverness of course. But, and this is important, left-wing polemics and right-wing polemics are treated in a very different manner. As the author tells us, his dissection of contemporary Britain was greeted by many critics not with a stalwart defence of a liberal establishment but by the implication that Hitchens was "nutty", "insane" and "in need of therapy." Kill the message by maginalising the messenger.

A shame and a sham, because Hitchens has given us a jubilantly intelligent and perceptive analysis of how Britain changed from being a very fine country indeed to a rather decadent and unpleasant land. For him the death and funeral of Princess Diana marked a social nadir, when emotion finally won the battle over intellect and everybody explored their feelings, wept on demand and turned their baseball caps the wrong way as they called their soap-opera addicted friends of the cell phone.

Hitchens' analysis takes no prisoners, and at times misfires, but his war cry is generally as eloquent as you'll find. There was mass civility in Britain forty years ago, he argues, where order and stability gave people fulfillment and contentment. Safe homes, clean streets, kind and clever language, common purpose, decent education, pride without prejudice.

A succession of governments and elites fixed what was not broken and played engineer to the wheels and cogs of British society. The liberal ruling classes decided in their egalitarian righteousness that they knew what the "ordinary people" wanted. The man has a point. I was one of those "ordinary people", living in an east London suburb, not much money, dad a taxi driver. At eleven I passed a national exam and was allowed to go to what was known as a grammar school, where a poor kid like myself could receive a first class education.

No, no, no, said the chattering classes. They abolished streaming and suddenly I was in the same class as teenagers who couldn't read. Nothing my parents could do. Much the rich chatterers could do. They had the money to send their brats to private schools. Hypocrites all. And this was the flavour of Britain in the 1970s and 1980s. Prime Minister Tony Blair is very much the natural product and prince of such a nation.

One of the ironies of all this is that in some ways the political right is just as responsible for the mess as the political left. As Hitchens points out extremely well, Margaret Thatcher's somewhat grotesque love affair with the free market ripped away many of the ropes and threads that had held together the British way of life. Her war against the labour movement destroyed the socialistic but morally conservative working-class communities of northern England. These miners and dockers sent Irish Catholic and English evangelical Labour MPs to Parliament.

"A man might be a militant shop steward, but that did not make him a social revolutionary", writes Hitchens. "Ernest Bevin, a former leader of the Transport and General Workers' Union, had led the anti-pacifist forces in the 1930s Labour Party and was one of the keenest supporters of a British nuclear weapon in the post-war Labour government."

There seemed to be something about getting your hands dirty that made you appreciate the timeless virtues. Little divorce, perversion and neurosis from the men and their families who dug black rock out of the earth's core every day. Thatcher tried to transform them into yuppie software designers. Actually most of them are just unemployed.

The New Britain of Tony Blair is every bit the sick child of Thatcher's brave new septic isle. The old Labour Party, a product more of Methodism than of Marx, was committed to economic justice, powerful unions and a high level of taxation. And to a stodgy but appealing patriotism. Their men smoked pipes, drank beer and told dirty jokes. They also defended the family.

Blair and his pals resemble some creation out of the town of Stepford. Programmed and robotic, they mouth slogans about gender, sexuality and so-called human rights. A Blair babe in a working man's club in Yorkshire? Think Svend Robinson and the Canadian Football League. The traditional party of the British working class has abandoned the shop floor for the boutique. Or perhaps for the sex store. Because the one issue that seems to obsess the new rulers of Britain is what they describe as sexual freedom.

"Our British Protestant sexual morality, which once required marriage as the price of pleasure, now treats any sexual activity as a recreation", writes Hitchens. "This allegedly liberates women from the slavery of the home, and men from the slavery of supporting a family. But in truth it imprisons children in a world where they always come second to adult pleasures, it imprisons women in endless competition with their sisters for fun."

What Hitchens doesn't give us are any solutions, or very much hope. Because of that this makes for sombre, even tragic reading. He finds more quintessentially British values in the United States than in England, and laments that there is no King Arthur in sight grasping for Excalibur. Better that way really. The poor old boy might be arrested for carrying an offensive weapon and then ostracised for having an all-male round table and an archaic attitude towards adultery and witchcraft. As for the Lady in the Lake, if she reads Peter Hitchens she might wonder why she ever bothered.

Katie

My sister Steph wants to write a book about her seven-year-old daughter. The title would be What Katie didn't do. Why? Because Katie is what society would describe as "handicapped". She was born four months premature and spent rather a long time in hospital. She came home accompanied by a nursing team, to a house wired for oxygen.

Katie had two strokes when she was tiny and is now classified as being Autistic. Which means many things to many people. I'll offer one example.

A large hospital in England. My dad lies is bed, having also suffered a serious stroke. We all sit around and do the usual hospital things. Make jokes that aren't funny, pretend that everything is okay, be abnormally normal.

Katie walks in. No inhibitions, none of our silly preconceptions and prejudices. She climbs on the bed, gets under the blanket, puts her arms around her grandpa and cuddles up to him. And for the very first time since he was hit by fate's cruelty, my father smiles. A smile as wide as the world itself.

Katie achieved that. Because that is what Katies do. What the physically and mentally challenged do every day. Cut through the nonsense and the fear. They are in the frontline of the battle for civilisation, teaching those of us who are without disability what honesty and simplicity are all about.

They are also the last people who have to fight for civil rights. Much as we congratulate ourselves on our liberal attitude towards those who are different, we regularly discriminate against the Katies of the world. Goodness me, her mum and dad have witnessed it for years. Even had to change church because their daughter was not accepted. We know the sort of thing. Don't we. Oh boy, don't we.

"Of course you are welcome here, as long as you don't get in the way, speak too loudly or make any of us, the lucky ones, feel in any way uncomfortable. There's a ramp out there so you can get in, but once inside you better conform and shut up. We'll fine people if they leave their cars in handicapped parking spots but won't turn a hair if they talk to handicapped people as if they were dumb animals."

Katie can do jigsaws like Super-Girl. She starts not from the outside but from the middle. The complex shapes that so baffle us take form in her beautiful mind. Wonderful pictures come alive and speak. Speak in a way Katie cannot. Hey, not like Super-Girl. She is Super-Girl.

She doesn't have an extensive vocabulary, even though her parents have added speech therapist to their many other roles. But sometimes words aren't so important. When I arrive in England she walks straight up to me, grabs my hand and takes me to a chair. She crawls all over me, showing me total and unconditional trust and love.

It's true that she doesn't always look you in the eye and that her attention seems to wander and that she appears to be distracted. Unlike, of course, those people who always look you straight in the eye and seem to take in every word you say. Then forget your name and care not a fig for your life and anything in it.

I sit down and chat to my sister. Has it been difficult? "Yes, but also joyous beyond belief. A new adventure every day and a new path of discovery. Wouldn't change it for the world. Katie has made us all grow so much, taught us things we didn't know about ourselves, about what it really means to be human.

"Yes we cry, but yes we laugh. Actually being a mum to Katie is about saying yes to things. Yes to life, yes to love. Yes. "

At which point Katie trots her way into our conversation, into our world. She wants to watch the video of The Jungle Book. She's seen it hundreds of times but that doesn't matter. It pleases her and she learns from it. Katie doesn't need expensive toys or fashionable luxuries. She's so much more than that. Perhaps so much more than us.

Fly Super-Girl, fly Katie. And never care about those who would clip your wings.

Pentecostals

When Jean Chretien attributed a shade or two of darkness to opponent Stockwell Day, and when Macleans magazine asked "How Scary" the leader of the Canadian Alliance might be, both were passing implicit comment of the man's religious faith. Day is a Pentecostal lay preacher. And to many people, and arguably to most politicians and journalists, a Pentecostal is a strange, exotic species rarely encountered and seldom known.

Odd, really, in that this particular Christian denomination is the fastest growing religious group in the world. Then again, not really that surprising. The majority of Canadian legislators and media figures have no religious affiliation, and most who do are associated with liberal Christianity. Pentecostals are more literal than liberal.

And therein lies the problem. Because this orthodox Protestant group believes in the truth of the Bible they often have the f-word thrown at them. That is, they are accused of being fundamentalists. Unfair and untrue. They are very much within the mainstream of evangelical Christianity, which would include Baptists, Christian and Missionary Alliance, Reformed, a surprising number within the United Church, some Anglicans and many others. In fact more than 10% of the population.

The evangelical position is largely that established by the Reformation four hundred years ago. Salvation by faith in Christ alone, and Christ to be found in the Bible alone. Everything in scripture is true, but scripture does require interpretation by believing Christians. There are some extreme variations on this and there are some Pentecostals who are fundamentalists and do, well, do fundamentalist things, but they certainly don't represent the mainstream of the movement.

Pentecostals would claim that their church has always existed, if not precisely in name. But it was given form and title in the early 1900s in Kansas and California. Central to the history of the church is what is known as the Azusa Street revival in Los Angeles led by an African-American preacher named William J. Seymour. He had been influenced by Charles F. Parham, a man who was convinced that the gifts of the spirit were being neglected by the established churches.

It is those very gifts of the Holy Spirit that distinguish Pentecostals, the most famous of them being the ability to speak in tongues. "Our roots are in Methodism or the Holiness movement, and speaking in tongues grew out of those traditions", says Brian Stiller, a noted author and broadcaster, President of Tyndale College and Seminary and an ordained Pentecostal minister since 1968.

"Speaking in tongues is speaking in a language that one has never learnt, in a heavenly or non-earthly language. In other words, speaking in a language that is not concurrent with any culture in the world. People can and do speak in identifiable languages that they do not know, but that's something different. But I don't believe that you have to speak in tongues to be a Pentecostal. It's a wonderful sign, but it's not essential."

There have always been Christians who have spoken in tongues, but they weren't always treated with any sort of understanding, let alone respect and brotherhood. This is one of the reasons that the Pentecostal Church came into being. It was, and to a large extent still is, a working-class, egalitarian body. Indeed, accusations of racism and sexism are somewhat ridiculous. The Pentecostal Church was racially integrated from its origins; at a time when such positions were so politically incorrect as to get your church burned down if you were not careful. The black influence on Pentecostalism, in worship, praise, music and style, is still obvious, even in predominantly white churches.

Most Pentecostal churches also ordain women, whereas Roman Catholics and many evangelicals still do not. Jean Chretien and Joe Clarke are Catholics of course, and the latter recently condemned Day's party for having an outdated view of women. Food for thought as well as for theology. In fact Pentecostals were ordaining women long before the allegedly progressive Anglicans had even considered the idea. The Pope has said that the proposition isn't even on the table.

The majority of Canada's Pentecostals belong to the Pentecostal Assemblies of Canada, a sister organisation to the Assemblies of

God in the United States. There are other denominations, such as The Apostolic Church of Pentecost as well as some independent churches but the flavour of Canadian Pentecostalism is very much set by the PAOC. The denomination has 1113 churches, with 3400 ministers and more than 260,000 members. In addition to this Newfoundland has its own church, the Pentecostal Assemblies of Newfoundland, directly affiliated to the PAOC. The total number of Pentecostals in Canada is something like 500,000.

Worldwide there are more than 400 million of the clan, making it the largest religious movement of the twentieth century and probably causing some sleepless nights to those who like their religion quiet, adaptable to changing moral codes and confined to a grand old building on a Sunday.

Peter McIntosh, senior pastor at Kennedy Road Tabernacle in Brampton, Ontario, describes Pentecostalism as "an orthodox Protestant denomination with a distinct emphasis upon the person and the work of the Holy Spirit." In other words, the faith is very much within what evangelical thinkers call "the pale of orthodoxy".

David Mainse has been described as one of the most admired televangelists in the world. Free from any of the gossip or sheer crassness of some of television's religious figures, he has hosted 100 Huntley Street for more than 23 years and is also chairman of CTS, a multi-faith television network. He was ordained as a PAOC minister in 1960. "A Pentecostal is someone who believes all the basic doctrines of the Christian faith, but is unique in that he doesn't fight about his beliefs. We hold the truth in love. I know that might sound optimistic, but I guarantee you won't find wars and violent revolutions started by Pentecostals. We've been at the forefront of building bridges with other denominations."

A pause, and an audible breath of frustration. "Some of this negative, critical talk about our religion, about my religion, shows a huge ignorance gap here. There's something anti-Canadian, anti-pluralistic, anti-decency about it all. And no way would it be accepted about, say, the Jewish or Moslem faith. Nor should it be."

It's an attitude shared by many Pentecostals, who for years have been worshipping, running soup-kitchens, and raising money to aid the victims of domestic and foreign tragedies, without any publicity. Suddenly they are in the news, and much of what they read leaves them more than a little sceptical about the press. "I sometimes wonder if that's us they're talking about", said the member of one Pentecostal congregation in Kitchener, and the dozen people around him all nodded their heads in agreement.

Interestingly enough, Stockwell Day is not the only Canadian leader to be an active Pentecostal. Matthew Coon Come, National Chief of the Assembly of First Nations, worships in a PAOC church. For some reason, however, the media has not speculated on his being "scary" and the Prime Minister has not alluded to "darkness." Perhaps they know how ridiculous it would all sound.

Harry Potter

I still remember it. We arrived at the store Friday night at 11.35, lined up for more than an hour and finally got the book. The kids started reading it in the back of the car on the way home, continued through the weekend and completed the hefty work by the end of Sunday afternoon.

The latest Harry Potter book. Of course. The one that a minority of parents, mostly Christians, find so unsettling that they have called for it to be restricted or even banned. The latest example of this lunacy is in Durham, outside of Toronto, where more than two dozen complaints were made. The result is that if the book is to be read in class parents first have to receive a note and give their approval.

Now you might know, and I hope you do, that I am a believer. An orthodox, faithful and, in theological terms, conservative Christian. But these antics shame and shock me to the core.

The parents in question allege that the book encourages children to indulge in witchcraft and magic. "It takes them step by step into a world of darkness which they may well embrace by the end of the books", is how one of the parents explained it to me. Had she read the books? Not really.

The Potter books do include references to magic and wizardry but they are also drenched in the triumph of good over evil and the traditional virtues. They are well written and intelligent. Which is not the case, unfortunately, for many of the end time novels that predict death and destruction and sell so terribly well within some Christian communities.

When I lined up with Daniel and Lucy to buy the newest Potter installment I heard the same comments again and again. "It's so good that children are here to buy a book, not to watch a silly movie or get a rap CD" and "They're reading serious books, it's just wonderful."

And it is. Because reading one book makes people read another. It expands the mind, not closes it. Indeed, research has shown that the books most commonly read by children after the Harry Potter series are the Narnia stories by C.S. Lewis, most notably The Lion, The Witch and The Wardrobe.

For the uninitiated, Lewis was probably the most successful popular Christian author and apologist of the past hundred years. His "Mere Christianity" still dominates the religious book lists and Lewis has arguably done more than any other commercial writer to bring people towards the Christian faith.

More than this, he is the hero of J.K. Rowling, the author of the Harry Potter books. So the woman who writes these things is a church-going Christian, her model is the purest and most convincing Christian voice many of us have ever known and the Potter volumes get children to read other books.

Look, the culture out there has declared war on our children. Violence, pornography, materialism and cruelty. These four stinking horsemen infect entertainment, media, advertising and even public policy. There are too many real enemies without us having to concoct others.

Satanism and the occult are a problem. But a small one. Most alleged cases of black magic turn out to be little more than hysteria and gossip. But judging by some of the e-mails I have received from my apparent brothers and sisters in Christ since I spoke out in defence of Harry Potter, you can't leave the front door without being taken away on a broomstick.

It's bad parenting more than bad books that makes bad kids.

Truth cries out to be heard. If you want darkness, just look around you. Children dying of starvation in the developing world, immoral wars, unjust sanctions and the diabolical exploitation of poor nations by the rich. Here at home we have poverty, homelessness, racism and despair.

Christian voices have dominated history in their fight for justice. The abolition of slavery, the end of child labour, universal education. All Christian victories. Now some believers obsess only about a book that they haven't even read.

As one fifteen-year-old, home-schooled Christian boy wrote to me. "You, sir, are as bad as the devil because you let him in." Well, at least he called me sir.

Prayer Power

I seldom write explicitly about my religious faith in this column. Secular issues demand secular language. What happened to me recently, however, simply has to be told.

My sister Stephanie is six years older than me and lives in Britain. We never really got on. We argued. A lot. Steph also argued with my parents. A lot.

Steph had a daughter, Tessa, but her marriage had broken down. After the collapse she had some dreadful rows with her family. Until after one particularly venomous episode she cut off all contact. Neither she nor her daughter, whom my parents had partly raised, would speak to any of us again.

This was all some years ago and in the meantime I married a Canadian and came here to live. So it wasn't so bad for me. But it was hell for my parents. Steph got married again and had a second child. Now there were two grandchildren living in Britain and mum and dad could see neither of them. One of them they had never seen at all.

As the years went by the tears dried up and a dark resignation replaced the feverish anguish that had been so difficult to tolerate. A scab formed over the wound. I had tried to make contact with Steph but I didn't even know her new married name. Hard to trace someone without their name. We didn't even know in which town she lived.

Five years ago I became a Christian. Which means I pray. Have to, want to. It's a conversation with my maker, a process partly of speaking but mostly of listening. I rarely pray for tangibles, although I am fully aware that all prayers are answered, even if the answer is sometimes in the negative.

But one day for some reason I felt the need to ask God to repair the bloody tear between my parents and my sister. Just a short plea. Then I forgot about it.

A week later the telephone rings. It's mum, in her wonderful cockney accent that makes me feel warm and safe. "Mike" she says. "You're not going to believe this. I've got a letter here from Stephanie." A long pause. "She says she wants to make up, to meet."

I listen, hardly registering what is being said. "I don't know what to do", she continues. "I'm frightened of starting all the pain again."

My sister has not spoken to my parents in fifteen years. Suddenly I pray for a resolution. My mother receives a letter from my sister four days later, meaning that she almost certainly wrote it the same day that I asked for help.

There is a phone number on the letter. I call it. A man answers. "Is Steph there?" I ask. He wants to know who it is. I hear him tell Stephanie and I hear her saying my name over and over again, as though if she stops I will no longer be there. She is crying, almost hysterically.

In between gulps for air she asks me why I didn't make contact earlier. I tell her I didn't know how to. Why, I respond, didn't she contact me? Because, she explains, she kept hearing that we all hated her. When I ask her who said this she can't remember, almost as though the thought was implanted.

I then ask why she decided to break the silence. "Because I heard that dad was very ill and I just couldn't have lived with myself if I hadn't spoken to him." At this point I choke a little. "But Steph, he's fine. He's not ill at all." Again, a thought implanted. This time from an entirely different source.

We chat, laugh, cry. Then I say to her that I must reveal something that is very important. I tell her that on a specific date some years ago I became a Christian. She doesn't answer at first. Then she asks me to repeat the date. "Mike", she says, her voice shaking. "So did I. Oh my God, so did I."

Mum, Dad, Steph and her husband John, Tessa and little Katie went on vacation to Spain together last month. They had a wonderful time. And they weren't the only ones smiling.

Assault with a Stick

Late last year a Leamington, Ontario woman was convicted of assault for beating her four-year-old son with a stick. She received a conditional discharge and almost a year's probation for repeatedly hitting the boy because he refused to do his homework. I shall not name this woman whom I interviewed for more than an hour for fear of further humiliating her. But I shall tell her story.

She home-schools her five children and has used corporal punishment on all of them, including her one-year-old. "But I didn't use a stick on the little one", she explains. I freeze at what she has just said. Then I ask why she would use a stick on any of them?

"When a dog is naughty or disobedient you use a rolled up newspaper or a shoe or something. The same with a child. They need to learn discipline, the difference between right and wrong. If I use my hand they don't really feel anything", she says in a flat, cold voice.

I ask how she feels when she gets the stick, orders one of her children to bend over and then starts whacking away. "I don't feel anything really. I'm not doing it to hurt them as such but to make them learn and understand. I'd asked my son to do his homework several times. He refused. There had to be consequences."

Did you leave any marks, I ask, and how many of them were there? "Well, I hit him once, twice, three times, four times. So there was one, two, three, four marks." A pause. "He had to do his homework, didn't he?"

Does she hit the children on a regular basis? "Oh no, not hit. I punish or chastise." What's the difference? I wait for some time but there is no answer.

Does it not occur to her, I continue, that the fact that she repeatedly beats her children with a stick shows that this sort of parenting

341

simply does not work. Indeed it was an older child who had left the home who complained to the authorities.

"That's a different story", she says. "How else am I supposed to make them do what they should do? I warn them, I don't use the stick right away. They know that there are certain limits."

Most children do what they are told, I argue, and almost every four-year-old in the world is a loving, innocent baby full of affection and wonder. Sometimes they need to be punished, but you abused your child.

"It was not abuse." How can assault not be abusive? "The judge didn't say it was abuse." Assault implies, by its nature, abuse. You can't have non-abusive assault. "It was not abuse." Will you do it again? "The judge says I mustn't." Will you? "The judge says I mustn't." I'll ask you once more, will you beat your kids with sticks?

"Well, the judge says I'm not supposed to and that it's wrong. Then I suppose I have to say that it's wrong." I'm sorry but I don't believe that you won't do it again. "I'm on probation and one of the conditions of my probation is that I do not do it again. So I won't."

What about when the probation period is over, will you do it again then? "The judge says I'm not supposed to." But will you? "I don't see what is wrong with it, I really don't." And so it continues.

I actually believe that a parent has a perfect right to use an open hand, gently, on a child's bum, thigh or hand. I also believe that this usually achieves very little. Any use of a stick, shoe, paddle or anything else is, frankly, repulsive to me. Spanking is an option, but one to be used seldom if at all.

There are zealots on one side who would make it illegal for a parent to ever spank their children in any way. There are others who want to beat their kids at the drop of a black hat. Perhaps we could put them in a room together, lock the doors, and let them work it out for themselves. In the meantime any mention of Leamington, Ontario will send a slight shudder through me. So it should.

Tramp

The corner of two of Toronto's main streets, on one of those cold evenings when people hurry everywhere so as to escape the punching chill. I'm about to cross the road. I don't notice the man sitting by a doorway until he speaks to me. Actually I thought he was a pile of rags, some abandoned garbage.

He talks in a quiet, frightened voice. As he does so his whole body shakes and he is too scared to make eye contact with me.

"Could you, could you, could you spare some money?" I turn round to answer him and this very gesture of contact makes him shrink back further into his hiding place. I ask him if he is hungry. He says he is. I tell him I'll buy him some food.

At which point I begin to walk to the corner store a few yards away so that I, well paid and well fed and one the world's privileged, can spend a tiny fraction of what I have to fill this guy's belly for a few hours.

As I walk I realise that he is following me. Of course he is. As I would him in such a situation. He walks a yard behind me, like some ancient servant in an archaic culture. As he walks he trembles and chatters. And stinks. The sickening odour of urine, muck and decay. The cologne I am wearing probably cost more money that he will see in a lifetime.

We walk into the store. Me with good clothes and good job. Him with ripped pants and genitalia almost exposed. I take some milk, chips, peanuts, any food that looks vaguely comforting and nourishing. I walk to the counter. He follows. I put the goods down and wait to pay.

The woman working in the store looks up at me. Then at him. Then at me. Then again at him. She seems bewildered, even nervous. A pause, and then:

"Are you two, are you, are you together. Are you together?" She was asking, of course, if I was paying for this man who looked as though he had not seen money in a very long time. Were we together? Was I together with this man? Were we together?

It seemed to take an eternity for the question to register. Only a second of course. But it was as if the whole world and all of its possibilities suddenly flushed and flashed though my mind. I steadied myself. "Yes", I said. "We are together."

I don't know what eventually happened to this man, don't know whether he is now dead or alive. Frankly, it could be the former. But I do know what happened to me and what is still happening. And I recount this anecdote not to advertise my meagre and pathetic display but to highlight a contemporary reality.

Simply, we don't really care very much any more. I'm sorry, but it's true. We've become tired of caring. "They bring it on themselves, they can get a job if they really want one, they made the wrong choices, they're all mentally ill anyway, everyone on welfare is a bum, the unions hold everyone hostage, it's time to get out of the compassion business, I can't stand those poverty pimps" and so on and so on.

Every time I write a column that deals in any way with the poor or the unfortunate I receive, naturally, some wonderful letters. But many others that use every excuse available to justify the writer's good fortune and to stereotype those less lucky.

They call me naïve. Hey my friends, I've seen almost everything. They call me religious. I have no time for religion, my faith is based on relationship, not organisation. They call me politically correct. You must be kidding!

They call me everything because they can't face calling the situation what it is. Repulsive. A society where we care more for the plight of a kitten than the purgatory of a Kate, more for the high life of a movie star than the hell of a Martin.

Yes, we are together. Pray God I will never forget that response and pray God I will live by it. That we all will, for ever.

Hopes for 2001

The prophets of gloom predicted that the world would end in the year 2000. But in spite of the number of books they managed to sell on the subject we are still here and, unfortunately, so are they. No Armageddon, no real change at all. The same old injustices and lies.

If only that could be transformed as we enter this coming new year. If only we could start to value a person for how much they care rather than how much they earn. If only we could value integrity over investment. If only we could turn off the cell phone and listen to the soul feelings. If only.

An end to homelessness. No more people living on the street and no more shelters distended to bursting. Every Canadian, and every person, with a full belly, a warm home, a place to call their own. Yes of course there are the mentally ill who will have to be helped into health and safety, but we have too long used them as an excuse.

Some of these men and women took to the street because they were mentally ill. Others became mentally ill because they were living on the street. They prefer a doorway or a park bench to a shelter, because in many of the shelters they are terrified by the sounds and sights and people.

The solution is not to let them die but to let them live. In their own spaces. Not in enormous mansions but at least in wholesome if simple homes with privacy and dignity. Nor must we think that it is only illness that causes homelessness. A great, dark, dirty lie. Many people in this country are never more than a pay-cheque or two away from being in such a situation.

We are a wealthy country and can afford to house and feed our citizens. And can certainly afford to forgive all of our Third World debt and try to persuade our allies to do the same. There are corrupt dictators in some of these countries but that shouldn't obscure the fact that there is not a nation in Europe or North America that has not grown wealthy through the exploitation of the developing world.

Eighteenth-century slavery to twentieth-century slave labour. Death by extermination to death by economic policy. We have much for which to answer. Fine, you say, but that is in the past. Yes and no. We do not inherit the sins of an earlier age, but corporations, arm dealers and bankers have been playing the vampire to the neck of Africa and Asia for a very long time, and they still do.

An end to the death penalty throughout the world and in particular in the United States. If proven guilty of a dreadful crime you spend the rest of your life in prison. But we cannot kill people simply because they are poor.

What do I mean? I'll tell you. If we look at the people who go to electric chair or receive a fatal injection we see a common thread. Poverty. The rich murderers can hire a good lawyer and get prison time or, in the case of famous sportsmen, even get off completely. The poor, both black and white, have no such luxury.

They tend to die in states where people scream for the privilege to own as many guns as they see fit and regard the right to own an assault rifle as something sacred and holy. Odd, really, in that the executed killers tend to have used the same weapons in their ghastly crimes.

Full employment, a safe environment, clean air and water, a stronger and more protected family, a moral foreign policy, an expansion of democracy, a fair economy, a better financed health system, an end to racism, a new respect for life, a fresh civility in public discourse, greater resources for victims of domestic violence, genuine equality for the handicapped, a reverence for children and childhood.

No I am not holding my breath waiting for it all to suddenly happen. But I am breathing deeply in the hope that we can all work together in the right direction. One last thing. A very happy new year to you and yours. From me and mine.

Coren can be booked for public speaking for the coming year at www.michaelcoren.com

Domestic Violence

She had no idea he was like it until she married him. He always seemed so gentle, so caring. And in a way he always was. It was just that he was a victim too. He had seen his mother beaten by his father and then by her various boyfriends. He had been slapped around as well. It seemed to him that this was the way you dealt with difficult situations.

The first major argument. He pushed her up against the wall, held her firmly and threatened her. The next time he grabbed her hair and pulled her. Why didn't she leave? She was pregnant, she loved him, she thought he would change, thought that maybe it was her fault. Nor was she a fool. A university education, a good mind and from a fine family.

There were some great times. Most times were great in fact. The baby came and he was loving, to both of them. Yes there were moments of pushing and hands around the neck but there was nothing she could really do now. No money, a small baby, the house being paid for by him.

Then the second child came along. Surely it would all change now. But it didn't. She wondered what to do, asked herself how all this happened. She still loved this man. She knew that others would wonder how she could have, when her husband hit and dragged her. But he was always sorry afterwards and it's much easier to be wise when you're not part of it.

Sometimes there were bruises and her parents and siblings would ask what had happened. She told stories about slipping on the stairs, walking into walls, having accidents. No more questions. Her husband? Of course not, he was so quiet and unassuming that the very suggestion was ridiculous.

It was when she was expecting her third child that she snapped. This time he wouldn't let go of her throat and she thought she was going to die. Thought her life, and that of her unborn baby, would be squeezed away. Dragged, punched, strangled, abused. A sudden shift in her mentality. A call to the police. He is arrested. Now it begins.

There is legal aid out there, police protection, a whole system to safeguard women thus treated and punish their oppressors. What nonsense! This frightened young woman with two small children and one on the way went to more than a dozen lawyers on the legal aid list and was told by every one that they were not taking on any such cases.

She phoned other law offices, and received the same response. When she went to a legal clinic she waited for three hours and was then told to virtually shout her story out above the noise. Humiliation, embarrassment, shame. They couldn't do very much, seemed less than sympathetic.

Tears and fear. It's hopeless, she thought. The police told her nothing, the Crown Attorney gave her just a few moments. Dad and brothers and sisters came round to help her, one sister gave her an old car. He had taken the one that belonged to her. Dad put another lock on the door.

The case came to court, a date was set for trial. Nothing said to her, nothing done for her. She just couldn't take it anymore. Eventually the family raised the $3000 to pay a retainer to a lawyer – the only way to get one. They worked together to find the cash. Many families can't afford to do such a thing.

The trial comes. He's not there. He has a lawyer, however, who has the date postponed. This, apparently, can go on for some time. She breaks down. The baby is due soon, he can go on his way, she has nothing and nobody seems to care. She keep saying that she did nothing wrong. That she did nothing wrong.

She didn't. But he did. So did the state. Every day, in every city, in every sort of family these cases occur. This young woman is someone I care for very deeply and have known since she was a girl. She has now changed the way I understand domestic violence. I'm sorry, my dear, that I didn't know before. I am truly sorry.

Gay Marriage

The issue of homosexuality is perhaps the most difficult one about which a Christian is obliged to write. It is about real, breathing, loving, often hurting people. More than this, to oppose the various demands of Gay people is seen by many to be cruel and uncaring. They have a point. Hatred and ignorance has been behind much of the opposition to homosexuality over the years and to a certain extent still is.

We're probably all guilty, and I know that there are some things I have written in the past that I would not say now. But to refine one's attitude towards a situation does not necessarily mean that one changes one's overall stance. For me the supreme position must be no compromise on truth, no compromise on love.

The latest cause for debate, of course, is the so-called marriage of two homosexual couples that occurred in a Gay church in Toronto early this year. The coverage has been quite extraordinary, almost all of its overwhelmingly positive. A few observations.

First, it is odd that people who routinely hurl abuse at anti-poverty groups, unions and social activists and who call for ever more attacks on welfare and public funding are so very liberal on issues like homosexuality. I have seen this time and time again. Journalists and commentators who make a living out of labeling people as extremists or as unrepresentative leaders of special interest groups, who champion banks and corporations, suddenly become all sensitive and sympathetic when sexuality is the issue.

It's the phenomenon of the lifestyle liberal. The campaign for supposed Gay rights is to a large extent a middle-class battle, one supported by money and the market because money and the market believes in low taxes and low morals. The neo-conservative rides again.

Protest the closing of a hospital or the shooting of a black youth by the cops and we'll call you a zealot. Ask for two men to be married and we'll cry for their pain.

Second, the bias shown by media in the reporting of the ceremonies in the Gay church was quite something even by Canadian standards. Interesting this, in that marriage is usually mocked and marginalised. People get married all the time, sacrifice for one another, remain faithful to one another, love one another, raise children together, nurse one another. Yet newspapers, television and movies seem to promote infidelity and laugh at the stable married couple. Perhaps it's just because they're boring old heterosexuals.

Third, it is truly ridiculous that Howard Hampton went along to the ceremony in person to show his backing. It seems that the NDP leader's desperation is showing. Having lost the support of organised labour and the poor he is now seeking the Gay vote. This could well be a waste of time. Many Gay people have higher than average disposable incomes and do not welcome the policies of the New Democrats.

There is the phenomenon of the Gay Tory. Some leading homosexuals claim that just because they are involved in one political struggle it does not mean that they have to embrace the political left. They may well be correct.

Certainly Hampton has given a slap in the face to every voter who holds that social democrats can still believe in the traditional family.

Fourth, there are crazy people on all sides. Some of those protesting all this have shamed the cause and the man they claim they represent. They evince venom and coldness and seem to be obsessed with this particular issue. Equally there are some in the Gay community who are horribly intolerant. I can show you the death threats and know all too well of the attempts to have me fired.

But these two groups represent the polarised borders. In between there is much room for dialogue and understanding. And dialogue and understanding there must be. Gay people live together, always will live together and, whilst we might disagree with their lifestyle, are entitled to name partners as legal and financial beneficiaries. Equally, marriage was conceived to describe only one thing: the union of a man and a woman.

A domestic partnership? A recognised civil union that does not in any way diminish or alter the unique status of marriage? I don't know exactly. I do know that currently the political and social fashion is with Gay people but that fashion has no answers. A genuine resolution please, with compassion and empathy all round. Shouting will solve nothing. We all need to be reminded of that.